The power to name the sac [barcode] y
Adam's silent partner. As if g
sleep, we women are slowly e
concepts from our eyes and looking at life as if seeing
it for the first bright time.

"Naming the sacred in our own experience is an absolutely essential theological task for women. For so long we have been afraid to do that, either because we thought we didn't know enough, or because we have internalized the message that our lives and work are trivial, or because our theological comments are not always in keeping with the classical theology we have been taught.

"This book is one of the most exciting books I've read for some time."

—The Very Rev. Dr. LOIS M. WILSON,
The Ecumenical Forum of Canada;
President, *World Council of Churches*

"Focuses on the 'ordinary' events in women's lives and finds there the luminous presence of embodied spirituality. These women are courageously speaking their truth. Brava!"

—CHARLENE SPRETNAK,
editor, *The Politics of Women's Spirituality.*

"An excellent book for reclaiming the holy everydayness of womanhood. Must reading!"

—ANNE WILSON SCHAEF,
psychotherapist; author, *Women's Reality.*

It is an awesome thing to find a voice within to express one's feelings, and then to shape that voice into words that utter one's truth for a first tentative time—and then to come to believe that one has the right and indeed the power to do this. It is like being present at the creation of the world.

ALSO BY ELIZABETH DODSON GRAY

Green Paradise Lost (1979)
Patriarchy as a Conceptual Trap (1982)

COAUTHORED WITH DAVID DODSON GRAY

Children of Joy:
Raising Your Own Home-Grown Christians
(1975)

SACRED DIMENSIONS OF WOMEN'S EXPERIENCE

EDITED BY
ELIZABETH DODSON GRAY

ROUNDTABLE PRESS · WELLESLEY, MASSACHUSETTS

Grateful acknowledgement is made for permission to quote from the following:

"For Strong Women" from *The Moon Is Always Female* by **Marge Piercy.** Copyright © 1986 by Alfred A. Knopf, Inc. Reprinted by permission of Alfred A. Knopf, Inc.

Portions from **With Child: A Diary of Motherhood,** by **Phyllis Chesler.** Copyright © 1979 by Phyllis Chesler. Reprinted by permission of the author.

"Fine Tuning" by **Janet Petersen** from *A Book of Yes.* Copyright © 1976 by Argus Communications. Reprinted by permission of the author.

Portions from **The Sacred and the Feminine** by **Kathryn Allen Rabuzzi.** Copyright © 1982 by Kathryn Allen Rabuzzi. Reprinted by permission of Harper & Row.

From **Waiting for Godot** by **Samuel Beckett.** Copyright © 1954 by Grove Press, Inc., renewed 1982 by Samuel Beckett. Used by permission of Grove Press, a division of Wheatland Corporation.

"Woman is as common as a loaf of bread" from *The Work of a Common Woman: Collected Poetry 1964-1977,* by **Judy Grahn.** Copyright © 1978 by the author. By permission of The Crossing Press.

Portions of **"We Need a God Who Bleeds Now"** and **"New World Coro"** from *A Daughter's Geography* by **Ntozake Shange.** Copyright © 1983 by St. Martin's Press, Inc. Reprinted by permission of St. Martin's Press.

The lines from **Chain** from **The Black Unicorn, Poems of Audre Lorde**, reprinted with the permission W. W. Norton Co., Inc. Copyright © 1978 by Audre Lorde.

Portions from Mary Barnard, **Sappho: A New Translation**. Copyright © 1958 University of California Press. Used by permission of University of California Press.

Portions from **Jack Winkler, "Gardens of Nymphs: Public and Private in Sappho's Lyrics"** in *Reflections of Women in Antiquity,* ed. Helene Foly. Copyright © 1981 by Gordon and Breach Science Publishers Inc. By permission of Gordon and Breach.

"When a woman feels alone." Reprinted from *Letters from Maine, New Poems* by **May Sarton,** by permission of W. W. Norton & Company, Inc. Copyright © 1984 by May Sarton.

Book design by David Dodson Gray
Printed in the United States of America at Nimrod Press, Boston, MA.

Library of Congress Catalog Card Number: 88-61742
ISBN 0-934512-05-1

Contents

General Introduction 1

1.
Women's Creativity

Introduction 8

There's No Kin Like Kindred Spirits
—Linda Weltner 12

Creating Sacred Emotional Space
—Carol Goldman.. 17

A Woman's Path to Power as a Sacred Process
—Lois H. Grace Stovall 23

The Sacredness of Our Spiritual Journeys
—Ann Thompson Traver 32

The Artist as Social Activist amid Adversity:
How the Job Is Done
—Corita Kent.. 37

Creating the Possible
—Judith Stone... 40

2.
Giving Birth

Introduction 48

Homebirth: The Sacred Act of Creation
—Sydney Amara Morris................................... 52

Born and Born Again:
Childbirth Rituals from a Mother's Perspective
—Myriel Crowley Eykamp 58

Pregnant with Peace—Anon. 65

3.
Caregiving

Introduction 68

The Labor after Creation
—Thérèse Saulnier.. 71

The Truth Will Set You Free,
But First It Will Make You Crazy
—Mary Guerrera Congo 76

Listening as the Language of Love:
Caring for an Aging Parent
—Marie L. Norton 85

4.
Creating Sacred Space

Introduction 94

Women as Creators of Sacred Order
—Elizabeth Dodson Gray 97

Creating Sabbath Space
—Terry Y. Goldstein.....................................103

Painting the Seasons "Sacred"
—Elizabeth Dodson Gray.................................108

Sanctifying the Home:
Ritual Art of the Women of Bengal
—Elinor W. Gadon 112

Sacred Solutions:
Afro-Brazilian Women, Ritual Power, and Art
    —Mikelle Smith-Omari 119
Coming Home Like Rivers to the Sea:
A Women's Ritual
    —Carolyn McDade & Lucile Schuck Longview 124

5.
Doing Housework

Introduction 138
Housework as Homemaking
    —Phyllis W. Harlow 142
The Zen of Housework
    —Marlane van Hall 147
Women's Work and the Sense of Time in Women's Lives
    —Kathryn Allen Rabuzzi 153

6.
Feeding as Sacred Ritual

Introduction 168
Cooking: Divine and Destructive
    —Sarah Hall Maney 172
Learning to Make Grandmother's Strudel
    —Marcia Zimmerman 176
The Tender Gift of Breastfeeding
    —Dana Raphael 181
The Meaning of Eating and the Home as Ritual Space
    —Sharon Parks 184

7.
Our Bodies Are Sacred

Introduction 196

Are Women's Bodies Sacred?:
Listening to the Yes's and No's
     —Emily Erwin Culpepper 199

"We Are Where God Is":
Sacred Dimensions of Battered Women's Lives
     —Laureen E. Smith......................................210

In Praise of Aphrodite: Sexuality as Sacred
     —Carol P. Christ 220

Body-Decisions as Sacred
     —Louise Hardin Bray 228

Our Bodies Are Still Ourselves as We Age,
and They Are Still Sacred
     —Jeanne Brooks Carritt 232

Why Do the Birds Sing?: Healing after Trauma
     —Elizabeth Dodson Gray.................................240

Acknowledgements

A collegial effort like this book is always an adventure. Originating, as it did, in a lecture series at Harvard Divinity School, it expanded through our women's networks to include friends and colleagues who had contributions to make to the tapestry we had begun to weave.

Our friend, Marie Cantlon, was an invaluable guide as we struggled to shape the contributions into a coherent whole. It was she who advised me in my first try at editing a volume like this, and I am very grateful for all her help.

My husband, David Dodson Gray, has walked every step of this book with me, editing and condensing chapters with a sure touch and a passionate commitment to our women's voice. His long hours on his typewriter and IBM-PC computer have made this book possible.

Reading an entire manuscript in order to write a comment for the book jacket is an incredible gift of time. We are very grateful to Phyllis Chesler, Elisabeth Schüssler Fiorenza, Naomi Goldenberg, Jean Kilbourne, Joanna Macy, Rosemary Radford Ruether, Anne Wilson Schaef, Charlene Spretnak, Mary Virginia Stieb-Hales, Lois Wilson, and Doris Anne Younger for giving us that gift in the midst of their busy lives.

It was Jeanne Brooks Carritt who fired my imagination with the possibility of pictures when she enclosed with her chapter the photograph of Imogen Cunningham that appears at the beginning of Section 7. Jeanne's copy of *Family of Woman* pointed us to four of the other photographs. So the visual character of the text owes much to Jeanne.

Publishing this book with a desktop computer led us out onto technological frontiers we were hardly prepared for, and our friend David Hill mentored us through the beginning stages. The final computer procedures in WordPerfect 5.0 could not have been accomplished without our computer consultant Marilyn Horn Claff. Her calm expertise made it possible to come close to our deadlines. The typesetting of the text was done with speed and competence by Richard Wilkes of Support Group, Inc. and the *WordPerfectionist* (McHenry, Maryland). Crockergraphics (Needham, Massachusetts) was extremely helpful with design advice, rapid evening and weekend turnarounds for laser-printer page proofs, and the typesetting of portions of the front matter, cover, and advertising materials.

This is our fourth book manufactured by Nimrod Press (Boston) and we want to thank them for the consistently superior quality of their work and the emotional integrity of their process. Jim Hamilton at Nimrod has been a total pleasure to work with over the years, and Norma Wilton of Nimrod's art department elegantly expressed our idea for the cover design.

Born out of a women's community, this book is offered to all women everywhere who wonder, and search, and come to know the sacred in their own lives.

—Elizabeth Dodson Gray

Wellesley, Massachusetts
October 1988

Introduction

To Name Reality

Throughout recorded time men have "named the sacred," from the standing point of the male body and male life experience. It is not accidental that in the Genesis 2 account of creation Adam "named" all the animals. Naming is power, the power to shape reality into a form that serves the interests and goals of the one doing the naming.

Today we are at a turning point in human history. The power to name is being claimed by Adam's silent partner. Woman for too long has been quiet, a submissive helpmate to the "naming" male, content to love and nurture, to support and assist, to give birth and care, endlessly to feed and remove dirt. For generations she has seemed content to live within the male naming of sacred reality.

But no more. Women at last recognize that male "naming" always fosters male power, privilege and status, while denigrating women's. As if awakening from a long sleep, we women are slowly shaking the film of male concepts from our eyes and looking at life as if seeing it "for the first bright time." [1]

Carol Gilligan entitled her important book about women's moral development *In a Different Voice.* [2] This book of ours is full of those different voices, the voices of women sharing our own lives, naming our own experience of the sacred.

A Different Naming

Do not expect this women's naming of the sacred to be like men's. Every time I read male theology I am newly impressed with the pervasive arrogance. There is no existential humility. Men immediately take private, personal ideas coming out of the particularity and specificity of their own lives and experiences (a fact which they conceal from readers), and they make those private, personal reflections into universal truths. I remember reading Paul Tillich's *The Courage to Be* [3] when it was first published. In bringing to bear his great theological and philosophical powers, Tillich never gave any hint of his own personal wrestling with actions or decisions that required of him personal courage. Their existence could only be inferred from his having deemed courage an important enough "topic" to write about.

Theologians have projected their intimations upon the cosmic skies with incredible insouciance, proclaiming to have divined eternal truth. And then they contend endlessly with one another in nimble wordgames. Like medieval jousters armored and mounted on horses, they attack and dislodge one another from presumed positions as King of the Mountain atop "the right way to think about truth."

That is *not* the way women in this book do theology. These writings are rooted in the particular. They are clothed in the subjective. They are luminous with the sights, sounds and feel of a real individual woman's life.

I think women are too aware of the diversity of our lives, and too affirming of that diversity, to forge universal generalizations from these personal reflections.

We respect the very different life journeys of each individual. When asked, we are however willing to share what we have glimpsed in the depths of our particular life journeys.

Renaming the Sacred

Male naming in patriarchal religion has given us a strange landscape of the sacred. A few places, a few people, a few occasions are seen to concentrate and to embody the holy, and these stand like sacred mountains, inhabited by the elusive power of the world beyond. Cathedrals, temples, churches, synagogues evoke religious awe with hushed darkness and stained glass. Priests, nuns, ministers, rabbis, saints and popes are sanctified with religious authority. The Bible, the Torah, the Koran are authoritative texts. Certain ritual actions are declared to be sacraments. The only moments in time which become hallowed by an aura of holiness are those which involve these places, these people, these texts and these acts. The rest of life is perceived as a vast desert of the mundane, the *un*holy. Here dwell ordinary people, our houses, our families, our everyday lives, routine moments, our physical bodies, and the natural world.

The goal of this old "sacred game" is to get away from the ordinary, the natural, the unsacred—away from women, fleshly bodies, decaying nature, away from all that is rooted in mortality and dying. "Up, up, and away" is the cry of this religious consciousness as it seeks to ascend to the elevated realm of pure spirit and utter transcendence where nothing gets soiled, or rots, or dies.

Shining with other-worldly splendor, that ethereal transcendence has allowed small shafts of itself to be captured like light and contained in those few conse-crated places, people, rituals and texts so that they shine with some of the magic of that sparkling transcendent stuff. These shining beacons point the way for us. In this old spiritual game it is clear that the movement of holiness is up, the direction is away, and the motivation is to escape from "here" to "there."

Women's renaming of the sacred is quite different. Our style is to peer into the richly woven texture of ordinary human experience and to find already woven there a golden strand of what we would name sacred. Instead of distanc-ing ourselves and withdrawing from the reality of life to find sacredness, we go toward that reality—toward bodies, toward nature, toward food, toward dust, toward transitory moments in relationships. And wherever we look, we find that which nourishes and deepens us.

Our naming of the sacred is thus life-affirming rather than life-separating or life-distancing. Our naming of what is sacred finds meaning in things that have never before been found important, much less sacred. Just as Anne Morrow Lindbergh describes in *Gift from the Sea*[4] how she would pick up a shell and slowly turn it in her hand as she pondered her woman's life, so each woman in this book picks up an area of her life and slowly turns it around in her mind, pondering its meaning for her. And like Anne Morrow Lindbergh they find subtle and quiet and new gifts of the sacred, here a double-sunrise of a caring relationship, there a delicate argonauta of creativity. Even that knobby oyster shell of housework yields grace to a wondering gaze.

Finding Our Own Voice

Some women in this book are scholars finding their authentic voice after being trained in scholarly "objective" writing in a chosen field. However most of the women writing here have invested their lives in marriage, child-bearing, child-rearing, and homemaking. They are breaking the long silence of traditional women too busy living their lives to write about them, women who, if they do write about their lives, usually have little access to publishers.

It is not easy to break a silence of generations, to find the voice inside that hardly knows how to speak. We have not been socialized by our culture to consider even reflections upon our lives to be important. Nelle Morton speaks about hearing each other into speech. [5] For many of us Harvard Divinity School has been the setting for such hearing. This book originated in a lecture series at the Theological Opportunities Program. Before there were lectures, there was an earlier beginning in the lives of the forty or fifty women of the Advisory Committee who meet each fall and spring to plan the lecture series out of their own life experience.

As the committee met in the spring of 1985, we realized that men had always declared whose lives, whose rites, whose space, was sacred, and the determination grew to take on the scary task of peering into the ordinary spaces of women's traditional lives and dare to ask, "Is there anything here we as women would name as sacred?"

This felt very risky to us. We were incredibly ambivalent about what we were doing. Now that we ourselves were declaring "women's work" sacred, were we consigning ourselves forever to the stereotypic servant role? We could not decide whether this was the most daring series we had ever planned or the most conservative. As many times as we turned away from this topic, we were drawn back to it. But we had difficulty choosing what topics to include. Which "ordinary spaces" should we peer into? A list finally took shape, a series of topics which have become the outline of this book.

Common Spaces

Like a woman moving from room to room, showing you her home, we have chosen to move through the "common spaces" of women's lives. All women may not do all these things, but the presence of these common spaces structures much of the reality of women's lives as we have lived them.

We begin with CREATIVITY that all women express in a myriad of uncelebrated ways. Usually everyone recognizes the creativity embodied in gardening, sewing or painting. Only recently have women themselves begun to value the relationality with which all women *create connection*—in families, in friendship, in support groups, in peace-making. Giving birth to connection in the midst of separation, or giving birth to our own empowered selves, or daring to ponder our own spiritual journeys in a culture that devalues women's lives—this serious task of creating "worth" is a task all women share in today. To bring into being that which is only potential is an art form of living which binds women together.

We move on to a very physical expression of women's creativity, GIVING BIRTH. A majority of women worldwide go through pregnancy and childbirth sometime in their lives. For most of those who do not choose to give birth, that awesome birthing power is still theirs, a gift given to them at their own birth.

Next we look at the reality of CAREGIVING, where all women experience themselves as the supportive web which holds human culture in place. The care of women links the generations in time, encouraging children into growth and assisting the elderly in their dying. But the caring of women—friend to friend, lover to lover, wife to husband—also functions as an invisible network, weaving together those who share the same generation.

Women occupy houses and make homes. We arrange furniture, we decorate with color and design. We make possible religious festivals. Usually we do not take these activities seriously, but when we stop to reflect, we realize what we are actually doing is CREATING SACRED SPACE.

Life in our homes requires that someone clean, dust, scrub, vacuum, and straighten up. Some women "don't do windows," but almost all women feel themselves responsible for the HOUSEWORK in their living space.

Then there are the meals women shop for, prepare, and serve. FEEDING is a major way in which women express their love to friends and families, and EATING together is a daily ritual of celebration and communication.

We come finally to our commonalities as women in our BODIES. In menstruation, in pregnancy, in giving birth, in breast-feeding, in menopause, we share the age-old journey of all women through the stages of reproductive female life. We also share a common vulnerability when we confront sexist advertising, pornography, rape, incest, battering, or the decision about whether or not to abort. Despite our great diversity of mind and psyche, it is the fact of our femaleness which places all of us on one side of the great gender dividing line set up by male culture; our bodies are what stigmatize us as "other" than male. Our women's bodies are the "given" which we all share.

These common spaces can be rendered in pictures, just as the daily lives of feudal people were portrayed in the great medieval tapestries. Here we see a woman sweeping, there a woman cooking, in between there is a woman taking a child for a walk. We know each of these pictures because we see all this in the life around us every day. But the question is, Is there a hidden thread of sacredness, a golden strand of holy meaning which we can identify if we look closely?

Who Are We?

The women who speak in this book have lived these pictures. We are as wondrously diverse as the many colors in that medieval tapestry. Our chronological ages range from the twenties to the seventies. We are Jewish, Roman Catholic, Unitarian Universalist, Quaker, Buddhist, Protestant, post-Christian, Goddess women. One is a columnist for a major newspaper. One is an anthropologist. Four are artists. One of our artists works in stained glass, one was commissioned to paint a giant rainbow on a large commercial natural-gas storage tank. One is a lawyer. Two are poets. One co-founded a women's retreat center. One has shaken up an entire denomination with her anti-sexism resolutions. One gained her Master of Divinity degree from Harvard Divinity School with a thesis in the form of a short movie about menstruation entitled "Period Piece," another with a thesis in the form of a play "Silent Sins" about the lives of battered women.

We are teachers, activists, scholars, writers, singers, theologians, composers, ministers, gardeners, a rabbi and a Buddhist priest. We are single, married, divorced, remarried, heterosexual, lesbian. We are daughters, sisters, wives, mothers, and grandmothers. One of us is black, one is Dutch; all of us are Western (although one of our scholars is steeped in the life and art of India, another in the life and art of northeast Brazil). In our diversity we bring you truth; where we are undifferentiated, we bring you limitation.

We have all struggled with our lives, seeking to find sacred meaning where our culture saw no meaning. Unfamiliar as we were with such a role, we felt more and more compelled to find within ourselves the power of naming the sacred, to call it forth from within. It is an awesome thing to find a voice within to express one's feelings, and then to shape that voice into words that utter one's truth a first tentative time—and then to come to believe that one has the right and indeed the power to do this. It is like being present at the creation of the world. As Hallie Austen Inglehart has written, "We are all creationmakers, and a new world is awaiting creation."[6]

And indeed it is. A new world of meaning is being created by women today. It will change everything, and not a moment too soon.

—Elizabeth Dodson Gray

NOTES

1. *To Be Alive*, a film produced by Francis Thompson, Inc., for Johnson Wax (New York: Macmillan Co., 1966), p. 1.

2. Carol Gilligan, *In a Different Voice* (Cambridge, Mass.: Harvard University Press, 1982).

3. Paul Tillich, *The Courage to Be* (New Haven, Conn.: Yale University Press, 1952).

4. Anne Morrow Lindbergh, *Gift from the Sea* (New York: Pantheon, 1955).

5. Nelle Morton, *The Journey Is Home* (Boston, Mass.: Beacon Press, 1985), p. 125.

6. Hallie Austen Inglehart, *Womanspirit: A Guide to Women's Wisdom* (New York: Harper & Row, 1983).

SECTION 1.

The Ribbon around the Pentagon (August 4, 1985)/Porter Stone

WOMEN'S CREATIVITY

1. Women's Creativity

A Different Assessment

Male creativity is expressed in what is permanent: books, paintings, music, sculpture, buildings, bridges. All are solid monuments to the male desire to leave sturdy (and autographed) footprints in the sands of time. Women's creativity seems quite different. We do have women authors who finally can publish under their own names. The work of women artists is finally being exhibited in the new Museum for Women's Art in Washington, D.C. But so many women have poured out their creativity and never looked for acknowledgement. Judith Stone in "Creating the Possible" cites the feminist aphorism (and book title [1]), "'Anonymous' was a woman."

Think of the anonymous designs for quilts, the patterns for dresses, the recipes for wonderful food, the table settings, the flower arrangements, the countless insights into better ways of childrearing and keeping house. Think of the knitting knots devised and the patterns of knitting ranging from argyle to cable that women have created. Think of the crochet knots and patterns, think of the needlepoint and embroidery stitches. All of these "women's arts" have been freely donated to the culture, and the originator never recorded. Searching for the reason for such "irrepressible" creativity, Judith Stone says, "We have constantly looked high, when we should have been looking high and low." She ponders the meaning of such creativity for our world today.

Creative Attention

The "women's arts" are but one kind of creativity. Women also are amazingly creative as we balance our family's daily life, juggling meals and mealtimes, jobs, laundry, car pools, doctors' appointments and shopping, while in and around our lists and appointments all the time encouraging and motivating ourselves and everyone else. A woman walks the tightrope of her life as an accomplished high wire artist, making it look easy to juggle many balls while riding a bicycle and keeping aloft a pink parasol.

Perhaps women's basic creativity is most clear in the serious but subtle care we give to human relationships. A woman builds relationships around herself with the commitment and devotion with which a monk prays. The care and attention of her heart's eye and body's hand are devoted to all the deeply felt relationships of her life. We women take relationships very seriously, and we invest some of our best creativity in building, preserving and deepening relationships. Linda Weltner writes in "There's No Kin Like Kindred Spirits" about the dedication women bring to the art of friendship. "Friendship, that state of intimacy in which two individuals reveal and share their inner worlds, can be even more than a priority. To both of us, it's a necessity."

Women seem able to take down their masks to each other and share the innermost journeys of their lives. Ann Thompson Traver describes such sharing in "The Sacredness of Our Spiritual Journeys" and tells what it has meant to her own spiritual growth. "Being the journey-teller that day was a heady experience, and the privilege of having a circle of some twenty women listening to my story for an hour was rare and wonderful. The details of that morning have faded, but the joys of being listened to carefully and taken seriously remain."

Carol Goldman in "Creating Sacred Emotional Space" describes the functioning of a support group that for its participants sometimes seems "like a cloud by day and a pillar of fire by night" (Ex 13:21). "Because I have heard women talk honestly about illnesses, losses, violations, as well as about their promotions, ongoing relationships, and adventures, I am encouraged to talk about my own experiences in these areas." All women are on a liberation journey, as Carol Goldman is. We are coming out of bondage in some Egypt, moving through a wilderness, on toward some Promised Land. The bonding of women as we tell one another more and more about our lives helps us unlock the energy, the rage, the power which we need to fashion a new life for ourselves and for the world.

Women give to others and to one another constantly. Yet we often find it hard to discover the kind of creativity we need in order to birth ourselves into power. We find it easier to do it for others. Attorney Lois H. Grace Stovall describes the kind of creativity involved in one woman's journey of coming into her own woman-power. "I remember my decision to have my babysitter bring my baby to court so I could breastfeed her during breaks in a lengthy trial. . . . On one occasion I asked the judge for a recess to go out and nurse."

Corita Kent used her unique art to make a statement which supported and nurtured the liberating social causes she cared about. She died of cancer in the summer of 1986. "The Artist as Social Activist amid Adversity: How the Job Is Done" is one of the few times she talked in public about her life and her work. "For the Hospice Society on Cape Cod I chose a watercolor, and then I tried to make words which would be helpful not only to the people in the hospice movement itself but also to all of us, because we are all in a sense in or near the hospice movement. The words I chose were, 'This day is given to us; from it we make life.'"

Bloom Where You Are Planted

Male creativity seems to build for eternity, while women's creativity is expressed in what is perishable, transitory, fleeting, ephemeral. Women's creative impulses are invested in perishable foods, fleeting flower arrangements, sensitive relationships with people who grow old and die, in rearing children who grow up and go away. Why do we women express our creativity in these fleeting ways?

Perhaps women sense that there is a beauty in these gentle creations that gives a vital substance and flavor to life. It is not accidental that many men pause in their mid-life (as Gail Sheehy describes in *Passages*[2] and Eric Segal recounts in his novel *The Class*[3]), feeling that their own investment in the upward mobility of career has left them emotionally impoverished. The abundant wealth of relationships many women have at this period in their lives provides a stark contrast.

Women's creativity is a different kind of life-statement, a different kind of spirituality. It is a valuing of the moment, a living in the immediacy of flavor, aroma, flower and child. A *New Yorker* cartoon by Ross pictures a male executive at a boardroom meeting. A male assistant at his elbow says, "Your wife's on the phone. The azaleas are out." Women know that our lives are like playing the childhood game of Cat's Cradle. We are weavers of delicate webs of impermanence. We learn to find satisfactions in the relationships and transformations of changing lives. We know that, like the azaleas, each moment is a good time to bloom.

The Birthday Party

The room is all prepared for the party. Colored streamers fan out across the ceiling like spokes of a giant merry-go-round. The table is set with matching tablecloth and napkins; a centerpiece features a large sparkling number displaying the age of the child. The fancy cake, iced by loving hands and complete with birthday message, sits nearby ready to be cut. A pile of brightly wrapped presents is close at hand. Everything is ready for the party.

Most of us can imagine such a party because when we were children, our mothers gave them for us. The moment the cake is presented to us and everyone sings "Happy Birthday" is a moment of incredible affirmation of our own being. For a brief moment we are at the center of a caring universe and it is wonderful. Year after year women pour out all the creativity which we as children received as the love and attention of our birthday parties. Such parties honor relationships and celebrate our growing up year by year. The parties are brief, transitory moments that celebrate children who themselves are in constant transition.

Birthday parties are like Fourth of July fireworks, huge pinwheels of bursting color and excitement which momentarily light up our skies. They are epiphanies, brief manifestations of the divine creativity which holds the universe in place. The power of relationship holds the earth in its astronomical course and on its center. Physicist and cosmologist Brian Swimme calls this power "allurement." [4] Carter Heyward names this "power of relationship" God. [5] Women's creativity as embodied in birthday parties is a perception and celebration of the essential nature and transitoriness of life itself. It intuitively grasps the reality at the heart of the universe, the sacred connection, ever changing and ephemeral but ever strong.

The Ribbon around the Pentagon, movingly described in Judith Stone's chapter, celebrates a birthday party for all the future children of our world. There was all the creativity embroidered or painted into each woman's panel, and then each panel was loosely tied on each end to two other similar panels, symbolizing women's connections with one another in a common concern: we must preserve the earth for all our children. That will be the best birthday party for us all!

—Elizabeth Dodson Gray

NOTES

1. Mirra Bank, *Anonymous Was a Woman: A Celebration in Words and Images of Traditional American Art—and the Women Who Made It* (New York: St. Martin's Press, 1979).

2. Gail Sheehey, *Passages: Predictable Crises of Adult Life* (New York: E. P. Dutton, 1976).

3. Eric Segal, *The Class* (New York: Bantam Books, 1985).

4. Brian Swimme, *The Universe Is a Green Dragon: A Cosmic Creation Story* (Santa Fe, New Mexico: Bear & Co., 1985).

5. Isabel Carter Heyward, *The Redemption of God: A Theology of Mutual Relation* (Lanham, Maryland: University Press of America, 1982).

There's No Kin Like Kindred Spirits

Linda Weltner

*L*INDA *W*ELTNER *writes a weekly column that appears in the "At Home" section of the* B*OSTON* G*LOBE. Each Friday her readers learn about the pleasures, pressures and conflicts she experiences being the mother of two and wife of a child psychiatrist, working professionally as a writer, and being active in her community. She is a graduate of Wellesley College, and in 1985 she was named "best columnist" by the New England Women's Press Association. Her most recent book is* No Place Like Home: Rooms and Reflections from One Family's Life *(1988).*

A Circle of Friends

Marilyn began the birthday parties with a simple invitation to her forty-fifth birthday, one of those out-of-date postcards of our local Preston Beach littered with women in old-fashioned bathing suits. She summoned all her old friends—colleagues from a nursery school board, co-workers on political campaigns, former skiing buddies—to a celebration of her own making, a delicious lunch, cold glasses of wine, a cake she had decorated herself. This being a small town, the faces were all familiar, the rapport instantaneous.

"Coming together and looking forward to the future and enjoying each other's company so much was a great surprise," remembers Lee, the baby of the group at thirty-eight. "That was why we decided to continue."

We leaped at the opportunity to gather together month after month and gave ourselves the birthday parties of our girlhood dreams, choosing motifs dear to our hearts. One invitation read, "Bring a favorite book to share," while others prevailed upon us to adorn ourselves with favorite political buttons, or to come in costume as the kind of old lady we hoped to become.

At one party in the spring, we each brought cuttings from our gardens to exchange, and even as I write this, deep purple irises bloom by the garden wall to remind me of May's event. I wrote a poem for Marilyn's birthday and was appointed by acclamation to be "poetess birthicus"; Marilyn collected all my rhyming tributes and copied them into a book she gave me when my party came along.

I have 8x10 prints from five of the parties framed and hung in our entry hall downstairs, for Lee always came with her tripod and self-timing lever and took photographs into which she leaped at the last moment. They have become what photographer Elsa Dorfman calls "magic relics," photographs with the power to resurrect people and moments that the passage of time has carried into a new reality.

The women in the first photograph smile directly into the camera. Marilyn, the guest of honor at her forty-fifth birthday party is in the center, facing forward. Sitting around the circular oak table in her dining room, ten of us are ringed like a halo above her short dark hair. The pleasure we took in each other's company fills all the empty space; we gaze ahead, fixed in an eternally trusting now, but with the vantage point of five years' hindsight, I see behind each smiling figure the turning points we did not see coming.

Hidden from the Camera

"It was a time of reaching out to one another," says Maria who has since given up her full-time teaching job to work in the environmental field. "When I look back I see our innocence. There was less awareness then of the underlying themes of one another's lives."

Marilyn has since moved away to Washington. Looking at the photo, she seems to be already slipping beneath the picture's lower edge. Her dark hair merges with the sweater of the woman behind her; she too has moved, on to another town and a new career, leaving an empty space. The woman to her right has been ill with cancer, now cured. Another has since lost her mobility to multiple sclerosis. Two long-term marriages have recently ended in divorce; one woman has been abruptly widowed.

As I scan the faces, I see the differences between our lives then and now. Though we were not conscious that our time together had any special significance, time has passed on, leaving us mindful of how much it means to us to have been present in each other's lives.

"When you add the changes you can't control, like parents getting ill and children moving away, then add in the changes you choose to make," says Dodie, whose son was shot on the streets of Berkeley last year, "the mid-forties are tumultuous." She has sold the house where we celebrated her April birthday.

We could control the ingredients of the chocolate cheese-cakes and almond tortes that appeared each month as the birthday cake of choice, but Fate had a recipe for each of our futures which it refused to divulge. It bided its time that whole year, then took us aside and, whispering "Surprise," revealed it to us one by one at a time of Fate's own choosing.

The women who shared their birthdays, treasure the artifacts from those parties, especially Lee's photographs. Her prints hang in bathrooms and bedrooms all over town and are collected in albums as proof that we were able to draw comfort from our whimsical gatherings. Even the pain that hovered on the horizon—the mother with Alzheimer's who would soon move in, the glaucoma that was only temporarily under control—was eased by our meeting. We are joined by a bond as real and tangible as Lee's pictures even as the moments they have captured recede further and further into our pasts.

Marilyn created this ritual from an impulse to weave the people in her life together. Her wish made our friendship a monthly celebration, the occasion for teasing, and laughter, sharing and remembering. We knew we were joined in a life-sustaining endeavor; our coming together became a ceremony of communion, an expression of mutual support, a statement of community.

Then, by a single declaration, Marilyn declared the parties at an end by deciding not to start another go-round when she turned forty-six. We protested, but somehow the circle of birthdays felt complete, as if the parties were the markers by which we would always know one another even as our friendships became a matter of individual choice once more.

Today the photographs reveal what we could not see at the time: events beyond our dreaming await us.

But the year of the birthday parties offered us all the reassurance we needed that growing older is eased by the company of friends.

Best Friends

My best friend Lynn and I threw our birthday party together that year; it seemed natural and fitting that we should both have been born in October. We have been best friends for twenty years now, so long that our sentences mingle, our memories merge, and our lives are so entangled that even our families accept that there are no secrets between us.

We spend hours together in any given week, despite Lynn's job as a high school math teacher and my deadlines as a columnist for the *Boston Globe*. We live within walking distance of each other's houses, and our friendship is one of our major commitments.

Most people think we're a bit odd. They tease us when I show up at the chowder party Lynn organizes for the Democrats each year; they laugh when I arrive to give a talk to some women's group and bring Lynn along for company. They think it's strange that I have picked up her husband after work, and that she has taken my brother to the airport. Unlike most of the women we know, we see our lives as a joint undertaking.

Americans may be among the friendliest people on this earth, but by and large they are fair weather friends, fair weather being that portion of time they have set aside to socialize. Friendship is expected to flourish at parties, over meals, and during arranged visits, but the rest of our time we are supposed to spend on individual pursuits. We're supposed to protect our privacy, to move through the major portion of our lives alone or within our nuclear family.

I could never live that way again. Not since the summer Lynn and I stopped the Marblehead Light Department in their tracks.

One of the reasons Lynn and I decided to actively oppose our town's decision to buy nuclear power from Seabrook was because it was a legitimate opportunity to work together. We had our separate lives—our own jobs, our own families, our own sets of friends—and still do. But that summer we found ourselves attending meetings together, lobbying town officials in tandem, and handing out leaflets outside the movie house where "The China Syndrome" was playing.

Our companionship energized us, creating new ideas and new strategies. We discovered an amazing ability to cooperate, to mirror and expand one another's vision. We were still our separate selves, yet in our interaction there occurred a doubling of female consciousness and determination. We felt twice as powerful, twice as wise as we ever had alone. To keep the home fires burning while we challenged the system, we did our grocery shopping together, pooled our errands, and joined forces in raising our families. Somehow the drudgery became fun and the work became play.

A Fun Quota

And that was only the beginning. Alongside our serious enterprises, we invented what we call a fun quota, our cure for that nagging sense that one's perfectly sensible life is less than satisfying. We are grateful for the essentials of our lives—air, water, food and shelter. We appreciate the extras—good health, our families, sufficient funds, interesting lives. Yet in addition to all that we choose to do as mothers, wives and workers, we have added to our list of obligations the commitment to make things *fun.*

Whenever we feel adulthood hanging too heavily around our necks, we think up something silly and irresponsible and light- hearted. And then we do it together.

For the past three summers, for example, Lynn and I have prepared a fleet of inner tubes. We live in a yachting community which has raised the art of staying afloat in the ocean to a fine art, and so Lynn and I work at making our tubes seaworthy, putting names on them in fluorescent paint and decorating them with tubes of glitter intended for T-shirts.

The first year we had the Pastry, the Boob, the Stomach and the Toothpaste, each of course fully illustrated. The next year we came up with the Eustachian, the Bronchial and the Fallopian. Last year we christened our tubes the Ampli-tube, the Pulchritube and the Scholastic Aptitube Test. Having determined that our posteriors are impervious to cold, we set off together or with a friend for a nearby beach to tie our tubes together and drift, to talk, to merge with the elements, to take hours in the day which could be put to good use and utterly waste them.

Once we told ourselves that our children needed other children to play with, and so we packed them up and took them with us to tidal pools, children's plays, museums, anywhere that appealed to us. Now however our grown children no longer need us around all the time, and we have expanded our horizons to include attending the dedication of a Buddhist pagoda in western Massachusetts, spending a weekend of protest in Washington, and studying Spanish for a week at Dartmouth College.

The Other Side

Our husbands look upon our friendship with mixed emotions. They enjoy being drawn into the larger circle of two families, but sometimes they feel left out of the smaller circle Lynn and I have formed. They see the benefits of not having to be the sole provider for all our emotional needs; at the same time they sometimes regret the limitation on their power and influence that a best friend represents.

Still when crises occur, we all turn to Lynn's husband, a lawyer, for legal advice and to my husband, a psychiatrist, for medical and psychiatric reassurance. Lynn's oldest son is my computer consultant; her younger son is currently landscaping my husband's office. When my older daughter visits the person who will cater her wedding, she is taking both Lynn and me along to offer advice. It is true that more people in one's intimate space increase the opportunity for conflict and jealousy, but they also significantly increase the number of satisfying human contacts.

Lynn and I have also been able to create a safe space for each other in the midst of tragedy. Lynn helped me through the summer one daughter lay at home bedridden with a slipped disc. She mothered me when my husband was in the hospital with an undiagnosed gall bladder problem. She kept me company when I lay in bed one spring with a broken leg.

Then there was the time Lynn discovered a growth on her leg. She insisted the dermatologist remove it, and he sent it to a lab only because state law required it. Almost by chance Lynn discovered she had a melanoma, the most virulent form of cancer there is.

A surgeon operated. He made a small cut with large consequences for Lynn's life, leaving her ten days at home to await the pathologist's report. That Saturday a friend and I dragged Lynn to a potter's studio an hour away. She sobbed in the car all the way there, sure that the news would be bad. She cried as I bought a set of dishes, convinced she wouldn't live to eat off them. She wept all the way home, heartbroken that she would not see her children grow up.

That afternoon, and all through the long sad days and evenings that followed, Lynn cried, but not alone. No one suggested she cheer up. No one chided her for overlooking the brighter side of life. We all grieved together and in doing so felt how precious was every moment of our connection. We mourned together and in our shared sorrow we felt the healing power of human contact.

A Necessity of Life

Our friendship created a miracle even before we received news that the disease had been caught in time.

There was, I thought, no way to explain this. Then I heard a lecture that described the Greek ideal of friendship as an indispensable way of attaining the highest good. The Greeks felt that through constant dialogue and honest sharing, friends could reach a higher level of truth together than if they searched alone. The Greeks, it seems, believed that in addition to providing high doses of mutual affection over a long period of time, true friendship could introduce us to the best of ourselves and bring us earthly happiness.

In contrast, the low priority given claims of friendship in contemporary America results in a "deadly emotional impoverishment," said Harvard Divinity School professor Ralph Potter as he expressed his concern that we are becoming so performance-oriented as a nation that we can no longer delight in simply being friends.

Unlike those who view friendship as a self-indulgence or perhaps a pleasant adjunct to a busy life, Lynn and I consider our friendship a sacrament, a celebration of all that gives our lives meaning and direction. We find in our friendship a reason for joy, a source of self-revelation, and a place of comfort. This dimension of our lives, like marriage and motherhood, claims our creative energy, stirs our enthusiasm, seems worth any degree of effort.

Friendship, that state of intimacy in which two individuals reveal and share their inner worlds, can be even more than a priority.

To both of us, it's a necessity.

Creating Sacred Emotional Space

Carol Goldman

CAROL GOLDMAN is an artist whose colorful abstract acrylic paintings have been included in numerous shows and in the collections of individuals, banks, hospitals and corporations. She has her B.A. from Wellesley and an M.A. from Harvard. She has gained administrative experience working for non-profit organizations and uses this in her marketing and public relations consulting for small businesses. She is the mother of two young adults and has been in her second marriage for fifteen years. She is active in her temple, a Rosh Hodesh women's group, the Manic-Depressive and Depressive Association of Boston, and self-help programs fostering positive eating habits and creativity. Her personal journey of liberation she symbolizes as leaving behind building pyramids as a slave in Egypt to journey through the wilderness to a promised land.

The Basics

The basic format of our support group that runs in connection with the Theological Opportunities Program [TOP] is simple. We gather chairs in a circle, and one after another we go in succession around our circle. Each of us in turn talks while the others listen. What each talks about is where she is right now in her life. Each one begins in the same way, identifying herself and her community, because often some of the women present are there for the first time. "I am Carol," I say, "I'm from Watertown." And then while the others in the circle listen, I talk about what is going on at this time in my life.

We talk about specifics. It may be something that has happened, or an issue in my life or an insight I have had. It may be about personal interactions or feelings. Or I may talk about an ordinary or extraordinary occurrence in my life. I may speak for five minutes or ten, or occasionally one of us may need half an hour to fill in complicated background. No one interrupts me; they just hear me out. They listen. I can explore the full range of my experience. I don't need to present a false self or a facade to be acceptable. I feel welcome and heard, whether that day I see myself as successful, self-sufficient, accomplished, creative—or as bumbling, inarticulate, inadequate. Or as somewhere in between. I find this freedom to speak from my inner self and be heard is a sacred experience.

Thursdays at Ten

Our support group meets every Thursday morning at ten. Except when the Theological Opportunities Program has its fall or spring lecture series in October–November and April–May. And we do not meet on Thanksgiving Day!

Women hear about the support group through the lecture series and from others who have attended the support group. We range in age from thirty to eighty-five. We are single, married, divorced. Some of us live by ourselves, some of us nurture husbands, children, and older parents. Some women are concerned about their careers, others about causes or organizations in which they are active. We include housewives, therapists, congregational leaders, activists, students, scholars, professors. One regular is a management executive in manufacturing for a major national firm. Many of us arrange our professional and personal lives to allow us to come regularly. This group is a priority in our lives. There are other women who come whenever possible or when they have a special issue or need to share with the group.

Meetings range in size from five to twenty; sometimes the group is as large as thirty. Whatever the size, everyone present has a chance to be heard. When your turn comes around, you can pass, saying "I don't have anything to say right now." But most of us do speak each week because that, and being heard, is a major reason we come. If the group is not too large, you can ask for a response if you want to. When we are asked to respond, we try not to judge each other. We know that each of us is doing the best we can and that we are all living different lives. We try not to come up with "pat" solutions. We are there to listen respectfully and thoughtfully to one another talking about what are often very personal aspects of our lives.

I have come to realize that outside the support group people often listen differently to one another. Sometimes I find myself with people who are intent upon getting a task done, and they are too busy either to "talk" or "listen to talk" about our personal lives. At other times I am with people who do not want to hear what I have to say about my life and act as if they have heard my story before and are not interested in my feelings. In our support group I find we listen to one another with enthusiasm, openness, and with empathy. Such "being listened to with love" I regard as sacred.

A Space Made Safe

I am willing to be vulnerable in the support group because I feel safe. The entire process of the group, its ways of doing things, is one in which I know I am included. Each of us is included. It is a safe and open process in which there is no hierarchical leader with authority or power-over. The guiding principle is that we listen to one another, and from this we decide together how the group will be conducted.

No one is the designated leader of the support group, but there is opportunity for individuals to exert leadership in the group. If something happens within the group that is somehow objectionable to some (or to all), or if someone wants to suggest we try a variation in our usual format, the group as a whole discusses this and together we arrive at a consensus about how it should be handled. At times I am disappointed at a particular outcome, but I know my ideas have been heard and considered. The group has evolved a structure which is firm enough to provide stability, but flexible enough to allow for experimentation and change.

There are no requirements for membership. We all come to the fall and spring lecture series (which have modest fees). But there are no fees or attendance requirements for the support group. It is literally open. Any woman who hears of the group and comes is included. I suppose that the fundamental requirement is that you are able to listen. That seems even more fundamental than being able to speak. We all attend as our time, desire, and energy permit. We do not gossip. We do not betray confidences. We are not in a rush. We are not getting together because we have to, but because we want to. We have no group goal such as making money, manufacturing a product, or dealing with a local or global issue —although individuals might want to talk about these sometimes. I note an enormous sense of relief and peacefulness in going every week to a place where my friends consider me for who I am, not what I do. I find this group process itself seems sacred.

Connecting Which Is Sacred

I relish the consistency and coherence which attending the TOP support group gives to my life. Because I have heard women talk honestly about illnesses, losses, violations, as well as about their promotions, ongoing relationships, and adventures, I am encouraged to talk about my own experiences in these areas. I have witnessed how the group responds with love and caring to one another. I am buoyed up as I approach my day-to-day routine because I don't feel isolated or stranded. I am inspired to take risks, try new behaviors, and share the outcome with the group. I find this opportunity to connect with other women whom I admire, respect, care for and enjoy is sacred.

Being a part of this support group has helped me to see my own life in a new perspective. I was not an isolated voice but an important part of a collection of voices. My feelings of invalidation as a child I found were not unique. I was not the only woman who believed that being sad, angry, grumpy, scared, sexual, or assertive made her parents uncomfortable. The sense of terror, panic and failure I experienced when my first husband left me when our son was seventeen months old and our daughter was six weeks old was not incomprehensible to others. In the support group I could share sadness and happiness—and feel heard and understood.

Within the support group I have explored for myself the Exodus metaphor of the Jews being freed from slavery in Egypt and then traveling in a desert until they arrived at Sinai and entered into a covenant with God. In my own past I clung to the equivalent of building pyramids in Egypt; I felt secure and comfortable doing only what was demanded and expected. As a child, wife, parent, employee, I wanted desperately to fit in. I believed abandoning the role of the slave would lead to my being totally rejected. I could not envision myself as an ex-slave. I was scared, I was afraid to cross the Red Sea and leave the life to which I had become accustomed. Could I exist as a nomad in the desert? Could I trust the guidance of the cloud by day and the pillar of fire by night (Ex. 13)? Could I leave slavery behind and claim the responsibility, power, freedom, joy, and community awaiting me at Sinai?

I was nourished on my personal journey across the desert by the positive response and attention I received from the support group, by the gentle challenges, the probing questions. Then when I told the group that I wanted to celebrate my birthday with my TOP friends, the next Thursday I was greeted with a marvelous surprise party which I felt honored my excitement at what I considered escape from slavery and my arrival at Sinai. This friendship, this encouragement, has been for me sacred.

Listening to Different Voices

Among those of us who come to TOP and to the support group there are many different theologies, values we hold important, lifestyles, viewpoints, histories, preferences, passions and choices about life. We sometimes irritate each other. Yet we come together as a group to hear and be heard, to tell one another our stories, and to hear the life stories of our friends. We speak in the first person, "I." We claim our own voices. One voice can connect with another voice to begin weaving a tapestry. As we talk together, we are spinning and weaving a collective oral history out of our individual lives and contributions. Sharing our authentic voices is to me sacred, and the community emerging from our shared ritual of listening is surely sacred.

I am an abstract painter, and I love to see lines and forms collide and interact with each other, forming various patterns and new designs. What follows now is a collage of responses by members of the support group. These were written by participants in the support group one Thursday in response to their hearing me read this description of my own experience of the group.

"In turn we give our name, speak our concern, our need, our delight. Slowly but surely with the naming, with the sharing, we become persons in our own right." The becoming of personhood is sacred.

"We meet because we each choose to. We create no group goals other than to receive with full attention what each wishes to share with us. We do this with the knowledge that each one will deal with our feelings and choices in ways which fit us individually and differently. I feel accepted, appreciated, and encouraged as myself, for the self which I can express at TOP and cannot often express in any other group setting, the self defined not by career and work but by being and by relating." Listening deeply and attentively to another woman is sacred.

"The discipline of attuning myself to another—looking attentively, listening hard, reaching out with empathy to someone who is suffering, sharing joy and accomplishment and laughter—all this feels to me like tuning in to the affirmation with which God sustains the entire universe. When I am away from the support group, it is the deep discipline of affirmative listening which I miss most."

"All aspects of our being and our living are acceptable to discuss in the support group, and our feelings about them are heard. Listening is valuable; what one woman says specifically to another so often provides insight and support to the rest of us as well." Creating a big pile of spiritual energy is sacred.

"I go out from our meetings revitalized by being involved and absorbed in the experiences of others which have been shared. I am not adept at sharing in this way at this point in time and where I am in my life-behavior span. Therefore, this revitalizing effect of being part of my friends' lives is vital to me and nourishes me."

"Having found TOP, I feel like a hungry person who is offered fine cake—it is what is wanted, and the more that is consumed, the more is wanted."

"It has been an inspiration to continue on my spiritual journey confirmed by the strength of the group and buttressed by the consistent loving that is a rare and unexpected gift to me." Weaving a tapestry of support is sacred.

"The sacredness of the support group is for me in the tapestry woven by my long-term participation. Often I listen long and speak short. Sometimes the opposite. But the piece of goods I have participated in weaving is a mantle of support that I keep wrapped around me all the time. The sacred support of TOP is very important in my life. I like taking my turn at being warp, weft, shuttle, weaver, and loom."

"My only daughter was in a severe automobile accident last year. I was held —or suspended—by the TOP organism which miraculously set in motion streamlined organizational support, hand-holding and inspiration. At the end of a long day sitting by my daughter hooked up to machines in intensive care and unable to speak, I was greeted by messages of acknowledgement, hope, concern and caring."

The Ritual of Our Circle

For many of us, the journey to Sinai is fraught with landmines and quicksands. We are adventurers in unfamiliar territory. We have had to function within patriarchal structures which treated women as invisible and subservient. We have managed to create an environment which allows us to reclaim and experience our own power and autonomy. In the safety of our sacred circle of companionship and sharing, we can gather our energy and spirit to try new ideas and ways of behaving. For many of us, we can share our deepest secrets, frustrations, hurts, dreams. We can dare to name our suffering and our striving and in the process begin our healing and begin our efforts to implement our visions. To name past traumas and to identify new challenges and opportunities is part of our effort to find our "voice" and make it heard.

For a time we tried to think of a closing ritual for our group meetings. We tried holding hands and passing along our energies. We sang moving songs such as Chris Williamson's "Song of the Soul." But what we did not realize until just recently is that we already were doing a powerful and meaningful ritual. We had neglected to see our process of sharing in our circle as the moving ritual it is. We had not recognized as a sacred ritual what we were already doing. We knew it was a very special time but we had not thought of sacred ritual as being as mundane and ordinary as our own talking and listening about our lives.

We have found that we do not need sacramental gowns, vested authority, exclusive language, formalized prayers, designated icons or special buildings, for our ritual to take place. Our ritual emanates from the core of our being and from the group process. Our ritual was developed gradually over the years by consensus, to meet our own needs.

Taking Part in a Birth

When I started out coming to the support group, I had really felt that the TOP lectures were intellectually and spiritually stimulating. I viewed the support group as more of an indulgence that I allowed myself. I enjoyed it and felt supported by the group but I did not see myself as doing something spiritually significant. But when I attended a TOP lecture by the authors of *This Way Daybreak Comes: Women's Values and the Future,*[1] I realized that ordinary activities can be extremely important. I often diminish, discount and belittle what I actually do on a daily basis. But I now feel that finding my own voice and listening and connecting to the voices of other women so that together we form a collective women's voice, is sacred work.

What I do today in the support group is no different because of this realization. What is different is that now I realize that what I have already been doing is extremely significant not on for me but for women in general. My actions have not changed; what has changed is the value I assign to my actions. I see my ongoing consistent commitment and participation in the support group as a sacred activity. I respect, admire and am in awe of the ritual I and the group create each time we meet.

What we do is important not only to us as individuals but to us as a group. It is important also as a part of women in general finding their voice. As we bring our experiences into words and find for them a voice, our voice, we are doing an important thing for other women. Women's values are being born here as we share our lives with other women. A women's process is being shaped. In our listening and in our speaking out we are fashioning together a women's culture. It is a culture that recognizes, attends to, supports, and honors women—women's contributions and women's experiences and women's perspectives upon life. To be part of such a birthing is a sacred experience.

Notes

1. Annie Cheatham and Mary Clare Powell, *This Way Daybreak Comes: Women's Values and the Future* (Philadelphia: New Society Publishers, 1986).

A Woman's Path to Power
as a Sacred Process

Lois H. Grace Stovall

Lois H. Grace Stovall is a southern woman "almost forty" who is a practicing lawyer, feminist, clergywife, and mother of a young daughter. She is "determined to have it all" and also be true to herself. "I am proud of increasingly having the courage to live my life my way—to satisfy my need and desire to have time with my child and still honor my need to continue my own inner journey AND have a career." She grew up in Atlanta, attended college in North Carolina, immediately went on to law school, and now practices law in Washington, D.C. Her religious background is Southern Baptist but she is presently active in an ecumenical Christian community in Washington, D.C. Of her leadership in that congregation, she says: "I am very interested in finding rituals and metaphors to help us and our children celebrate life events in a non-sexist, non-racist, liberating sacred space. I have designed some pretty wild child-inclusive worship services!"

No Longer "Girls"

I began to name and claim my woman-power many years ago in North Carolina when I was a college sophomore. The year was 1969. During an open forum for both faculty and students I protested the curfew hours imposed on female students but not on males. In my impromptu statement I referred to the female students as "women." Afterward the chaplain of the university remarked that, by calling the female students "women" rather than "girls," I had named a new social reality on that campus.

This naming sprang spontaneously out of my own journey. It was a part of my defining who I was. It grew out of my personal family history as well as out of the social circumstances around me. I had not planned that naming but somehow I was open to expressing in this way the energy which I felt welling up within me and around me. "Women's experience, expressed in [such] ferment," writes Elizabeth Janeway, "is not just a measure of change but also a sensitive guide to the future." [1] Across my campus and across America "girls" of all ages were renaming themselves "women."

As I reflect today upon the process by which I have come to claim more and more of my own power, I realize I experience my creativity being released as I live out of my core self. I recall a recent job interview after we moved to Washington, D.C.:

"I wonder whether a woman will have the same commitment to this job." A senior partner was interviewing me for a position as a family law specialist in his Capital Area law firm. "Women like you have so many distractions, children and all. And I am disturbed by the word 'part-time.'"

I was taken aback.

I didn't know whether he was serious or baiting me. Probably both. After ten years being successfully self-employed as a lawyer, I knew I had good skills. But I also knew my chances of finding part-time work as a trial attorney were slim. Other lawyers told me it could not be done. But I was convinced that the right option for me was combining lawyering, childcare and parenting. What I did not yet know was whether any firm in the Capital Area would give me the chance to show that I could be effective with a less-than-full-time schedule.

"Sir, our society calls what I want to do 'part-time.' But I assure you that when I practice law, whatever the number of hours, I am committed to high-quality performance. However if you are looking for someone who lives and breathes this job, then don't offer me the position. I have other very important interests in my life, especially my child and family. I not only believe my priorities are right for me. I think the whole world would be a better place if we began giving more time and space to our whole lives, not just to our paid work."

I could sense my energy flowing through me as I claimed once again who I am. Whether I got the job offer or not, I recognized my words as declaring a growing integration of my personal pilgrimage as an individual and my calling to help make the world a better place.

Power, as I am using the word, is the exercise of who I am as I act out of my most authentic self. I know that the forces released when I use my power can be demonic, that sometimes use of my power constricts others in their discovery and exercise of their gifts. I can see this with my daughter when I impose my need for control and direct her toward goals that are exclusively mine (rather than ours), or when I use my power to satisfy my need to acquire more and more possession of things, people, myself. Other times, though, the energy released as I claim my power and use it can be simply bursting with creativity. This occurs when I embrace my own capacity to be whole and to be fully human with all its joy and suffering. Then my individual power is transformed into a meaningful moment of grace-filled creativity contributing to the whole planet's movement into wholeness and well-being. In such moments I am engaged in a sacred process. Claiming my power becomes transforming not only for me but for others as well.

Experiencing the Dark Side of Coming into My Own Power

I had been prepared by my family and my educational opportunities to become a lawyer. I became a partner in a small law firm in a medium-sized city in North Carolina. I was also a political and social activist. I nurtured political connections and I paid my dues in various social-action enterprises. After a number of years I was asked by several politically strategic men to run for judge. I was primed and ready to climb the ladder of my professional world.

I was also suffering from recurrent bouts of depression. I think now that the reason I could not capitalize upon the traditional power I was amassing was because I had not yet done the inner work on myself that I needed to do to sustain and inform me in my social quest. [2] I began to realize that my peers were almost all men and that my path to success was indistinguishable from theirs. Being a judge—or a legislator, or president of a company, or President of the United States—needs to be within our vision as women and be made a reality. But I was finding that the path I was taking to such power in society was not one that was true to who I was as a woman. It was not the *power* that felt off-center, but the *process* I was following to claim the power. My depressions were telling me this. I knew it, for I was somehow not at peace with myself. I had many regrets as I turned down the offer of help from the men who wanted to support me politically.

Perhaps I lost forever the opportunity for political office. But as important as full political and social power is for women and for the world, I am convinced that the time was not right for me. I had neglected developing a grounded self. I think I had done this partially out of my fear of becoming the type of woman who is a nurturing caretaker and who never moves to claim her rightful place in the world. I was disdainful of such women, who feared the dark side of their power and were afraid that exerting power meant controlling and hurting other people. Today I am able to accept more readily that the dark destructive side of power is inevitable whenever we lose touch with our authentic selves, and that women's power needs to keep in touch with women's connectedness to other women (and men) so that we exercise our power with accountability and in community. I will come back to this later.

Naming Myself and My Power When Married

Ten years after I first named my social identity as "woman," I stood at the brink of marriage. At this point I began another, more individual, naming process. This one also helped me clarify in a new way who I was (and am). I was engaged to be married and my maiden name was not something I was willing to give up. What would my name be after I was married? Patrick and I both believed our marriage had great creative potential, and we wanted to communicate to the world our new shared identity as a couple.

We considered various alternatives. Patrick finally suggested we both take a new additional name. I was concerned that, with any name we chose, the society we live in would soon convert mine to Mrs. Patrick Newname, and I would still lose my birth name. So we decided to adopt a shared name but to place our new "married" name in front of our individual last names of birth.

We designed a process for choosing our name that protected each of us from exerting any pressure, real or suspected, in favor of a name that might not be the real choice of the other. We each made a list of potential new names and exchanged them without comment. We prayed about the list and marked off names we could not live with. We added to our own list a name the other had on hers/his that we liked and exchanged lists, again without comment. Eventually we narrowed our choices to three names that we both liked a lot. Only then did we discuss our feelings and partiality for a certain name. We chose the name "Grace," and each of us legally changed our names to add Grace, while keeping our original birth names. I became Lois Helena Grace Stovall and he became

Patrick William Grace Conover. When our daughter Samantha was born, we gave her our "married" common name, her last name becoming Grace.

We continue to receive raised eyebrows and rolling eyes from peers in our respective very-traditional professions. But our family name of Grace gives us ample opportunities to testify to the importance of naming. Grace is that part of my name which symbolizes my own call to the sacred empowering process that is a daily part of my life. It also symbolizes to me my calling to be creative in the face of options that otherwise are unacceptable.

Respecting Our Fears and Choosing Our Sacrifices

Naming, as important as that process can be, cannot by itself enable us fully to claim our power. We must also deal with our fears and learn to distinguish between "transformative sacrifice" and what Carol Pearson has called "mere suffering caused because we are too cowardly or too unimaginative to think of a more joyous way to live." [3]

Some women allow their fears to immobilize them. They then turn away from the sometimes painful process of remembering who we are in our personhood and as a part of a larger social group. Others of us ignore our fears in an effort to accomplish goals at whatever the cost. We do this by blocking off from ourselves crucial information that our bodily fears can provide us.

Several years ago I had to be carried off a ski slope when at the end of a long day on my very first day of snow skiing I took some careless risks and fell. I remember telling a friend immediately prior to the accident as we were going up on the ski lift how tired I was, and that perhaps I was being foolish to go on this slope one more time. In my fall I seriously damaged my knee. Knee surgery followed, and I went through a long recovery and lots of pain. I had time to reflect upon the circumstances around the accident.

I realized that I had been afraid. But I had ignored my own body signals and even my own words. If I had paid attention to them I might have made the same decision. I might have decided the risk was worth taking. But I would have had the benefit of knowing, acknowledging, that I was tired and I could have taken that into account. I gradually began to connect this experience with other times in my life when I had steamrollered over my fears. I had done this particularly in the early years of my law career. It was no wonder I was so exhausted after those early successful career years. In my climb up the ladder I had lost touch with my center. The result for me was frequent depressions.

My skiing accident happened at a time in my life when I was more conscious of my inner journey. But I was seeking to control even my body's awareness of danger. I had blocked the very senses which I needed to use my skills and capabilities responsibly. I am now learning that it is only when I respect my fears and listen to my body that I have access to information that helps me discern whether the sacrifice or suffering I am contemplating will be transformative or will involve me in giving away a part of myself which needs to be protected and nurtured. [4]

Naming ourselves, respecting our fears, choosing our sacrifices—these are all part of the sacred process of claiming our power in the midst of relationships. As we become attuned to these aspects of ourselves, we develop into autonomous individuals capable of nurturing ourselves in the midst of nurturing others.

Transforming "Poisoned Apples"

In *Kiss Sleeping Beauty Goodbye* Madonna Kolbenschlag writes, "A woman who gives birth to a child long before she has given birth to herself faces the impossible task of raising an autonomous daughter."[5] Like Snow White and the Queen mother, we are condemned to repeat the pattern of presenting our daughters with poisoned apples because of our damaged egos, and having our daughters accept our poisoned lack of self-love and respect. The creative alternative is that we break out of our destructive interaction through transforming its hold on us as we reach for what Kolbenschlag calls "ethical autonomy."

For me, breaking the pattern has involved a step by step process—not always forward or backward, but sometimes around and through—a process of expanding my self-image so that I am capable of managing my own power.

I need to open myself to the healing of the wounds to my self-respect and to my self-love which I have suffered in the environment of our culture. Otherwise my unresolved rage and rebellion will hinder my creative use of my power in my most intimate relationships, especially with Patrick and Samantha. Without this painstaking work, my power can indeed be destructive. For a woman lacking sufficient self-love and respect, her rage too often turns back upon herself, reinforcing the culture's voices, as Marge Piercy suggests with these echoes of words many of us have heard:

> . . . ugly, bad girl, bitch, nag, shrill, witch,
> ballbuster, nobody will ever love you back,
> why aren't you feminine, why aren't
> you soft, why aren't you quiet, why
> aren't you dead?[6]

A Breast-feeding Lawyer

As I expand my view of personal power, I know it to be inseparable from the ordinary processes of living. I remember my decision to have my babysitter bring my baby to court so I could breastfeed her during breaks in a lengthy trial. Unfortunately the breaks did not always correspond to my body's schedule and the baby's. On one occasion I asked the judge for a recess to go out and nurse.

I worried about the effect my request would have on his respect for me and for other female attorneys. However I believed my choice to be the correct and authentic one for me. I was balancing as best I could the demands of court and my own needs and those of my child. How delighted I felt several months later when the same judge announced to all waiting lawyers and witnesses, "We will be recessing early today because I am going to attend an event very important to my children. If nursing mothers can ask for recesses, so can I." My actions had come out of my own very personal struggle to meet competing demands in a creative manner, and now they had somehow freed up this male judge so he was acting according to his own search for balance. We cannot control how our actions will be received. But when our choices reflect a clear and honest response to a given set of circumstances, our actions can sometimes take on transformative power and surprising creativity.

Confronting (and Being Confronted by) a Husband's Work-setting

For many women our lives are inextricably entwined with a male partner. Even if we are fortunate enough to have a partner who is on a compatible journey, sometimes other people or the institutions of which we are a part and which we serve may seek to limit our free expression of who we are. At such times our being participants in a supportive community of understanding and encouragement becomes especially important.

Several years ago my husband was asked to leave the church he was pastoring. We had been warned that his active role in efforts for world peace and nuclear disarmament education in our city had evoked criticism from certain church leaders. Problems escalated when our child was born. My husband cared for Samantha in the mornings while I worked, and he then worked in the afternoons and evening and weekends. This situation became intolerable to the governing board of the church, which sent representatives to forbid my husband from "babysitting" in the mornings. This pronouncement came despite many positive words from elderly and shut-in members of the church who were delighted when my husband brought our baby along on morning visits to them, and despite the back-up arrangements we had made to provide for the possibility of emergencies affecting parish members.

My husband was understanding through all this and sought to use the confrontation with the church leadership as a means of helping people to grow. But I was furious. And I knew that to vent my rage, to be who I was, would only add to my husband's problems. Already I had heard rumors suggesting that it was I who was causing my husband to lose his job by my insisting that he "babysit" (Why is male parenting called baby sitting?), by my ordering him to use inclusive language in the worship services, and by my refusal to fulfill the role of minister's wife properly.

I recognized that I should "rise above it all," but I felt threatened. Patrick and I were committed to caring for our child without day care for her first two years while each of us continued our careers. If my husband lost his church job, one that by definition had to be flexible but that was thereby compatible with our complex career and childrearing commitments, we knew our options in all these matters would be severely limited. It seemed unbelievable that the church would force my husband out because of his stands on peace and family! And I felt insulted at the criticism he was receiving for parenting four hours a day for only five days a week, as though he were the primary parent rather than I who was caring for Samantha every afternoon and most evenings and weekends.

I had so many things I wanted to say and do, and I felt powerless to do or say any of them. My rage towards the institutional church and the patriarchal aspects of Christianity had simmered at the boiling point for years, and it surfaced now without any appropriate outlets. Most of my feminist friends discounted anything religious and could not be sympathetic to the grief that was mixed with my rage. I felt alone. My church friends could not understand the importance to me of maintaining my career when I had a baby at home. If ever we needed understanding and supportive friends it was then. Both my husband and I were trying so hard to be true to ourselves, and we felt punished and alone.

Gathering a Core Community to Help the Emerging Core Self

We began to identify among our friends some who were also engaged in struggles over issues of religious faith and personal liberation. We invited them to meet at our house weekly in what grew to be a dynamic and highly committed group of four women and two men. We met every Sunday night for the next two years. This group became a setting where I could voice my frustration and anger when finally my husband did lose his job. I received support from this small community and encouragement to explore the complex sources of my anger. We became what we called "spiritually accountable" to one another. In time this group of six enabled several of us to take risks in our work and political spheres because we knew we were not alone. We had become for one another a corporate expression of our collective power.

What I have learned as I grow in community is that the sacred process of claiming one's power is not reserved just for a person's individual pilgrimage. The transforming element of courageously creating options can also be present as together with others I take on the evils of our society. To act together provides sustenance. To always fight alone is to risk our sanity and our ability to remain true to our identity and central commitments.

The confirmation of my choices by friends in a core community has been essential to my discovery and application of my powers. My core community has provided me with accountability as well as support and understanding. I have found new gifts and new powers being called forth from me by the combination of challenging circumstances and the presence in my life of those who really see me and can name who I am.

For Ourselves—and On Behalf of Others

Creating new choices for myself, not just accepting the culture's definitions of my choices, must evolve into more than fierce individualism. Otherwise transformation cannot occur. [7] Integration of my personal pilgrimage as an individual and my social one as an activist lawyer is an arduous task for me. It is still far from complete. I sense that women as a group are at a critical point in our quest for personal and social power. We have nurtured and given to others for so long and often to our own detriment. It is our turn now, we want to say. Now we must take care of ourselves. And yes, we must.

But we cannot afford to forget our sacrifices, and those of our mothers and grandmothers. Sacrifices have been made for us and for the world we have today, and there are sacrifices that we, in our power, must also be prepared to make. We must by trial and error determine the "appropriate and courageous response"[8] to the actual needs of our specific situation. We must not yield to the temptation to claim our power and, like the yuppie stereotype, grasp it only for ourselves. We certainly must enter every hallowed hall of the corporate and political power brokers of our society. But our world community cannot afford for women to accept its traditional benchmarks of power; our world remains too close to social disintegration and self-annihilation for that.

Many of us tremble on the frontier of innovation where we know we are being challenged to integrate our collective social identity as women and who we are as individuals, discovered and claimed through painful journeys. Tremendous energy (or power) is being released for each of us personally and for our world as this integration begins to occur. Whether this power transforms us and our planet remains beyond our control. Such transformation is a matter of grace and mystery. But the process will be sacred and meaningful if we accept our responsibility for our power and seek to create with it choices which are liberating and life-giving. When I make such choices, I align myself across economic, geographical, age and other barriers with all others making such choices.

We need to acknowledge with joy our heritage as nurturers and caretakers but balance that inheritance with our developing skills as managers, inventors and world leaders. We can learn to flow between our inner hunger for authenticity and our outer yearning for visibility and the capacities to bring about change. We must remember that it is not our power itself that is sacred. My power emerges from the wellsprings of who I am and reaches out to touch and connect with the lives of other women on similar journeys. This empowerment differs profoundly from the hierarchical control which imposes unity on all for a predetermined goal formulated by the powerful few. A woman's path to power is more like engaging life's energies in a swirling movement filling us up, out, into wholeness. That movement embodies the sacred, and it prepares our bodyselves[9] and our earth for the gift of transformation.

NOTES

1. Elizabeth Janeway, *Powers of the Weak* (New York: Morrow Quill Paperback, 1980), p. 11.

2. Carol Christ, *Diving Deep and Surfacing* (Boston: Beacon Press, 1980), p. 11. Her words about a woman's spiritual quest supporting her social quest were important to me when I felt burned out from my activist involvements.

3. Carol Pearson, *The Hero Within* (New York: Harper & Row, 1986), p. 109. She helps me name myself by writing about the different phases of our personal journey that weave in and out of our lives.

4. Pearson, p. 111. She helps me understand the positive aspects of the martyr and the need to choose our sacrifices.

. 5. Madonna Kolbenschlag, *Kiss Sleeping Beauty Goodbye* (Garden City, N.Y.: Doubleday, 1979), p.46.

6. Marge Piercy, "For strong women," in *The Moon Is Always Female* (New York: Alfred A. Knopf, 1986), pp. 56–57. Another portion of this poem that relates to my perception of woman-power: "Until we are all strong together, a strong woman is a woman afraid."

7. Robert N. Bellah, Richard Madsen, William M. Sullivan, Ann Swidler and Steven M. Tipton, *Habits of the Heart* (Berkeley and Los Angeles, Calif.: University of California Press, 1985), esp. pp. 275–296. The cultural mythology about individualism is another tradition women need to help transform for the good of the earth.

8. Pearson, p. 104.

9. "Bodyselves" is James Nelson's word in his book *Embodiment* (Minneapolis: Augsburg Publishing, 1978).

The Sacredness of Our Spiritual Journeys

Ann Thompson Traver

ANN THOMPSON TRAVER takes spiritual journeys seriously because she herself has been on one. Married twice, with two grown daughters, "I reached the place where I believed I was a woman with a story worth telling, a story uniquely mine and yet filled with universal truth." She says of herself, "I don't think of myself as a fascinating person. What I like about myself is that I keep developing all aspects of myself. I work hard at balancing lots of different parts of me in my life." She designs and builds stained glass windows in partnership with her second husband. "My proudest moment professionally came when we installed a series of four windows at my alma mater, Mount Holyoke College."

My first introduction to TOP came five years ago when I went to hear a lecture by Krister Stendahl on "Violence in the Biblical Tradition." I had heard Krister speak in Andover in the fall of 1981, and the impression of his kindness, wit, intelligence, warmth and wonderful spirituality stayed with me long after I had forgotten his exact words. Then a friend told me that Krister was lecturing in Cambridge and, being free that lovely spring day, I went to Harvard Divinity School, wondering what I would encounter. While I was pleased to reconnect with Krister's presence, what I found was that the real pull of the Theological Opportunities Program for me was to be not the lectures but the kindness, wit, intelligence, warmth and wonderful spirituality of the faith community of TOP women.

When a flyer came in the mail describing a mid-winter TOP program, I was intrigued. The idea was simple: women sharing their personal life stories, their spiritual journeys, with each other. The words of the announcement rang a bell for me, and I knew I was being called softly but surely to a new pathway, a sacred space.

I remember still the wonder and power of those first stories that I heard:

- Carolyn, who is now in her eighties, recounted wonderfully colorful stories of being an adventurous woman in the 1920s, of her China travels with her sister, and her very happy long-lasting marriage. My inner self resonates still as I remember Carolyn telling how she, a rather traditional woman in her family relationships, welcomed into her home her daughter-in-law who needed a place to heal and to live after divorce from Carolyn's son.

- Marlane's story was filled with fascinating accounts of her early adult life in Paris and her work in theater and music, but the part that touched me most deeply was her account from her childhood memories of the first bombers flying over her Holland home in the early days of World War II.

- Argena told of the color and joy brought into her life as the devoted wife of an artist. I was particularly moved by her stories of how she was spiritually enriched when sharing her love and understanding of life with others, especially young people.

- Charlene showed a program of slides that she and her daughter had created. Their work on comparing the early suffragist movement with the contemporary struggle for adoption of the ERA was a wonderful example of how mothers and daughters can work together and complement each other. I have often held up the model of Charlene and Jan as a guidelight when I have been searching for better mother/daughter harmony in my own life.

- Alice shared perhaps the most moving story of all. Her sacred journey took her from the depths of horror during childhood abuse to the place where she could lead workshops the world over, teaching others a message of love and ways of peace.

As I got to know many of the TOP women, I realized that on the surface we were a very average, normal group of middle- and upper-middle-class mostly-white women. So it was that we had the privilege of being able to carve out a piece of time on Thursday mornings to spend together. But even as I knew we were ordinary as individuals, I was awed over and over again by the power of our group. It was my first experience of the way power *with* is different from power *over*, and watching the way we were able to empower each other as we shared and listened and grew together was a real eye-opener.

The positive energy I gained (and continue to gain) from the group came in large measure from the deepening sense of belonging that I felt as I listened to the spiritual journeys of other women. I knew that for me a desire to deepen my own spirituality was both at the center of my own life and my life with TOP. At first, I was very hesitant to think of telling my own story, fearing that mine might not be sacred or spiritual enough. Nonetheless, I felt constantly drawn to participate in the cyclical nature of the group: lecture series, planning process, support group, spiritual journeys, and then a new lecture series. As time passed, I came to know and be known by others while sharing steadily in the group process. I hungered for nourishment to my own spirit, wanting to hear more and more accounts of the life stories of other women. Finally I came to understand that the most effective spiritual nourishment for me would come when I was ready to tell my own story. It took three years for me to get to that place.

In January of 1986 I was beginning my fiftieth year. As I looked forward with great joy and anticipation to the milestone of turning fifty, it seemed the perfect time to look back over my own life and reflect on my spiritual pathway. But the questions came tumbling out. What *is* a spiritual journey? What is unique to *my* story? Setting my doubting questions aside I hoped I would find some answers as I went through the process of preparing to share my own story with this group of women who had become such an important part of my life. My father, an English teacher, had died two and a half years earlier, but I could still hear him suggesting that a good first step would be to go to several dictionaries and check various definitions of spirituality. What joy I felt when I realized that my parental tapes were not the only source of information and inspiration available to me. I found I could also look inside and trust me to define spirituality for myself. Perhaps for the first time I dared to believe I could do it in my own way and that way was fine.

After coming to that realization I felt ready to start recalling my own life story. I found the process was a satisfaction and not an ordeal. My spiritual journey was my attempt to trace the journey of my spirit. My spirit was and is my essence, my inner self. I gave myself permission to search for this real "essence" within, and to let myself discover and rediscover the real Letitia Ann Thompson Bedford Traver. I was able to go back over my childhood, my teenage years, my college experiences, my early marriage, the birth of my children and my child-rearing time, my learning about love and sexuality in a new way, my divorce, the rebuilding of me, and my remarriage. And I saw all this with new eyes.

I found myself recapturing some of the pure pleasures of childhood: the image of little Annie with the daisy chain in her hair dancing in the fields. I found I had the strength to relive some of the dark moments such as the lost feeling I had at fifteen when my sister left college to be married and I felt so alone with no one to talk to about the huge moral decision I was making never to "disappoint" our parents, as I perceived she had done. I also found that I could look at motherhood, finally admitting that though both my daughters had been very much wanted children and had brought me huge measures of happiness, I had not been prepared for the difficult and constant demands they would make on my life. I found I could accept the fact that my marriage of seventeen years had ended for reasons I was still struggling to understand, but that nonetheless our divorce was a forward movement on my spiritual pathway. During that January of reflection, many new perspectives on my own journey came to light for me and I saw emerging a more well-balanced pattern of mind/heart and spirit/body.

I truly loved the Ann who was developing. I used that time of soul searching to decide to work on shedding some burdens that had been with me for years: the burden of trying to be perfect and the burden of needing to be a super-achiever. I also began to celebrate some current joys: the ever deepening relationships with my two wonderful now adult daughters, the blooming love and friendships in my well-tended closest relationships, and the creativity that I could unleash as I grew in depth of spirit and self-acceptance. The process of formulating my spiritual journey had helped a seed of spiritual understanding to grow and begin to flourish.

The last Thursday in January 1986 came and I was ready. I went buoyed up by the support of several visual aids that I had prepared, dressed in a favorite outfit, wearing jewelry given to me by a few of my dearest mentors. Being the journey-teller that day was a heady experience, and the privilege of having a circle of some twenty women listening to my story for an hour was rare and wonderful. The details of that morning have faded but the joys of being listened to carefully and taken seriously remain. I had been inspired to look at my own life-journey by listening to other TOP women share their stories so openly. Preparing and sharing my own reflections with those same women was a wonderfully growth-filled experience. It was an added comfort to me to realize that this inward journey had brought me closer to an inclusive God, a wider deeper wisdom than my own. Where would this path of deeper self-understanding and closer connection to God take me now?

In the preface to *Picturing God* Ann Ulanov writes,

> It is scandalous to many that an infinite God should move into the trivial world of the human psyche to speak. Better to put God at a safe distance in pulpits, in political ideologies, in obscure biblical texts. We resist God touching us intimately in dreams, in myths, in our bodies, in our social groupings, in all our little worlds. Yet depth psychology drives this fact home: that God does touch us in the flesh, in the least of our moments as well as in the largest, in all our private and shared experiences. [1]

I had discovered the sacred in my private and shared experiences, and the fear of emptiness I had felt when I first contemplated telling my spiritual journey was soothed. What were the sacred spaces, the private altars that I had found? A small room in our home where I feel secure surrounded by treasured drawings, photographs and posters; the pleasure of sharing food, wine and talk with loved ones at our round kitchen table; times of quiet at a retreat center near my home.

My small room is a sacred place I created for myself at a time when I was feeling fenced in by my life. My second marriage was rocky then, my self-confidence was low. I felt up tight and was not sure why. So I decorated one of our extra bedrooms all for me. My husband wanted to help, but I was unsure whether I wanted him to have any claim at all on this new space. Partly because of his gentleness in offering and his understanding of what I was doing, I "let" him paint the woodwork. I think that was a sign, which I did not fully accept at the moment, that he and I were starting to refashion our relationship in a new healthier, growing way. This room of my own is a place where I love to go, and it was there that I was able to do most of the preparation for the telling of my spiritual journey. A painting by Agam, a French artist, hangs over the bed, and the beauty of its geometric rainbow and central glowing light provide a wonderful God-image that is there with me in all my deliberations.

Our often cluttered kitchen is very different from my small room's meditative quiet but I cherish our kitchen too as an equally sacred space. Sometimes a group of us wallow collectively in the sensuous enjoyment of my husband's gourmet cooking; sometimes I am with a friend quietly talking, smiling, sharing, crying; sometimes there are eight of us laughing uproariously over a game of Trivial Pursuit; sometimes my husband and I enjoy the intimacy of a candlelit supper. In each instance the companionship in our kitchen is special and treasured.

Madeleine L'Engle, an author and a delightfully creative thinker, speaks often of her favorite private altars. She has become an integral part of another of my sacred spaces: the retreat center at Adelynrood, about 25 miles north of Boston. I recently spent a weekend there, and Madeleine's meditations were the focus for our own times of silence. Having the courage to slow down the pace of my life and believing I will find the inner voice, both mine and God's, to keep me company in the silence, has been one of my most recent experiences of the sacred.

Rilke speaks of growing into the answers to our questions. Madeleine L'Engle speaks of the really big questions having no answers. I believe them both. I am learning to stop asking many of the trivial questions that used to block me from acting. I am able to live more creatively with some of the medium questions that take work and patience to deal with. I am willing to ask life and God to share the burden of some of the unanswerable questions. At least some of the time I am. Sometimes I still say, "Why, why, why," and "Damn, damn, damn."

The first fifty years of my spiritual journey is complete but my search for the sacredness in life continues, and my willingness to share my journey with others has just begun. Thank you, my favorite authors, my dear friends both inside and outside TOP, thank you universe and God, for putting out the signposts directing me to a path of deeper spirituality. Thank you, Annie, for choosing to follow.

NOTES

1. Ann Belford Ulanov, *Picturing God* (Cambridge, Mass.: Cowley Publications, 1986), p. 2.

The Artist as Social Activist
amid Adversity:
How the Job Is Done

Corita Kent

CORITA KENT was a graphic artist, painter and printmaker whose limited-edition silkscreen prints can be found in thirty-seven museums. During her lifetime Corita's graphic designs were also readily available in the popular media: on posters and greeting cards, as book illustration, in advertising and on billboards. In Boston each day more than 100,000 commuters see her Rainbow, the largest copyrighted painting in the world. Rainbow was commissioned by Boston Gas Co. for one of its harborside gas-storage tanks. For thirty-two years Corita was a nun and, as Sister Mary Corita, she taught at the Immaculate Heart College in Los Angeles. In 1968 she resigned from her religious community and moved to Boston. Corita's art is unusual in combining luminous color with provocative words from poets and writers, and she often integrated her visual images with statements about commitment to social justice. Her chapter is a rare self-interpretation of her life and work. Corita died in 1986.

Art Amid Adversity

From my long training I have been taught not to talk about my adversity. But I can talk about a kind of global adversity which I think is our personal adversity today. I think we have to have the awareness that everything is sacred, and when we lose that awareness we lose connection with the whole, with the cosmos.

Art is one of the means amid adversity of reestablishing the connection. A picture may be a symbol for the whole if we look at it as a small cosmos.

Let's try to look at a picture as though there is absolutely nothing outside of it. This small world stops at the edge of the paper. Here within this frame, everything belongs. Everything is in a satisfactory relationship with everything else. Try to see all the colors and all the shapes supporting each other, loving and complementing each other. There is no discussion about which is the biggest shape or the most privileged color. Even the smallest section is important in the balance of the whole, and the white shapes are acting just as importantly as the colored shapes.

So in the little cosmos of this picture, everything is sacred. And this wholeness (or holiness) makes a good symbol of the great cosmos which is beyond our comprehension. We are taking here a small taste of the greater whole, which is why we like to see pictures and to look at films and listen to music. The great works of art work this way.

The Burden of the Artist Being An Artist

The responsibility to try to make pictures that work like this for others is a very heavy burden. It is like always aiming for the top quality, and then having to go on making, creating, at your own level. So the artist is never satisfied, never sure, always frightened to begin each new piece. Even if it is only in the depths of your own unconsciousness, there is in you the awareness that you are attempting the top level.

I have over many years put words and other images together. This causes some people to regard my work as not serious art. They regard my work not as art but rather posters (as they like to call them). I think of it more like a singer putting words and other sounds together, which doesn't make it less music. I try to avoid all these distinctions.

Johanna Gill said it in a way that really pleased me. She said,

Since 1951 Corita has been doing the serigraphs for which she has become famous, using the paper as a matrix for graphic imagery that included words and text. The rich surface became a powerful tool for expressing her remarkable fusion of social, political, religious, educational and aesthetic concerns. To a degree rarely found in this cautious world, she refuses to make a distinction between her own work and commissioned work, between art as aesthetics and art as political statement.

All of these things are really not separate for me, nor can I as a plain human being stand apart from any of them.

Earlier I was speaking about the artist hinting at the cosmos. In this shrinking world, and with our growing sensitivity to a global consciousness and a greater realization of how interconnected everything is, it becomes for the artist intensely difficult, almost impossible, for even a small-size hint to be made. But we can look on it as a challenge. And we can build up our hope by making, by creating.

Preserving This Wonderful "Room"

It is very difficult for an artist not to have space. Not to have a room of her own. Not to have time to create in, and the materials and the energy to create, to make. Perhaps the greatest adversity we have is living with the realization that all of these—all of our equipment and all of our lives—can be taken away from us in a matter of minutes by a mistake of technology or a mistake of judgment by another human being.

So I consider it a part of my life as an artist to work on preserving this wonderful "room" in which we work and preserving the materials we use and preserving our very lives. So I make prints and posters to benefit organizations that are also aimed in this direction, as well as contributing financially to them. These groups are working on behalf of our making-space. Without their resistance to the arms race, I feel that life as we know it would already have been blown up.

I am working with the Physicians for Social Responsibility on a billboard project. This will spread around our world a peaceful landscape and the words, "We can create life without war." We have these words also on bumper stickers, T-shirts, posters, cards, postcards, also on the flags, trucks and 5000 people marching in a pro-peace march from Los Angeles to Washington, D.C. The hope is that the words in all these places will empower individuals who read them to join in the work of saving our "room" and our lives. What we want to do is reach more people who are not creatively aware of the danger and to enable them to create. You may even have seen the 52' billboard with these words "We can create life without war," which is appearing along major highways.

Working for the Common Good

I also do posters for organizations and groups to benefit specific occasions. Sometimes my way of approach is to go through my watercolors and think, Which watercolor would be exciting to be used with this particular set of words? So for the Hospice Society on Cape Cod I chose a watercolor, and then I tried to make words which would be helpful not only to the people in the hospice movement itself but also to all of us, because we are all in a sense in or near the hospice movement. The words I chose were, "This day is given to us; from it we make life."

For the Abraham Heschel Memorial Lectures I used his words, "Who lit the wonder before our eyes and the wonder of our eyes?" I chose "To be open to the vision of the new" for the words of a poster for the Kendall Center for handicapped children. When the Girl Scouts had a fund-raising drive I was asked to do a poster. It said "Good for you" and at the bottom used their appeal slogan, "Keep the Girl Scouts in the green."

I did a poster for the Governor's Commission on the Status of Women that read, "Opportunities for women are as great as the hope that leads to action." For the Action for Soviet Jewry "Unable to leave and unable to live as Jews" summed it up. Another reads, "Love is a canvas furnished by nature and embroidered by imagination." Leonard Bernstein did a benefit concert for Amnesty International and I did the poster, "To be fully human is to work for the common good."

One of the things which has been most detrimental to art (and also, I think, an adversity to artists) is when people separate the making of pictures from art. Art really means making something well; in that sense we are all artists. We may not be top-level, but there aren't very many of those. We have two or three maybe in a century who are really great, and the rest of us try. But we are all artists. So when I talk about artists, I am talking about your process too, whatever you may do amid adversity for the common good.

Creating the Possible

Judith Stone

JUDITH STONE is a traditional corporate wife, mother and homemaker. Her artistic capabilities are multifaceted: she sings and plays the piano, gardens and restores gardens, knits, sews wedding dresses, caters weddings, teaches gourmet cooking, paints murals, designs and restores houses, rescues partially finished quilts, collects dolls, and works old lace into her new art forms. She sees the creativity· of women as making an enormous and unacknowledged contribution to the survival and continuity of the human family. "I am a conscious celebrant of the possible."

Looking at a Summer Meadow Ablaze with Wild Flowers

I had never been comfortable with the explaining away of women's creativity —that since there were no women composers, novelists, historians, musicians, poets or architects, etc., women were just uncreative. So as I began my research for women's creativity, I discovered over and over that grace did abound where I had least expected and that these millions of women whose talents never saw the light of poetry, music or architecture had nonetheless expressed their creative force, their spirituality, to light the way for their children. I found that the truest answer to a question that really matters can be found very close.

Questioning the source of my own essential spiritual self, I found the answers were so close that for most of my life of some fifty-five years I had failed to recognize them and take them seriously. Instead I had often regarded my talents and gifts somewhat suspiciously, sensing the lack of real dollar value, the undisguised envy of other women, and the pulls and scattered directions in which these very gifts sent me. Should I be a dress designer, open a restaurant, go on stage, or just what?

The search for other women's creativity actually forced me to look again and again at my own. Slowly I began to honor and accept it. Because I chose to work in my home, I had discredited my contributions, my creativity; it was "woman's work." I have restored and brought to life with pain and paper and love countless homes, especially the one I now live in. With the help of Alice Walker's account of her mother's garden I was able to accept commitment to restoring the gardens here, and I have finally planted a perennial garden. A forever garden—my cooperation with nature, my sacred work. I read somewhere that most perennial gardens are planted by women who have passed forty, and that the joys and sorrows of living forty years are somehow mystically rendered in this particular art form called gardening. So we plant, and plan, with the past and the future fused with vision and hope and expectation and, oh yes, patience. And acceptance. The delphinium isn't quite happy in this spot, so I will move it over by the stone wall in the fall.

As my creative spirit expanded with the restorations in the gardens, my husband and I undertook a major expansion of the original 150-year-old kitchen. Working with a skilled and patient builder, and without plans or blueprints, we created a space where I could conduct my business of catering weddings, teach my cooking classes, grow seedlings, soak in a hot tub, and yet provide a nurturing place for family and friends who come to our New England village to ski or canoe or swim or just sit on our porch and visit.

After many years of avoiding paint, brushes and canvas, I recently felt compelled to start painting pictures. My daughter, who had just finished restoring an old stone barn needed some art for the bare walls, and I was moved in a strange way to connect with this long-buried aspect of myself. After my first two flower paintings, I couldn't stop. I painted more flowers, and sent them to my other daughter in New Orleans, then several interiors, and finally I gathered up my paints and brushes and went to my daughter's barn in Woodstock where I painted on the newly plastered walls of her barn-become-house. I painted a hat rack in the hall, complete with straw gardening hats trimmed with ribbons and flowers. I painted an old umbrella leaning in the corner, an urn of geraniums by it, and an arch covered with morning-glories, with a wren perched in the top. It was great fun, and I learned something of the value of my paints and brushes when the listing realtor saw my work. She added $10,000 to the asking price of my daughter's house.

Learning Where to Look for Women's Creativity

Women's creativity has for the most part been born in those few moments when there was no other work to be done. As Virginia Woolf points out in *A Room of Her Own,* for a woman to write fiction (and, I would add, to be a composer or musician or artist) she needs a room of her own with lock and key and enough money to support herself. This is an unheard of dream for the vast majority of women, and lacking these essentials, such genius never did get itself on paper, on stage, on canvas. So it is that we must look in different places for that creative spark—in diaries, in long forgotten recipes, in needlework, in homes and gardens.

Continuing with Virginia Woolf, "When . . . one reads of a witch being ducked [and drowned], of a woman possessed by devils, of a wise woman selling herbs, or even a very remarkable man who had a mother, then I think we are on the track of a lost novelist or a suppressed poet or some mute and inglorious Jane Austen. . . . Indeed I would venture to guess that Anon., who wrote so many poems without signing them, was often a woman." [1] Alice Walker in her essay "In Search of Our Mothers' Gardens" recalls these words of Virginia Woolf and says, "So our mothers and grandmothers have, more often than not anonymously, handed on the creative spark, the seed of the flower they themselves never hoped to see: or like a sealed letter they could not plainly read." [2]

Alice Walker tells of her mother making all of the clothes they wore, the towels and the sheets, and spending summers growing and canning and the winters making the quilts for their beds. "Her day began before sunup and did not end until late at night. There was never a moment for her to sit down undisturbed, to unravel her own private thoughts, never a time free from interruptions by work or by the noisy inquiries of her many children." And yet it is to her mother and to all the mothers who were not famous that Alice Walker goes when she sets out in search of what fed "that muzzled, vibrant creative spirit that the black woman has inherited."

When did her overworked mother have time to know or care about feeding the creative spirit? "The answer is so simple that many of us have spent years discovering it. We have constantly looked high, when we should have looked high—and low." It is in her mother's gardens. Like Mem, a character in *The Third Life of Grange Copeland,* her mother adorned with flowers whatever shabby house they were forced to live in.

Her mother's gardens were watered in the early morning before she went to work in the fields, and she would be hard at work on them in the evening until it was too dark to see. These were ambitious gardens—"not just your typical straggly country stand of zinnias"—gardens of color, of unusual design with over fifty varieties of flowers. They bloom profusely from early March until late November and people from three counties would come to drive by or ask for cuttings.

"I notice," writes Walker, "that it is only when my mother is working in her flowers that she is radiant, almost to the point of being invisible—except as Creator: hand and eye. She is involved in work her soul must have. Ordering the universe in the image of her personal conception of Beauty. Her face, as she prepares the Art that is her gift, is a legacy of respect she leaves to me, for all that illuminates and cherishes life. She has handed down respect for the possibilities—and the will to grasp them." Being an artist was a daily part of her mother's routine of life, despite all hindrances and interruptions. "This ability to hold on, even in very simple ways," says Walker, "is work women have done for a very long time." [3]

I look back now at my own mother's artistry. I can only say that she was a gifted cook long before the days of kiwis and strawberries in the store in January. For years I have watched her do it. I have written down her recipe along with her detailed instructions. And after years of my trying, I have never yet reproduced the baking powder biscuits that at ninety she is still making in batches to fill my freezer. I will never make an apple or blueberry or lemon-meringue pie, for I know that pie perfection exists only in my mother's fingers. Her fried chicken, her stew from leftover Sunday roasts, her meat loaves and her potato salads—all are truly acts of creative genius. And this was my daily fare growing up. I knew—and know—how food could and should taste.

Despite Constraints

Women's creativity pops out irrepressibly. No amount of muzzling or lack of opportunity or time can keep it below the surface. In college I was a fine arts major and I graduated about the time of the so-called Color School of stripes and geometric forms painted in never before dreamed of color combinations. I was shocked to find that these "innovations" had decades earlier been the province of Amish women in their quilts.

Amish women are forbidden any exposure to the outside world. Without any empirical knowledge of advanced geometry yet limited to the use of geometric forms, and confined by a severe patriarchal society to a routine of cooking, washing and cleaning, the Amish women create. They reorder the universe in brilliant reds and pinks and cobalt blues, intense greens and purples and blacks. The Amish woman brings her creativity to something of lasting value and proceeds to exhibit her own creative spirit. When the top surface has been completed finally, she joins with other women to do the actual quilting. This aspect of women's creativity is something that is so known to us that we often overlook its creative potential, the ability and knowledge that is mobilized by women's connecting, cooperating, contributing. Again, shall we look high or low —at the countless quilting bees, church suppers, women's auxiliaries, PTAs, Junior Leagues and hospital volunteers, or at one woman just plain being a good neighbor? Yes, women have always known that many hands really do make light work, and with no particular need for heroics we just go about getting the jobs done.

Creativity As Standing Against the Loss of Hope

While I have been living with these thoughts, the words *women, creativity* and *adversity* became one. The concepts fuse and took on an archetypal character. What I have come to see is that in our ability to live our creativity daily and in our search for such creativity, we can look as high as our creating life itself and living, and as low as the table set, the meal cooked and consumed, the dishes washed and put away. And we begin in this creativity again and again and again.

Looking back at my life, I realize I have taken my gifts lightly, and myself less than seriously. But illumined by the insight of such writers as Alice Walker and moved by feminist theologians such as Mary Daly, I have learned to rename the sacred and to honor my own creativity and what it produces. My creativity is the truest aspect of my self, the essential source of my being, the whole and holy nature of my human experience.

But as I was enjoying the fruits of my search I began also to understand the darkest side of oppression, the deadening of the spirit, the numbing of the senses, the loss of hope inflicted upon all those who, like women, are both conscious and unconscious, by living under the threat and coercion of this nuclear age. Such deadening, such numbing, is to me the ultimate oppression.

Yet one woman, Justine Merritt, dared to think the unthinkable—the destruction of all life on this planet in a nuclear war. After attending a retreat and asking for guidance she began to create a vision, a woman's vision, a vision of both peace and protest. In her vision she saw the Pentagon building in Washington, D.C. wrapped in a ribbon made by many women and tied together in a spirit of cooperation. Her vision was of a gentle reminder to us all that life is precious and that her grandchildren (as well as yours and mine) could be an endangered species in a nuclear war. In her vision the ribbon would be made of segments made by women and tied together, each segment depicting what each person cannot bear to see lost forever in a nuclear war.

It began with notes from its creator, Justine Merritt, to each person on her Christmas card list in 1981. It began with the Sisters of Loretto distributing 2000 flyers at Lafayette Park across from the White House in May 1982. It began with a Unitarian-Universalist friend taking 200 fliers and distributing them during the New York City Peace March on June 12, 1982. It leapt forward with an editorial about the Ribbon in Robbie Fanning's stitchery magazine, *Open Chain* in December 1983. It leapt forward when Church Women United created 1-1/4 miles of segments for their quadrennial celebration at Purdue University in July 1984 with the quadrennial theme "Pieces to Peace."

The Ribbon was getting longer and longer for three years as Justine Merritt traveled to 31 states and British Columbia, stayed in more than 200 different homes, traveled thousands of miles by bus, train, car, plane and ferry boat, all the time encouraging people in groups as small as three or four to make a statement about nuclear war. From the first newspaper article in an Alamosa College paper in Colorado during 1983 to a *People* magazine article on July 8, 1985; from a small mission church on the southern Ute reservation in Ignacio, Colorado in 1982 to Washington's National Cathedral in August 1985, the Ribbon had grown to be 25,500 pieces (15 miles) in length. [4]

On August 4, 1985, the 40th anniversary of the dropping of the first atomic bomb and the opening of the nuclear age, the Ribbon was linked in a human chain that stretched from the Pentagon to the Capitol building and back.

My husband and I went to Washington to witness and participate in this miraculous event. I went thinking about Justine Merritt's original expectation that about 400 panels could be forthcoming, knowing that instead these expectations had been multiplied by the concern and the creativity and the participation of so many, many women. I thought about all the people who made them and the ones who carried them. I thought about the sacred nature of the things the panels portrayed. As I watched the women pick up their panels and go out onto the mall to join up with thousands of others, and joining in myself, I knew my own humanity and experienced it illuminated and affirmed and built up and expanded.

The panels sewn by so many women were like so much of women's work. They were created to be given away. Their power came finally from the shared efforts of many women, saying again and again that life and living must continue, must go on. It is my deepest conviction, the core of my faith and hope for a future, that the subtle, irrepressible, glorious day-to-day creativity of women will inevitably light the way.

NOTES

1. Virginia Woolf, *A Room of Her Own* (New York: Harcourt Brace Jovanovich, 1929), p. 49.

2. Alice Walker, "In Search of Our Mothers' Gardens" in *In Search of Our Mothers' Gardens: Womanist Prose* (San Diego: Harcourt Brace Jovanovich, Harvest Books, 1983), p. 240.

3. Alice Walker, *In Search of Our Mothers' Gardens*, pp. 241–242.

4. *The Ribbon: A Celebration of Life*, ed. Lark Books staff and Marianne Philbin (Asheville, N.C.: Lark Books, 1985).

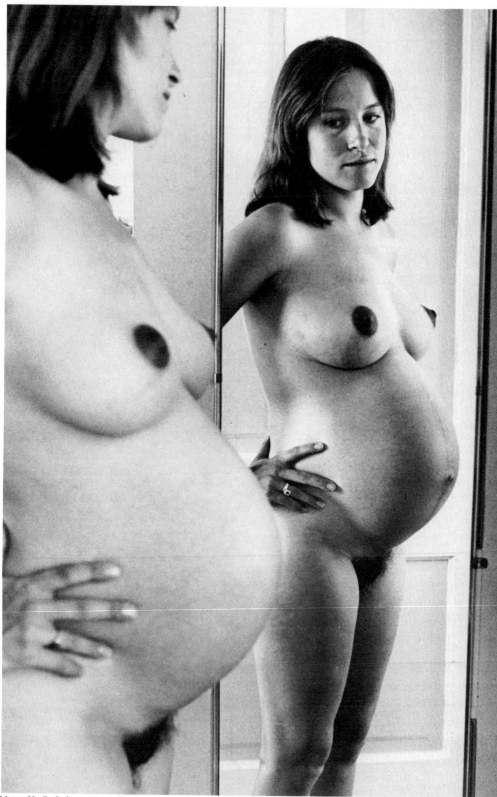

Monte H. Gerlach

SECTION 2.
GIVING BIRTH

2. Giving Birth

A Power Not Our Own

Men have always had problems with women's awesome capacity to give birth to new life. Women bleed and do not die. When women become pregnant with new life, our bodies change and grow, our bellies stretch, menstrual flow stops, and then finally, with a great crescendo of water and blood and pain, a new human being emerges from the circle of a woman's vagina, which has stretched from a circle around the male penis to a circle around a baby's head. An awesome process brings humans into this life.

In the prehistory before patriarchal society, women's powers to give birth were celebrated in those many "little Venuses" with their pregnant bellies and full breasts. But the historical religions of Judaism and Christianity have insisted that the *important* birth, the one that is sacred, is not the actual physical birth from a woman but what happens later in the male rituals of baptism or circumcision.

Myriel Crowley Eykamp describes this strange reversal in "Born and Born Again: Childbirth Rituals from a Mother's Perspective." She reminds us of the implications for women of Christian leaders' assertions that baptism is when you are really born—into God's family, the sacred group, the Church. Circumcision is when males (only) are really born into the sacred covenant of Judaism between God and his chosen people. She concludes, "The necessity of being born again is a widespread religious and cultural phenomenon." To be alive, to have been born of a woman, is viewed as insufficient.

Myriel Eykamp's chapter highlights for us how women give new life in childbirth and that achievement for humanity is not celebrated in ritual. U.S. soldiers who fought in Vietnam had a similar experience when they returned— "without ticker-tape parades"—to a society which was deeply divided about that war. There was no ritual or celebration appreciating what they had done, and they felt diminished.

A similar displacement of ritual attention away from mothers' role in birthing can be seen in our everyday celebration of birthdays. By cultural agreement, birthdays focus only on the one who is born, and seldom (if ever) acknowledge and celebrate the long gestation and labor of the mother that brought this child through birth to life.

The need of male religion to put down physical birth as unimportant is pervasive, as is the need to elevate to sacred status imitation birthing ceremonies. The put-down extends to women's reproductive blood—the blood of birthing and menstruating—declaring that it pollutes male sacred spaces. In both Judaism and Christianity for many centuries women have been declared unclean after giving birth. In Judaism there are ritual cleansing practices to follow before women are allowed back into the male-defined sacred space of the synagogue. In the Episcopalian and Roman Catholic churches there have been prescribed rites for the "churching of women" which functioned as cleansing rituals.

Male Fear and Awe

Evidence of male fear and awe before women's birth-power is everywhere. The Genesis myth of creation is distanced from any crude reference to women's bodies and the way babies are actually born. It substitutes instead a creation by a disembodied Male Spirit who fashions, as a potter would, humans from the dust of the earth. Feminists have noted the curious way Eve seems to be born from Adam, fashioned by the Male Spirit from a rib taken from Adam's side. The Genesis account thus reverses (and denies) the natural order of things in which males are born, as women are, from women's bodies.

Learned biblical scholars have always contrasted the "higher" spiritual monotheism of the Hebrew Bible with the pagan fertility cults of surrounding tribes, cults featuring temple "prostitutes" and loathsomely connecting religion to women's sexuality and fertility. There is a primal fear and awe of women's power to create new life.

A Journey through Ambivalence

Because of this ancient overlay, it is not easy for women to lay claim to our life-giving power. How are we to reclaim that which has been declared fearful, polluting and yet unimportant? How are women to name as sacred the actual physical birth, which comes with no sacred ritual, while lurking around the corner of time are the long-established meta-physical rituals of circumcision or baptism?

But even that is not the entire story of the ambivalence a woman experiences along the way to claiming the sacredness of her own birthing process. There is the reticence she feels about possibly offending other women by seeming to elevate her own birthing experience. How is one woman to claim her own experience of an "easy" birth when she knows other women labor for days in pain and some women die giving birth? How is she to name as sacred her experience of having babies when, for whatever reason, other women are childless? How is she to claim her own experience of "conscious" home-birth (as Sydney Amara Morris describes), when other women may now regret having been unconscious with medications? Or if you had a "bad" experience giving birth, how are you to name that when women around you are happily anticipating a successful culmination to their Lamaze classes? Women's naming of much in their own birthing experiences is silenced by their sensitivity to other women's feelings.

But despite these many reasons for reticence, there is a bonding of women who have given birth. It is deep and silent. You can see it in Sydney Morris' post-childbirth vision of a silvery shadowed path between life and death down which all "the birthing mothers on the planet" have moved, those "mothers of all times without whom no one walks this planet." Women who have given birth reach out to one another, just as Sydney Morris does, saying to all those mothers whose birthing experiences were different than hers, "Don't feel badly. 'Rejoice in the incredible, joyous, astounding fact of creation. . . . Every moment a child is born is a holy moment.'"

Women today also are aware of laboring to give birth to a planet of peace and justice. The author of the poem in this section was for a long time unknown to me. Like hundreds of photocopied pages of women's writing, this came into my life and found a place in my files and in my consciousness. These words of Dorothy Fadiman need to find a wider audience because they sum up so vividly the deep "soul-pushing" I sense in many women who are laboring hard to bring a new world down the birth canal of today into the light and air of tomorrow.

When Women's Lives and Bodies Are Laid Waste

The rejoicing of a woman at the birth of her child is made difficult when continual and prolonged childbearing without birth control wastes the mother's body, spirit, nutrition and well-being. The 1984 Zimbabwe Reproductive Health Survey reports that on average a woman in that country spends 18 to 20 years of her adult life pregnant. By contrast, her counterpart in a developed or industrialized country invests only three to five years. Reproductive patterns such as those in Zimbabwe (the report says) erode women's health, exhaust women's energies, fragment their time, and greatly hinder women's participation and contribution to the wider community's development. [1]

Women's fertility, when it is without the protection of birth control, can make the blessing of birth seem like a curse. Thus women who try to claim the sacredness of their own birthing process have to move through and overcome their own fear of constant pregnancies. A woman may honor her own birthing process but still fear her own vulnerability to male sexual desire and its nine months later consequences (whether wanted or not). Women's bodily capacity to gestate new life is a sacred resource to be gently and tenderly preserved, not squandered thoughtlessly in constant childbearing. And a woman's choice to bear or not to bear children must be affirmed and elevated since hers is the subjectivity which is at the heart of the gestating and birthing process.

We Cannot Affirm Life without Affirming Women

It is well past time in human history to push aside male dread and boldly claim the sacred woman-centeredness of every human birth. The Christmas wreath, standard now on the doors of American houses and apartments during the Christmas season, is the circle symbol known to the Hindus as the yuni, signifying the circle of the woman's vagina which stretches to give birth. The wonder at new human life cannot be separated from the sacredness of women's bodies or women's lives. We will be involved in a profound betrayal of the gift of life itself as long as individual men and male culture "freak out" before women's power to give birth. Men betray the sacred gift of life when they withhold from women the means of birth control so that women can *choose* to give life. Men betray the gift of life when women's bodies are denigrated in advertising. Or when men desecrate women's bodies by pornography or incest or rape. Or when they kill women's children in war.

If we cannot affirm women and women's bodies and women's birthing and women's choice, we will go on bringing death to the planet and to ourselves. We cannot affirm life without affirming women.

—Elizabeth Dodson Gray

Ann Grady, C.S.J./"The Spirit of Life," Cyrus E. Dallin sculptor, Brookline, Mass.

Notes

1. Sally Mugabe, "High Fertility Hampers Women's Status" in *Popline: World Population News Service,* vol. 9, no. 6 (June 1987):1–2.

Homebirth: The Sacred Act of Creation

Sydney Amara Morris

SYDNEY AMARA MORRIS combined birthing with her graduate studies in theology. She writes of a long home-birth which was for her a time of spiritual revelation. She graduated from Harvard Divinity School in 1986 with her M.Div. degree and gave birth to her second child just before graduation. She has been a hot-line staffer, a drug and runaway counsellor, a therapist, director of a conference and networking center, and now, in addition to her work as a full-time ordained minister of the Unitarian Universalist Church in Ames, Iowa, she is a member of the PTA, works with a shelter for the homeless, and is on the board of a socially responsible investment company.

"You'll Never Guess What!"

Once I knew I was pregnant, I began the long search for a doctor. I knew I wanted a home birth. On one level it was because that's just what was done in our community—everyone had their babies at home. We were all working to build an alternative culture. The food we ate, the clothes we wore, the way we related to one another, were all manifestations of a lifestyle we had chosen and believed in and for which we put our bodies and our minds on the line. I had attended several births, and they had all been relatively short and uncomplicated, with friends and family in attendance; they were very moving experiences.

I was also hearing, as you always do, stories which validated my own perspective. Another friend had gone into the hospital for a routine exploratory operation and had awakened to find an entire ovary removed. Neither her permission nor a medical emergency was involved but rather, she was told, it was done "as a matter of precaution." My husband and I dutifully toured many hospitals. But all had some rule I could not get comfortable with: taking the baby away for a required period of observation, putting stinging medicine in the baby's eyes, or not allowing husbands or children to be present.

On top of all this I was told I would be categorized as a high-risk patient, which would require me to be in the hospital and have extra precautions taken. It sounded as though I would be given a Caesarean section the minute it seemed anything was amiss.

I just did not buy all this. I decided medical practices were slanted toward procedures which would create more of a hazard for me than they were preventing. It seemed obvious that I had a very different idea of what constituted "necessity." I was receiving a lot of support from a group which supported natural childbirth for women who had conditions like mine, and given that my prenatal course was extremely smooth, I was determined to do the birth at home.

The Most Natural of All Conditions

So I began to look for a midwife. At that time midwifery was illegal in my state. But we found a woman who had been the head of obstetrics in a hospital for ten years. I got to know her by her pseudonym since, if she had been discovered practicing midwifery, she would have lost her nursing license. I also found a doctor nearby who was willing to cover me if I did have to go to his hospital. He was someone I trusted medically and who understood my proclivity for the least amount of intervention possible. He was willing to have both the midwife and my husband be with me no matter what happened.

When I came to Harvard Divinity School after a good 15 years absence from school, I was already three months pregnant. I went to my adviser, an older man. Feeling somewhat intimidated by the Harvard ambiance, I asked him if he thought it would work out for me to be pregnant and beginning graduate studies. "Well," he replied, "in the days of Dean Sperry"—some thirty years previous— "you would have been invited to leave, but then of course as a woman you wouldn't have been allowed here in the first place."

Fighting back tears I fled to the Women's Studies Department of the Divinity School, where the director, a woman, told me not only were two other pregnant women currently enrolled but others before me had managed quite successfully. She assigned me to a new adviser, a woman who had herself taught and gone to school throughout her three pregnancies. The difference between the two responses was amazing. To the one person I was a pariah, an oddball. To the other I was part of a community of people that included women living both biological and intellectual lives, lives which once had been separate but now were being integrated by a new generation of women.

The Surge from a Great Source That Comes Up From Down Under

My husband and I attended natural childbirth classes. I decided that I was going to breathe through my pain, experiencing it not as pain but as strong sensations, relaxing and going with the flow. (I can hear you, if you've been through childbirth yourself, laughing at my innocent resolves.) I read everything I could get my hands on about birth. I had my pictures of holy people lined up to look at, and my orange-juice ice cubes were ready for my refreshment. None of this really prepared me for the actual event.

Rosemary Ruether has said that we need a new body of scripture that reflects the truth of women's experience. I think we need to hear about women's experiences of giving birth. As we study birthing we study the act of creation and we are given glimpses into the mystery, the profound, the deeply human. In birthing we confront that which ultimately connects us with every sentient being and with the essential nature of the universe. My own addition to scripture would be these words of Mary Livermore, who was a suffragist in the 1860s:

Women . . . go down into the valley of the shadow of death and win the child of love by struggling for it with death itself. And then this dearly bought child is part and parcel of their own nature. [1]

I could spend a whole book expounding upon the meaning I have found in this short passage by Mary Livermore. She says: "Women go *down* into the valley. . . ." In birthing one does go down into the valley; I also went down into my own body, into the core of my existence, down, it seemed, into the very core of existence itself. Nelle Morton talks of finding a theological wholeness in this kind of downward movement:

Whole means . . . a oneness of body and mind, a oneness with one another in our helplessness, in our powerlessness, in our great pain. . . . Some of you know how to be at home in your bodies. You have a theology of the birthing process—of Creation itself. Some of you must teach the rest of us how to plant our feet in the earth and feel the surge of energy from a great source that comes up from down under. [2]

Lifting Up a Corner of the Universe

What do we know of the surge from a great source that comes up from down under? This is a question for all of us to answer in our new scriptures. Mary Livermore says we go down and then win the child of love by struggling for it with death itself. We go down into another realm of existence, and we struggle for life with death. I am awed every time I think about this.

As part of our everyday life—of what it is like to be a woman and have a baby—we struggle with death itself. Sometimes we win, sometimes we do not win. Sometimes the baby is lost, and sometimes we are lost. But when we survive, there is a triumph. Initially created by an act of love—or of deep affinity, even if only physical—life is manifested only by wrestling with death. If you are looking for metaphors for the nature of reality or the ground of being, if you are looking to see the face of the Goddess, here is a clue: love brings us face to face with death, and then beyond into life. This is the sacredness of everyday life, the common life of a common woman, who as a matter of course fights with death on the side of life.

I think it is a universal human need, the need to face death and wrest from it life. Lacking the experience of being near birth, or being close to a woman who is birthing, men have often turned to war in order to come in contact with death. In his article for *Esquire* magazine William Broyles, Jr. says:

The love of war stems from the union, deep in the core of our being, between sex and destruction, beauty and horror, love and death. War may be the only way in which most men touch the mythic domains in our soul. It is, for men, at some terrible level the closest thing to what childbirth is for women: the initiation into the power of life and death. It is like lifting off the corner of the universe and looking at what's underneath. [3]

I think we women must claim it as a fact that we have lifted up a corner of the universe and gazed at what lies beneath. Every mother, through birthing, has this knowledge. There is a community of understanding, a body of wisdom and revelatory experience, which we must begin to acknowledge. We must learn to speak the words, dare to reexperience the feelings, help one another claim the awareness which is within all birthings. Let us read our scriptures of birth and let us ask ourselves, Is there a way this metaphor, this information, this art, can help us rise above the message of death and of war?

Is there a way to include people in these events so that they may find a way to struggle with death not by reaping more death but by finding new life? I once had a fantasy of going, nine months pregnant, to a command post of an army about to begin World War III, and giving birth on the big central command table, coordinating this act with pregnant women in command posts the world over, thus diverting everyone's attention from war to life.

Becoming a Pushing Machine

I was in labor for three days. At a hospital, had I been in one, I would have been induced, with the excuse that the baby was not coming fast enough. My son took his own sweet time and, given that no waters had broken, I was content to go through the labor as it came. Many friends gathered at my house, about fourteen in all, some of them children. All gathered in my living room to chant, pray and eventually play cards while they waited for me and with me, taking turns coming in to massage my back, bringing things to eat, encouraging me. Their love sustained me.

The pain of birth is the worst pain in the world. I despised it. I hated the pain of contractions and of pushings, the loss of sleep and youth. Nothing makes up for the pain, nothing except the love of the people around me who offered me, and continue to offer me, their love no matter what I have gone through, no matter how I feel or how I look. Nothing makes pain okay, but community transcends it.

The breathing techniques worked fine until the baby descended onto my cervix, which was only four centimeters dilated. The pressure made my cervix bruise and then freeze, unable to dilate any further because of the swelling. Breathing didn't help then. I tried talking to the pain: "Pain, I just can't make friends with you. I really want to work together. Pain, please speak to me." All my talking to my pain didn't put a dent in it. Finally I was counting out the seconds as each contraction came, raising my voice in correlation with the intensity, louder and louder, screaming and singing the numbers out with my friend Lyra whose birth I had attended. That did help. Only a woman could be with me wholly, fully, to the peak of each contraction and back down again to its denouement.

At the hospital they would have operated. My midwife put me into a warm bath to relax my cervix. She had me do a few T'i Ch'i movements with my hips. While I was becoming fully dilated, all there was to do was to breathe and not push, not try. I just floated on top of each contraction. It felt just like all the books I had read said it should. It was a strong sensation; my attendants and I were riding on top of it like surfers. I was like the Queen of the River riding the waves, as if the river, the waves, my breath and my life were all the same thing. People seemed beautiful as they all crowded in to be with me. I saw medieval saints among my friends and Hindu goddesses and peasant wise women and the children of the entire human race, all with me, breathing together with me and letting life come through.

The sun came through my window, pulsing with breath; my midwife said, "You're fully dilated." Everyone helped me push, taking deep breaths and grunting with me. I was a tunnel, a cavern. I was a pushing machine, a vessel of sacred water flowing out, out, out to the sea of faces and life and breathing and push!

The baby had emitted and then swallowed some meconium in the last moments, and came out covered with green. Jon, my husband, solidly in his own metaphorical reality, saw him as a dark green DeSoto. I thought he looked like a fish coming out of the primordial ooze.

Damon was born at 5:30 A.M. He didn't cry at all. My first words were, "Don't die, baby." The midwife said, "He's fine. He's blinking at me. Hello, darling." She put a tube down his throat to suction out any meconium in his stomach, which did start him crying. But then, instead of him being taken away, she gave him to me to fondle. After saying hello, I handed him to Jon while I attended to the afterbirth. Jon took the baby in his arms and said, "Hello, baby. I'm your father. You've had a long journey just now, but you are out and everything is okay. We're going to love you forever, little baby. I promise we will take good care of you." My friends cried, I cried, the midwife cried. Then they all sang a song a friend, Robbie Gass, had written after his daughter was born.

Welcome to this world, dear child, welcome to the earth.
All our love surrounds you at your birth . . .

Looking at the Moon That Night

That evening when everyone had finished their discussion of where to go for a celebratory dinner, and the midwife had done her final check and the house was full of sleeping breathing, I went alone to look out the window at the full moon. The air was gray and fuzzy, illuminated with slivers of silver and black shadow. I felt myself in a world of soft gray light and warmth. Slowly, peripherally, it seemed as if the clearest of clear blue began to appear, blue like a New England October sky, until there was only the softest of gray lines in the middle of my vision separating, but oh so gently, the two blue sides of life and of death.

It was as if I could look down that line, a long and infinitely thin silver-gray line so bright; an endless blue was all around me. I felt myself walking on the silver path, between life and death, between this world and the gracious gorgeous world beyond. A voice came that was very like my own voice or my mother's, but bigger and wider and more sense than sound: "I am the Mother, the channel and the gateway of life. It is I who gave you birth, I who births all things that come into creation, I who am you, with, of you, the Mother of All." I stood there listening, the soft gray air cradling my body. "Let us give thanks, you and I," the voice murmured, "gratitude to all those who have suffered, to all those who love, to all those who have been born, to all those who die. Thank you, thank you, birthing mothers on the planet now bringing life; thank you, mothers of all times without whom no one walks this planet." I heard echoes of the divine: "No one is here but through the Mother. It is I among you, the woman, the mother, the locus of the divine within you. It is I, sweet love, sweet life, forever birthing, dying, and bringing forth anew."

There was more. But it is not in words but in moonlight and darkness. What lasts for me is the sense of calmness and wide assurance that between death and life there is no conflict, no war. I remember that, and the strong solemn sense of gratitude.

Finding Our Peace in a Holy Moment

Sometimes people become sad when I tell about Damon's birth; their own experiences of giving birth or being born were so different and marked by powerlessness and fear. And mistakes. There is an unfortunate backlash occurring which makes people feel guilty if they didn't get through their birthings totally naturally, even if they ran into dangerous situations in the delivery. I think that is a shame, because on some level it does not matter how it happened as long as you are still alive. You are a part of our human story, and this is good news: that the incredible, joyous, astounding fact of creation is among us and in our lives. Creation is right here among us in the human community every time a child is born. Every time a child is born is a holy time.

Notes

1. Mary Livermore, cited in *American Universalism,* by George Huntston Williams (Boston: Beacon Press, 1976), p. 45.

2. Nelle Morton, *The Journey Is Home* (Boston: Beacon Press, 1985), pp. 67–68.

3. William Broyles, Jr., "Why Men Love War," *Esquire,* November 1984, p. 61.

Born and Born Again:
Childbirth Rituals
from a Mother's Perspective

Myriel Crowley Eykamp

Myriel Crowley Eykamp is a Roman Catholic laywoman and mother of two sons who is interested in ritual and its power to enhance or diminish life experience. She has her master's degree in library science and her M.Div. from Harvard Divinity School. She has been a science librarian at MIT. Now she teaches undergraduates about women and religion, and coordinates an adult literacy program. She sees her work as ministry even though her church will not acknowledge that. She is active in WomanChurch and in the Boston Women's Ordination Conference. She says of her chapter: "Three middle-aged mothers were asked in a class at Harvard Divinity School to prepare a class session on rituals of childbirth. Everyone was surprised when we reported how little ritual celebrates the actual birth to the mother. Most 'childbirth' ritual celebrates the handing over of the new baby to the FATHERS!"

A Prayer for Colin

At the birth of my second son, Colin, my doctor asked if he might say a prayer of blessing for our child and of thanksgiving for his safe delivery. My husband and I were taken aback. We had not expected this conjunction of science and religion in a twentieth-century hospital. We said yes, and the doctor spoke a brief prayer aloud.

I have come over the years to attach increasing significance to that doctor's simple ritual. For no logical reason and certainly through no particular manifestation of Colin's character, I have come to regard Colin in my heart as "the child who is blessed," rather like some reluctant prophet in scripture. Like other unsuspecting prophets who are genuinely surprised at their summons, I trust that Colin will speak some word of God's truth when his time comes.

Ritual, writes Edward Fisher, [1] helps us sense holiness, or the possibility of holiness, in the familiar. That doctor's prayer, offered so immediately after Colin's birth, helped me sense the holiness in the moment, the holiness in the age-old work of carrying on the species, the holiness in my own body.

This story is the only story I have that celebrates my giving birth as a sacred event in its own right. It is the only story I have for Colin that locates him, however remotely, in a sacred landscape. There are few events which evoke what Fisher calls "the ache of existence" more than the birth of a child. New mothers and fathers long to be celebrated and sustained in their new status. There is a yearning for ultimate connection. At the same time there is a need of confirmation that this particular birth is unique.

Ritual Expression of the Ache of Existence

While it is easy for most of us to rejoice at the birth of a desired and intended baby, it is more difficult to acknowledge that accompanying many, if not most, births there is also loss. When the spectrum of birth situations in our culture is considered, the wanted and the unwanted babies born into families of diverse configurations and means, and babies born to mothers who are still veritable children themselves, the ache of existence can be overwhelming.

It is at moments of change and often crisis, such as the birth of a child, that the old ways of interpreting life no longer hold. Then there is possibility, often because there is necessity, for discerning new patterns and meanings. It is precisely on such occasions as births and deaths, marriages and divorces, and other significant beginnings and endings, that people are most in need of rituals.

I am not speaking of ritual which endorses the status quo in a world that cries out for change. Nor am I speaking of ritual which romanticizes motherhood and silences women's articulation of the ambivalence which motherhood often entails. I am speaking of ritual which can keep us connected with one another when we feel most alone. I am speaking of ritual which can help us authentically name our experience and which can help us incorporate new understandings into the patterns of our lives. I am speaking of ritual in which we can actually act out —practice, if you will—new ways of thinking and living.

Diana Eck tells of a high-school class that was studying marriage and the family. They decided they wanted to act out a marriage ceremony, and so a student bride and groom and a student minister were selected and the student community gathered around. When it came to the point in the ritual where the couple exchange their marriage vows, the student couple found they were unable to respond to the questions, "Do you John take Mary . . . ?" and "Do you Mary take John . . . ?" They suddenly became aware of the power of the words "I do" to change reality in a way they were not prepared for.

No single ritual can be expected to hold the many meanings of the childbirth experience, but a careful ritual might at least begin to honor new life and help a new mother to integrate into her life, whatever joy or loss the birth means to her. A ritual can give a new mother interdependence with other women and a communion with them. It can help the gathered community to begin passing on its store of wisdom to her, and it can give a story to tell a child.

Baptismal "Rebirth": A Mixed Message to Women

Baptism! I neglected to mention that both of my sons were baptized. By habit or out of a sincere desire to make something sacred of critical life-events, people turn at decisive moments of the life-cycle to religious institutions. Consequently churches have variously loaded the sacraments which were originally instituted to express faith events, with meanings related to life passages, often with what seem to be ambiguous results.

Baptism, for example, is popularly requested and celebrated as a ritual of childbirth by members of churches which practice infant baptism. Churches which practice adult or "believer's" baptism offer a service of child-dedication which is viewed similarly. When one examines the many actual meanings of baptism, however, one finds little acknowledgement—and less celebration—of the actual birth of the child to the mother. *Baptism is not a birth ritual; it is an initiation rite into the Christian church.*

Consider what is acted out in the baptismal service and what experience is created. The initiate recapitulates the death and resurrection of Jesus (see Romans 6:3–5); he or she dies to sin and is *re*generated with the life of God, or grace. In baptism one is born *again* (see John 3:5) and one is clothed with the robe of *new* life.

My family and I were travelling this past summer when my son Colin (the blessed one) encountered a street preacher who handed him a pamphlet. If he would but embrace Christ as his savior and be born again—and send his name to a certain Ohio address—my son could receive an actual spiritual birth certificate. Colin already has a birth certificate, for *I* gave birth to him.

To Be Simply "Born" Is Not Enough

The necessity of being born again is a widespread religious and cultural phenomenon. The Hindu *samskara* [sacrament] of *upanayana* combines elements found in Christian baptism and ordination. *Upanayana* is received after the age of eight, so it is separated in time from physical birth. The child (male only) is ceremonially separated from his mother and placed under the care of a special teacher, or guru, who initiates him into communal life and instructs him in a regimen of spiritual discipline and study. The most striking feature of the *upanayana* is its association with cultural and spiritual rebirth. After the initiate has "died" to his mother, symbolized by a final meal eaten with her, his teacher vests him with the sacred thread, the wearing of which marks the student as "twice-born."

Baptism shares many characteristics of initiation rites in general. In the anthropological literature I found that rebirth is a universal metaphor in rites of passage or initiation. Victor Turner writes extensively about "liminality," which he describes as a "threshold state" analogous to the catechumenate that in the early Christian Church preceded the baptism of adult believers. Turner describes liminality as the state of being in the womb, from which the neophyte is to be fashioned anew, or reborn, into a new and better station in life. [2] Mircea Eliade makes brief reference to tribal female rituals which celebrate childbirth, but these are clearly not the dominant pattern. The usual pattern in rituals surrounding childbirth is initiation, conceptualized and constructed around the idea of new birth, which is to a culturally or spiritually "higher" life. [3]

Thus, while birth itself is the initial and primordial passage, and while the birth moment is recapitulated in baptism and countless other rites of initiation, the actual birth to the biological mother is rarely celebrated in ritual. On the contrary, there is attached to birth through a female a legacy of pollution, and the ancient original purpose of baptism (like that of circumcision in the Jewish tradition) was to wash away ritual impurity, to drive out evil spirits, and to purge from sin.[4] In the Hebrew Scriptures Leviticus 12 prescribes a rite of atonement to be performed on behalf of the new mother. She is to offer a pigeon or turtle-dove as a sacrifice for sin. The practice of "churching" women, which dates back to the eleventh century in the Western Christian church, included at various times elements of thanksgiving and reintegration of the mother into community. But the dominant emphasis in the churching of women after childbirth was always on the purification from sin.[5] Contemporary Roman Catholic church documents assure us that through baptism men and women "are raised from their natural human condition to the dignity of adopted children."[6]

Ritual Rebirth by Males

What these rituals suggest is that the actual physical birth, being of the flesh and of the female, is not only not valued, but is insufficient. If you read these rituals closely, you can see that they are a reappropriation or taking over of the birthing-act by the male priest. Through baptism the birth experience is usurped from the mother and reappropriated by the fathers. One must not only be born again, but born again of the male.

A Hindu scholar describes in similar terms the significance of the *upanayana,* the rite of the twice-born. "The physical birth of a child is crude, as it is associated with animality; but rebirth through discipline and learning [available, of course, only through the male teacher] is considered exalted and holy."[7]

I do not find re-birth as a metaphor used in the literature describing the Jewish rite of circumcision, but the appropriation of the child (again, only the male child) by the fathers in that custom is clear. At times the mother is not even present at the *bris* or circumcision ritual. Similarly the traditional Jewish naming ceremony for a daughter often occurs in the absence of both the mother and the child.

Phyllis Chesler expresses the ambivalence of some Jewish feminists about handing over their babies to the fathers for initiation into the Covenant. She writes on the morning of the circumcision of her son Ariel:

Ancient One: Today is your *bris.* Am I doing the right thing? My innocent Isaac: Why do Jewish men need to do this, before accepting a male child into their protective custody? Proclaim love of God first, family second? A ritual wounding, to ward off a more personal one? Patriarchal tampering with what Woman and Nature have made?

I have agreed to it. Your father's desire to do this is so strong, I dare not deny him. I'd be afraid for you—if I did. I'd be afraid—for my sake, for our sake—to protest my anger so firmly. This quarrel is very old. I am so powerless.

Baby: Forgive me. *I'd be guilty too.* I cannot cut you off beforehand from this people. *That* severing is your choice, not mine to make for you. (May you never make such a choice . . .)[8]

The precedent of the male appropriating for himself the birth experience is ancient, at least as ancient as Gen. 2:21–22:

> So the Lord God caused a deep sleep to fall upon the man, and while he slept took one of his ribs and closed up its place with flesh; and the rib which the Lord God had taken from the man he made into a woman and brought her to the man.

Zeus gave birth to Athena from his skull. Hephaestus created Pandora (as a punishment to men) in his smithy at the command of Zeus. The Hindu Vishnu produced a lotus from his forehead, and on the leaf was his future consort, Lakshmi. There are many, many more such stories in the mythological literature. In the absence of a vagina the means of birth range from head to penis to thigh to sweaty armpit. Adam and the Lord God were but following a well-established pattern.[9]

I do not want to point the finger exclusively at religion. One can find a variation on this theme in Freudian theory, specifically the Oedipus complex. In this paradigm of what constitutes appropriate psychological development, the child must separate himself from the mother, who is identified with nature, and align himself (again the system actually applies only to males) with the father, who is identified with culture or civilization. This is the same pattern that Eliade found in his studies of tribal initiation rites. Separation from the mother is followed by an ordeal or testing which results in symbolic death, and is then followed by rebirth with the help of the male priest or guru. Eliade characterizes this pattern as metacultural and transhistorical. He sees the underlying philosophy as universal—that *true* man is not given or born but made by culture.

And aren't we fortunate that, if your mother really botched it up and things have been going badly for you ever since, you may employ a trained instructor from one of the rebirthing movements and be born again, or re-birthed, right down to the re-utterance of your primal scream—without even calling your mother!

Regaining a Lost Piece of the Sacred Landscape

My point is not that re-birth is a useless metaphor, for surely change and growth and regeneration are qualities of life to be sought and cherished. But consider what has been overlooked in the religious and cultural emphasis upon re-birth. What has been neglected in ritual and story and celebration is our initial and biological birth by our mothers. In this neglect, what has been disparaged and even detested is what pertains uniquely and most intimately to the female. Women have lost something here, the power to name our own reality and to make our own meaning of this widely shared women's experience. We as women have lost a parcel of sacred landscape, and I am suggesting that we can take it back.

Phyllis Chesler in her diary describes a second ritual following Ariel's circumcision. In spite of a snowstorm thirteen women have gathered to welcome and bless Ariel in their own ritual. "It's over," writes Chesler of the circumcision. And she continues:

> Time for the women's Ceremony. We go into my study. We sit in a circle on the floor, on large pillows: grandmothers all.
>
> The women will bless you, each in her own voice, each with her own wish. The room is filled with flowers: roses, anemones. I've laid out candles and matches. Miriam holds you. The men watch. Some stop, voluntarily, at the door. Your father joins us.
>
> Miriam begins. She lights one of the candles.
>
> "Women. Let us each, in turn, light a candle for Ariel. Let us bless him with a wish. Let us each give him something of ourselves—a strand of hair, a nail, growing. I'll paste it down for you in this little Book of Life. To seal the wish."
>
> She takes a pair of scissors, Scotch tape, a folded-over piece of red oaktag. The women are silent. We all watch the first flame.
>
> "May you never know any more pain than you've known today."
>
> "May you never be as lonely as I've been. May you have strong friendships."
>
> "May your parents have the courage to allow you to be yourself. May they love you for it." "Good health."
>
> "Long life."
>
> "May you be blessed by women all your life, as you are today." "I wish you playfulness. And laughter." "I bless you with musical talent."
>
> "Never turn away from your mother. May you know her as we do. I bless you—and her—in lifelong friendship together."
>
> "May you love and be loved by your father. May you be blessed by his sensitivity and his gentleness."
>
> "I hope you have the courage to be the child of feminists. The strength to be 'different.' I bless you with trusting your own instincts."
>
> "I bless you with luck. May you be lucky." "May you honor women in your life, as we honor you today." [10]

I allow myself the luxury of imagining what I might have said had I been there, or what blessing I would offer to a child born today, or with what prayer I would grace my sons Christopher and Colin, should they ask. This would be my blessing:

> To the mother: May you not look back on your life to find that you have worked for the Army.

To the child: May you never be a soldier; may you never know war. I bless you as a peacemaker all the days of your life.

Chesler continues:

Ariel. Are you listening? You're so quiet in Miriam's arms, on Frances' lap. You know, we should be naked, garlanded. We should each kiss you on every part, every limb. We should spend the day reclining, eating. Telling stories.[11]

We could do worse. We could do worse than celebrating the birth of our own children with our own rituals. We could do worse than spending the day reclining, eating and telling stories.

NOTES

1. Edward Fisher, "Ritual as Communication," in *Roots of Ritual,* ed. James D. Shaughnessy (Grand Rapids, Mich.: Eerdmans, 1973), p. 176.

2. Victor and Edith Turner, *Image and Pilgrimage in Christian Culture* (New York: Columbia University Press, 1978), p. 294. See also Victor Turner, *The Ritual Process: Structure and Anti-Structure* (Ithaca, N.Y.: Cornell University Press, 1969).

3. Mircea Eliade, *Rites and Symbols of Initiation: The Mysteries of Birth and Rebirth* (New York: Harper, 1958), p. 128.

4. Julian Morganstern, *Rites of Birth, Marriage, Death and Kindred Occasions among the Semites* (Cincinnati, Ohio: Hebrew Union College Press, 1966), p. 81.

5. Walter Von Arx, "The Churching of Women after Childbirth," in *Liturgy and Human Passage,* ed. David Power and Luis Maldonado (New York: Seabury Press, 1979), pp. 63–71.

6. *The Rites of the Catholic Church as Revised by Decree of the Second Vatican Ecumenical Council and Published by Authority of Pope Paul VI. Rite of Christian Initiation.* (New York: Pueblo Publishing Co., 1970), p. 3.

7. R. B. Pandey, "The Hindu Sacraments, (Samskaras)," in *The Cultural Heritage of India,* 2nd ed., vol. 2. (Calcutta, India: The Ramakrishna Mission Institute of Culture, 1962), p. 403. See also Pandey, *Hindu Samskaras,* 2nd rev. ed. (Delhi, India: Motilal Banarsidass, 1969).

8. Phyllis Chesler, *With Child: A Diary of Motherhood* (New York: Crowell, 1979), p. 126.

9. Barbara G. Walker, *The Woman's Encyclopedia of Myths and Secrets* (San Francisco: Harper & Row, 1973).

10. Chesler, pp. 127–128.

11. Chesler, p. 128.

Pregnant with Peace

I am pregnant with Peace,
  aching to give birth
    to the child of tomorrow.
My fear of labor
  gives way to the urge . . .
    an urge to push.

Part of me wishes for drugs,
  a numbing injection
    of unconsciousness
to block the nerves
  to my feeling center . . .
Or to be able to sleep,
  and awaken with the baby
    already born.

But I know too much
  to allow myself to be drugged.
The birth of this baby is to be
  a conscious act.

Like a birthing ward, I see around me
  many pregnant beings . . .
    each of us becoming ready
    in our own way.
I pray for guidance,
  the courage to push at the right time
  the wisdom to rest
    between these contractions,
  the love to bear the pressure
    of this birth
    with the joy of knowing . . .
  not that I have no choice
  and must endure
But that I choose freely!*

This comes from one of the innumerable unsigned peace pamphlets that women have produced and distributed widely, usually without attribution as to authorship. As this book was going to press, someone suggested Dorothy Fadiman, a filmmaker in Palo Alto, might be the author. She is indeed; she originally launched the poem as an anonymous piece, in keeping with the spirit of the times in which it was written. It is printed here with her permission.

SECTION 3.
CAREGIVING

3. Caregiving

A Continual Presence of Care

Women are caregivers the world around. Images flood the mind: women caring for children, for the elderly and for the sick, stark pictures of mothers and children in African famine, pictures of mothers and children napalmed in Vietnam. Photographers record in terrible split-second images that which flows in ordinary times unnoticed all around us. Women caring for others is part of the taken for granted invisible life of the planet, like the rains that in their coming and going nourish the earth and its plants.*

Our culture idealizes a selected few caregiving women—from Florence Nightingale to Mother Teresa of Calcutta—and then it idolizes them. On Mother's Day children send dutiful cards and flowers. Most often people simply accept, count on, and take for granted a continual fountain of care flowing from wives and mothers, sisters and daughters and daughters-in-law, lovers and friends. Sophisticated discussions of social policy about children and the sick elderly still assume that some woman, somewhere, will be giving care. The numbers of children far exceed the number of places for them in daycare centers; the millions of sick elderly needing care far exceed the capacities of nursing homes. Always women are counted upon to make up the difference.

A Male God as Caregiver?

The classic defense of male-gender language about God, epitomized in the phrase "God the Father," is that God loves us as a father does. This is surely a strange patriarchal reversal,[1] since we all know that most of the care in childhood did not come from our fathers.** Rather, in sickness and in health, our nurturing almost invariably came from our mothers and from other women. Dorothy Boroush, a Unitarian Universalist minister, says she is going to produce another communion service, one which celebrates the nourishment we have all received from the body and blood of our mothers, blood poured out over the years for us.

There is yet another even greater theological oddity. Male religion has always stated *from a child's point of view* its central image of God-the-Father as caregiver. Caregiving has always been reflected upon from the position of the one *receiving* the care. Once again male theology discloses how it is permeated through and through by the limitations of male life-experience.

The truth is that since males usually do not give care, they are severely limited in their capacity to reflect upon how caregiving may be sacred. They can

---

* Caregiving is so invisible that the word *caregiving* does not even appear in *Webster's Eighth Collegiate Dictionary* (1973) or in the *American Heritage Dictionary* (1982).

** We now know that many of us also experienced alcoholic fathers, abusing fathers, and incestuous fathers.

only and have only reflected upon the sacred nature of *receiving* care. There has not yet been a theology imaged and written by those who *give* care.

Sin, Grace and Caregiving

Judith Plaskow has written, "Sin may flourish and grace abound where they have not yet been suspected."[2] It is not easy to express what is sacred about caregiving. To speak the truth about what caregiving actually involves is to challenge basic cultural assumptions. Male culture assumes that the sacrifice of self which is demanded in caregiving comes naturally to women. Therefore all the mixed feelings of real women about caregiving must be pushed down inside ourselves, lest we be labeled "bad mothers." Mary Guerrera Congo in "The Truth Will Set You Free, But First It Will Make You Crazy" writes about her painful struggle with this internalized cultural voice. "I had so wanted to be a good mother. But could I be one if at times I found myself hating my kids? Could I love my kids and hate mothering? All the images and messages and voices of my past and my culture today told me, 'No.'"

How strange it is that a male-defined Christianity can contemplate and name the "cost" of the crucifixion of Christ but cannot bear to hear women name the true cost of mothering: the years of effort poured out into other people's lives, the sacrifice of other talents and identities which never enrich the world. Perhaps it is too painful for children to know. As a man once said, "It is like Chinese women unbinding their feet in public."

The bittersweet dimensions of caregiving are explored by Thérèse Saulnier in "The Labor after Creation" and by Marie L. Norton in "Listening as the Language of Love: Caring for an Aging Parent." Each feels driven by urgent needs —of her children or of an aging parent—into the total demands of caregiving. Each finds a sacred resonance finally in the experience; what they feel is a glimpse into the nature of life itself. Thérèse Saulnier says, "Beneath me, I feel an abyss of care open, and I let my tears fall into it. Supported, I know I am not alone. It is life that is supporting me, I realize." Marie Norton says, "In these moments of deep harmony together as mother and daughter I was slowly becoming aware of the healing presence of the sacred."

A Deep Sounding

At first the moments of spiritual illumination in the midst of the constant giving of oneself seem fragmentary. Yet they take on the role of a deep bass voice in a full chorus. Easy to miss in the multitude of sounds from other voices, they are always there, sounding deep resonances within your soul, reminding you of the structure of giving which is built into the life of the universe itself. In those moments of illumination and in those profound soundings, the caregiver is aware of being connected to the heart of all being.

—Elizabeth Dodson Gray

NOTES

1. Mary Daly, *Beyond God the Father: Toward a Philosophy of Women's Liberation* (Boston: Beacon Press, 1973), pp. 95–7, and *Gyn/Ecology: The Metaethics of Radical Feminism* (Boston: Beacon Press, 1978), p. 8.

2. Judith Plaskow, *Sex, Sin and Grace: Women's Experience and the Theologies of Reinhold Niebuhr and Paul Tillich* (Lanham, Maryland: University Press of America, 1980), p. 175.

The Labor after Creation

Thérèse Saulnier

THÉRÈSE SAULNIER is thirty-eight. She is a Roman Catholic who married at twenty and had five children in seven years. Her intellectual curiosity and extraordinary creative talent for writing both prose and poetry have had to compete vigorously for her time in order to find expression within her life-context of intensive full-time mothering. On the surface Thérèse seems to live the life of a very traditional woman. But she says that on the inside she feels very detached and more a philosopher, a poet, or a writer. She has always known that her life's real connections are to those other mysteries.

Pre-dawn Feeding

Three A.M. (1971) Sitting on the couch with my feet propped against the edge of the coffee table, I wonder if I should try my hand at hypnotism. My newborn is laying on my legs; her head is at my knees and her feet are resting on my stomach. She is wide awake, but quiet. "You are getting very sleepy . . ." There is no putting this one to bed; she has her days and nights mixed up and does not want to be left alone. Looking into her eyes, I think: Little one, you look at me so placidly, yet you have so much power. You have controlled my life since the moment you were conceived. Your occupancy disrupted my system, throwing it off balance, making me feel sick and nauseous as my body responded to your intrusion. The adjustment made me ill for weeks, and for the next nine months, as I carried you, I noticed changes in all the organs of my body. Changes I could only watch, adapt to and wait out. Your presence made me a partner in your life and I began to know and experience how little control I have.

Nine months were an offering I willingly made, but I thought that total sacrifice would be completed with birth. Once you were born, I expected things to be different. I thought, for one thing, I would regain control of my body. Now, five weeks later, I still bleed, and ache, and wish I could recover myself. I still feel out of control. I ache with exhaustion and long to be in bed, giving my body sufficient time to recuperate from bearing and birthing you. How will I ever be able to make enough milk to nurse, if I do not have this time?

The Sacrifice Is Our Lives

No one tells us the sacrifice is our lives, our whole lives. They make remarks, the old ones, those mothers who greet us in church and supermarket, "Oh, she is so adorable . . . God love her. Enjoy her while she's little; it's when she gets older that your troubles will start. God love you." Enjoy? All I want to do is sleep for longer than four hours.

So, here we sit. We are tied together, no longer having the choice to be separate. We have set a power, an energy, in motion that will eternally continue. Could I have ever envisioned how it would be? Could I have ever anticipated the whole-life alteration I would experience, and I expect will continue to experience? Never have I known the body-numbing exhaustion that drives me to the brink of madness, and rage, and panic, and despair.

Deliciously, I have contemplated walking away—insanity is what I'll plead, and who would doubt it? Desperately, I keep the desire to murder at bay—I'll just stay here, I've thought, locked in the bathroom, until the feeling passes, covering my ears to block out her wailing. I know what those mothers feel, the ones I read about in the newspapers. Abusive they are called. Understanding fills me. I've thought the very same as they, and walked along the edge that separates the thinking from the doing. I have become a stranger to myself in these few weeks; one who considers violence and abandonment; who is capable of hating so passionately the life I have proclaimed to be my joy; and then the cramps of revulsion set in as I think of who I have become.

Ashamed, I hide these thoughts and feelings from my husband. He is in bed. "After all," he states his case, "I can't very well nurse the baby, can I?" He needs his precious sleep to do the important work of earning a living for us. The baby must be kept quiet; he has made that clear. And I collude in that crock of crap, never daring to reveal what thoughts crowd into my days and invade my nights. "She slept four hours," is my report when he asks, "How was your day, sweetheart?" And amazingly, irrationally my anger washes away when I see him sweep her up into his arms. I want him to love her. She needs someone to love her with that carefree joy a mother cannot give.

No Walking Away

There is no walking away for me. There is, right now, only care. Care that must be given tonight, tomorrow, and in the days beyond. Care that is gift and burden.

Little one, I see that you need me for your survival. You will die if left alone. You need me to be patient for awhile, until you can sort out things for yourself. You need to see love and delight in my eyes, just as surely as you need the milk from my breasts, and you need my experience and strength, and the gentle touch of my skin against yours. I look into your serious eyes and see a world of infants in their mothers' arms—there by accident or intention, looking at their care givers, needing to trust that their survival will be aided and ensured.

I imagine the question "Can you be trusted?" in your eyes. A question that scares me more than all the tabulated chores I'll ever be required to perform for you in the next eighteen years. Who will aid me? Who will instruct, comfort, nurture me? I begin to cry, because I know the answer: no one. Not the partner I chose to share my life. He draws back into a role we swore we would be free of, and I do not know how to demand he act differently. I feel the desolation of loneliness overwhelm me and I feel guilt for my wants.

Dawning

Beneath me I feel an abyss of care open, and I let my tears fall into it. Supported, I know I am not alone. I realize it is life that is supporting me. I am part of that nurturing system, as are all mothers, doing the never-ending labor of creation.

I look into the eyes of my child, now drooping with sleepiness, and see that she too is supported by other than me. We both are buoyantly carried by the life force that swirls around us.

Moving to place my daughter into her bassinet, where she finally sleeps, I whisper a prayer that she will sleep for more than a couple of hours.

In the living room, at the window, I watch the sky begin to lighten. The night is over and I feel at peace with my place in the world. I have unanswered questions; I have fears that make me feel like a child, and hopes that inspire me to work. I am exhausted, yet I feel I have retrieved a cord that connects me to life. There is an energy I can tap into that links and flows through all creation, and a wisdom that reveals the mysteries. It occurs to me that this is God's work, and I have gained a little understanding of it tonight.

Times I Wish Myself Away

Five-thirty P.M. (1987) The family has finished supper and I stand at the kitchen sink washing dishes. I will not give up this task to the children, though they all know how to do it. They scatter to their interests, and I do my mental sorting while sloshing in the soapy water. Above the sink is a window I can look out to watch another world affected by the season's passing. Inside, my third child is wrestling with the physical changes and conflicting emotions that mark the thirteenth year. He snaps at his brother and sisters, putting them down for their ignorance. He picks fights to test his growing strength and then cries when he is hurt through miscalculation or clumsiness. Speaking with negative, snarling answers when I remind him of his responsibilities, he is mystified that I object. Tonight, he is moping at the kitchen table complaining that he can't finish his homework, because he has left necessary papers at school. My youngest is crying because someone found the last Pudding Pop that she had carefully hidden in the freezer. My two oldest are fighting over the use of the telephone. And my youngest son is off somewhere, probably eating a Pudding Pop.

This hour is so wearying, there is still much to be done and hours to pass before the children go off to bed. Tonight is one of those times I wish myself away as I watch the traffic speed past my window. I regard the autumn leaves swirling in lazy patterns to settle in my yard. They are so like my emotions, caught in passion's gusting winds.

Sacred Times and Sacred Places

"Patience is a virtue," echoes in my mind. It is my talent. I am patient, and slow to anger, but sometimes I wonder if patience is a quicksand that suffocates and robs me of opportunities, when the natural response of action or fury could change the course of my life for the better, making me richer in vitality. Perhaps that is what I need, instead of iron-fortified vitamins.

"Marc, you are not going to get out of doing your homework. Stop moaning and do it."

"Girls," I shout up the stairs, "stop fighting this instant, or you'll lose your phone privileges for a week."

"Come here, Dani. Let me give you a hug. Come on, I'll even let you help me do the dishes." Surprisingly, she acquiesces, and now I must share this treasured time alone.

Like a miser I guard these few moments of contemplation and reverie. My thoughts and emotions unravel and re-sort themselves as I lather and scrub away crust and crumbs. It is my communion time where I am fed wisdom and revelation. There are two other sacred places in my home where I can go when I am wounded, weary, or when my mind spins with confusion. One place is the shower, where I can lock myself away and stand under a hot spray revitalizing my body, draining away my concerns, and find them replaced by fresh, clean insights. The other place is "my" chair in the den, where I go to be surrounded by the dark quiet of a sleeping household. There I sit, so many nights, with a notebook to capture what swims in the well on my imagination. I find grace and peace, knowledge and forgiveness in these places: I find myself. These are my prayer times—secret, sacred gifts to myself when, often, I sense the presence of the Creator.

I have learned also to cherish the unexpected embraces of my children. Their looks of love, and the moments when they are gentle and kind with each other warm me. They cause me to think I am doing right my job of raising them. But if I were to depend on these scarce moments for affirmation to balance the overabundance of grumbling and complaints, I would be lost and mired in despair.

There is a time for all things, I believe, and this is my children's time to take, and my time to give. My life is about giving. I have learned what is necessary and what is favored; I serve my family well.

Suburban Conspirators

Daniele and I make the dishes a game and are soon done. In a few minutes I will call my friend and suggest a walk. She will easily recognize my need to get out of the house and away from the children for awhile.

When I do call, my friend knows just by my hello how much I need to be with her. "I was just trying to reach you," she answers. When I suggest a walk, she responds with a chuckle and a "That bad, huh? I'll meet you half-way in ten minutes. I'm dying for a walk myself."

Always she meets me half-way, bringing all of her energy, compassion, understanding, and humor. She brings to me the touch and healing of the Divine.

We walk away our exhaustion. We feast on a dripping cone of chocolate chip ice cream that we stop to purchase, and we talk of our frustrations, complaining about every little thing.

Supporting each other, we plan our escape from the craziness of our lives, and laugh at the world's absurdities. Railing at our confinement, raging at the injustice of our isolation, we vow to break the silence of the suburbs that webs its women in captivity, commanding we curtsy and simper, uttering no challenge or defiance. Together we grieve for the loss of our girlhood expectations and struggle to be free of the guilt and archaic "shoulds" that bind us in the trap of confusion. We map a battle plan to reclaim ourselves and stake out a territory that cannot be invaded by those who would take more than we have to give—husbands and children, expecting ceaseless wealth from a store that is depletable.

The Only Direction Is Tomorrow

Although renewed by our walk, we are not content with this little interlude, lying to each other that this is all we need. We return home changed. Passions spent, verbiage expended, we have cleared the way for a new course. After wishing each other courage, we head back to our homes.

Back in the kitchen, I look out the window at the huge maple in my yard. Loosing its leaves, it is prepared for another winter. I muse at its majesty and think I, too, must let go of the past season's fruit and growth to meet empty-handed tomorrow.

In the ordinariness of my life, I experience a spirituality that strengthens me, like the daily meals I serve my family. Coloring my world, grace and blessings blossom in the private gardens of my life, like delicate spring flowers emerging from under the winter's snowcover, sometimes just a perfume's presence, and other times, a rose, lover-sent.

> I am of two worlds
> mysteriously entwined.
> I journey instinctively
> parting the myths
> that mar and blur my vision.
> The only direction is tomorrow,
> the only time, today.
>
> I shout my words
> into the darkness
> and blindly follow.
> Leaving behind one world
> I step into another,
> braiding the two—
> my lifetime work
> and labor of creation.

The Truth Will Set You Free, But First It Will Make You Crazy

Mary Guerrera Congo

MARY GUERRERA CONGO is a thirty-eight-year-old mother of two children ages six and twelve. She has been a Peace Corps volunteer (West Africa) and is a social justice activist on issues of hunger, peace, and women's demands for a new church. She characterizes herself as a "feministically critical Catholic." She has always had an ambivalent relationship to mothering, struggling to integrate the many idealized pictures of mothering (her mother's, the culture's, the church's, and her own) with the actual day-to-day realities of child care she experiences. "I feel like a puzzle piece which doesn't fit," she says. She is now relishing the expression of her artistic creativity in painting, ceramic sculpture, and, as a part of her elementary school teaching, leading children in singing.

The Struggle With Truth

Let me write down quickly what I must tell you before this moment of lucidity leaves me, before I am overcome once more by the numbness of giving all day long what I do not have to give, before I am overcome by guilt for speaking my truth.

Things are not all that they seem in my mothering. I find myself, often against my will, worrying that certain friends and acquaintances of mine who are mothers will think that I don't love my kids because I no longer hide the fact that I need the kids to be in school—any kind of school—where they will be safe, because I cannot be with them all day long. I cannot be with my children day after day without risking the limit of tolerance that might cause me to lash out uncontrollably in anger and do something I might regret.

I balance this worry by remembering that another of my friends asked me to be godmother to her newborn because somehow to her I fit the image of one who is an instrument of God's love in a parenting sort of way.

Struggling with Love That Will Not Let Me Go

The sad truth for me is this. I have experienced new wonders and perceptions of God through my role as mother, and I have felt the love of God for my child (and all children) as a result of this experience of being a mother. But mothering itself has been for me a catalyst: it has released until-now dormant conflicts, and it has launched me into what is sometimes a life and death struggle over who has what rights and claims to my own self.

Underneath my woman's smile always ready to affirm, there frequently lies a feeling of pain and uncertainty that, since I became a mother, has been almost too acute to bear. So it seems a paradox, that experiencing anew the love of God for my child and other children, I myself have often never felt farther from God's loving care. This, I am told, is the demonic side of mothering.

I can tell you about the lessons of trust and openness and innocence and curiosity and playfulness and adaptability and compassion and fidelity which my little ones have taught me. I have found the wonder of a flower, a bug, a garbage truck—commonplace things—by seeing them, as though for the first time, through the eyes of one of my children. But I have found that there is also a dangerous flip-side to these dimensions of our mother-child relationships.

I was deeply moved by the miracle of connectedness when I had to cope with too much connectedness, for I was mistaking my own needs for my child's. I was learning that living vicariously through her was for me a trap that was easy to fall into. I could not let her become for me an escape from responsibility for myself and my own well-being. It was not good for either of us for me to burden her life with what eroded me. Both she and I needed me to be strong, happy, healthy.

Exhaustion and the Well

With the birth of each child I responded with wonder at the sudden appearance of a well within me from which gushed forth love for the new little being. As a new well appeared with the birth of my second child, I wondered about this phenomenon. Were these wells of affection there all along? Was it just that I now tapped into them? And is this what would happen with successive births? It seemed such a miracle of love and free grace.

But I also learned that this well of affection could suddenly go dry. It was most unexpected. It was like a sudden drought. For brief periods it would be gone, and then, just as suddenly, there would be water again. That is how my love seemed to work. But I was bothered by it. I could not anticipate when the well would run dry, and I often had no defenses except my loyal and committed husband, who often would recognize my exhaustion before I did and invite me to get away and take some time off.

I observed that my well appeared to run dry more often than the wells of other mothers. They acted as if everything was all right with their lives. I thought there must be something wrong with me. I berated myself for not trying hard enough, for being lazy, for not caring enough. Underneath it all, I felt I was a complainer. At such times I felt committed to seeing this mothering relationship through, but my heart was elsewhere, listening to these now-inner voices from long ago. I was miserable.

My pain surely had something to do with my desire to be a "good" mother. It felt painful to me not to be able to live up to my original images of what a good mother would be—and could be. It has been a painful process, this learning that motherhood isn't what it was "spozed to be."

My Version of "The Good Mother"

I wanted to be a good mother. I had a picture in my mind of twelve kids. I would be jolly, imaginative and energetic like the father in *Cheaper by the Dozen.* I would be wise, patient, smiling, noble, and unquestioning in any sacrifice. I would be like the Virgin Mother of my Roman Catholic childhood. And I would make my own mother proud of me for being so "good." That would somehow atone for what I sensed had been her sacrifice and suffering in mothering me.

My house would not have to be exquisite. But it would be orderly, neat, clean and an attractive welcoming space. I would be a frugal, creative homemaker and with the gleanings of my resourcefulness, I would strap the baby in a backpack and go off traveling through Europe with my husband. Motherhood wouldn't stop my self-actualization. It would *be* my self-actualization. I would be great (and feel great).

I did not foresee that nature and technology would unite to take over the birth of my first child, who was born critically premature. This abruptly severed my expectations and left me in confusion and off-balance for a long time to come. I had not expected that my giving birth would usher in a period of grieving in which I mourned my daughter's lengthy hospitalization and her necessary separation from me and my mothering. I was mourning also the dashed images of what childbirth and my beginning parenthood would be like. I was mourning, though I did not recognize it at the time, the loss of my old autonomous self. Post-partum depression would become a way of life for me.

The Transformation of Religion and My Marriage

I did not foresee that what I had previously counted on for comfort and for a sense of direction—my faith and religion—would soon become questionable because of my new perspective and status as a mother. It would gradually become painful and then intolerable for me to sit in church and watch robed men, who had cooks and housekeepers running the rectory for them, playing out the supposedly sacred roles of giving "new life" to children in baptism, children they had never labored to birth, and feeding such children with sacred bread they had never labored to bake. [1] My experience of mothering would eventually lead to a crisis of faith and a break in the easy connection I had with my faith and my church.

I also had not foreseen that, while becoming a parent would strengthen the trust and tie I shared with my husband, it would also erode our relationship as we both suffered exhaustion and frustration with the strain of growing within the bonds and responsibilities of parenthood. I did not foresee that I would come to feel resentment towards him for his being with adults all day. Or resent the recognition that came to him through promotions. Or that I would come to feel resentment for his being served meals in his company's cafeteria without his having to prepare them. My anger towards him resembled that of a prisoner towards her jailer. It was as if he were personally responsible for my irritability at five o'clock each afternoon.

Surprises, Surprises

Mothering heralded a commitment of my life that in many ways I welcomed. I also welcomed the way mothering slowed the pace of my life. But there were many surprises, things I had not foreseen which were to become problems for me.

I had not foreseen that my sacrifice of energy and time to parenting would result in a continually widening gap between my own ability to advance in a financially sustaining career and the comparable ability of my husband and some of our single women friends. I find that comparing myself to them inevitably leads to self-doubt. It also leads to anxiety and resentment and even to a resigned sense of being trapped, as with the passing years I see it becoming less and less financially feasible simply to switch with my husband.

I was repeatedly frustrated in my attempts to "go back to work." I found it required constant reassessment of my priorities. The very ground beneath me seemed to shift and then shift again and again, as I tried to balance my work, my energy, my confidence, my own sense of purpose and direction, and of course the child-care needs of my children. What I finally have found is that trying to weave mothering together with work—work that will ultimately result in my work satisfaction, work security, and financial independence—is an ongoing and nagging and unresolved puzzle in my life.

To summarize, I did not foresee that my entering motherhood would demand of me a completely different kind of work after creation from what I had envisioned for my life. I knew others who were mothers, and who were mothers who worked. But I had not anticipated that grappling with how to parcel myself out among my new responsibilities would finally demand of me a total reassessment of my identity, my talents, my strengths and weaknesses, and of all my relationships. I never dreamt that this reassessment would require of me nothing less than the clearest truth about my deepest and most protected feelings and hurts. Nor did I realize that this analysis (plus the rest that mothering requires) would be so totally exhausting.

A Larger Network of Dependencies

I spent two years of our married life in the Peace Corps in a remote village in the third world. I also did not foresee that this experience would forever challenge my previously comfortable image of the serene mother/wife/homemaker in pursuit of the best for her children. I now saw myself and my children as part of a larger world, a larger network of dependencies.

No longer could I take for granted the American dream of the affluent suburban "Leave It To Beaver" home equipped with the toxic-free neighborhood full of beautiful children, well-dressed, well-fed and being driven to completely equipped schools in the latest model cars. I know now that this vision is unobtainable for most of the world's population, and also that increasingly this vision is maintained in the United States at the expense of poor and third-world peoples. [2] As I look around me I see that if a white woman has found her own liberation in the midst of mothering, it is frequently the case that someone else, often a woman of color, has left her own children in order to earn wages by taking care of the white woman's house or children.

So I can no longer assume that doing the best for my children does not cause other children to suffer. I know I live in a world that almost seems as if it cannot wait for needed social justice. I always feel the pull to help. And yet it has become more clear with time that I, like the earth, am in danger of running out of resources. I am aware, as never before, of my own need to be nurtured.

Earlier I did not anticipate the never-ending giving without replenishing that motherhood entails. Only now am I coming to see the sources of replenishment for me. Like the earth itself, I am renewed and sustained by the functioning of fragile ecosystems and delicately balanced food chains in which all *consume* and are replenished but also *are consumed*. I recognize that as a breastfeeding mother I am literally a part of that food chain.[3] I have come to respect how one small change in an ecosystem can reverberate dramatically throughout all the other parts of a fragile ecosystem. I feel I have experienced all that in my own body and in my own family by my becoming a mother and doing mothering.

So for the moment I maintain my balance in this much larger network of global dependencies by vigilant and conscious monitoring of my needs along with those of my kids. It is a necessary habit, but I have not learned it easily for it is contrary to my family upbringing and culture of origin. At times all that this engenders in me is guilt.

Listening to Other Women's Voices

I so wanted to be a good mother. But could I be one if at times I found myself hating my kids? Could I love my kids and hate mothering? All the images and messages and voices of my past and my culture today told me, "No."

If I grieved over my "road not taken," did that mean that I didn't love my kids? My voices chanted mockingly and cruelly, "You shouldn't have children if you can't take care of them." Or "You shouldn't have children if you want all these other things you seem to want." "Why don't you just take a vacation?" "Why don't you stop being married?" "Why don't you just get a job?" "Why don't you just go back to Africa and the Peace Corps experience?"

What I finally learned is that for many of us there are rules that go along with motherhood. These rules are not written down, nor is there any one voice of authority proclaiming them. We carry them within us as soft voices that repeat what the girl-child has heard from all the messages and voices around her. While she is young she can consciously choose to adopt or repudiate a particular message or voice. But the voices and the messages as a whole remain inside as she grows up. They are often mute, until the arrival of her first child. At that moment it is as if a tape recorder hidden in some mental closet starts playing these voices from the world and culture of childhood on a self-winding reel, over and over again. They are the voices of mother and grandmothers, the voices and messages of ethnic background and socioeconomic class. They are the voices of religion, and the songs and images and plot-lines of television and popular culture. The voices chant the rules and the rules tear her apart.

"Well I had *five* kids—and I never had any babysitter."

"I know a woman who is glad to be scrubbing floors to keep her kids in private schools. "

". . . maiden mother, meek and mild . . ."[4]

"I had *eight* children, and I *never* had time to *my*self."

Some of us have more rules than others. "A good mother does not need rest." "A good mother does not leave her children to go to work." "A good mother does not fulfill herself except by being a good mother." "A good mother does not divorce her husband for the kids' sake." "A good mother does not have nice things for herself." A good mother, a good mother, a good mother. There are lots and lots of things a good mother does (or does not), is (or is not). She does not give up her children for adoption, or give up custody to her husband, or have an abortion. She is not a Lesbian, she is not a single mother. On and on, and these are just the more audible voices.

Amplifying the Powerlessness

There are other voices which are not consciously heard but which are received by vulnerable young female ears. These voices whisper sharply, "You must really love being a mother." "You must not tell a soul if you don't." "And you must not complain." "*You* are not a true mother, a real mother, if you don't just love being a mother every moment and if you don't love your kids every hour of the twenty-four-hour day." [5]

The voices make the rules, and the rules are demonic. My tapes play on and on, and I can't seem to shut the voices and the rules off. Sometimes I can turn them down to soft, sometimes I can shut the door on my mental closet and muffle the sound of the voices. But they are always speaking, always there, and while they speak I doubt my own wisdom, my own truth.

I was (and still am) uncertain about my adequacy. I am pained by the absence of anyone to tell me, "It's okay, this happens to all of us." If I had come into mothering looking for an identity for myself or with no self-esteem, the voices would have had even greater authority in my life. Balancing all the claims of this still-new way of life has been complicated by the times I have had other children in my care, or the times I have been worrying about bills, or when I was trying to maintain another job. And I have been indecisive throughout because I have been looking for approval from those voices. I felt isolated from other young mothers in similar circumstances by a tacit competition with them to appear the perfect mother.

Motherhood not only exacerbated the powerlessness I already felt, but pregnancy—and labor itself—shocked me into the realization that forces in my body could be cruel and could wrest control from me. I was left feeling vulnerable and dependent in a way I never anticipated. I have not yet made my peace with this truth, but I have since learned that I am not alone in experiencing it. For some, conception, pregnancy and birth is a crowning achievement. But for others, like myself, it is an event fraught with violation, pain, and loss of a sense of self. Women still experience miscarriages, still-births, and maternal death in childbirth. I read statistics about rape and rape within marriage, about incest and sexual abuse of children, and about women seeking abortions. I shudder at what is done to women and at women's experiences of powerlessness. It is small wonder that so very many women wrestle with an inner climate of depression. [6]

All is not as it seems in mothering. There is much of the demonic here.

A Woman Is Born

I have gradually moved away from this world of the "good" mother. It has been with the help of good friends, the support of other women in various growth groups, and the gentle and nonjudgmental probing of a supportive therapist. I have come to understand that my questions about "Am I good enough?" can be themselves questioned. I have learned to ask whether anyone can ever be "that good" or "good enough." And I have come to realize that being *good* enough is, at its root, akin to that other preoccupation of women in a patriarchal society that values women as ornament, "Can one ever be *thin* enough?"

Now I ask, "Is motherhood a relationship or is it a patriarchal institution?" Now I can think about where all those destructive images of "Mother" came from. I can ask whether this society really values children. (It does not, if you judge by how as national social policy it provides and cares for them.) I can ask, "Does this society really value mothers?" "Does it value women and what women do?" I think the answer is, "Not very much."

I have learned to look at the way *I* have valued myself as a woman and valued other women. Do *other women* value *them*selves (and other women)? Too often we have to say that we have not valued ourselves very much. Who then is it who gains from these romanticized myths about motherhood? Who gains when women are isolated from one another by their competition to be "perfect" mothers? Who gains when women don't have full reproductive rights and consent over their own bodies and lives? Who profits when the largest portion of the malnourished and impoverished are women and children?

I am conscious of new voices now, voices that challenge the authority of the old voices, voices now which speak for me and for my sisters as we get in touch with ourselves, with one another, and with our truth and with our God-given powers as mothers and women. It is in the spirit of these times that all the demonic aspects of mothering are giving rise to these questions. I am no longer alone, isolated by the taboo against speaking the truth about my self and my life-experiences. I am joined by other women gathering and sharing the facts of our lives. We are raising hard questions and demanding new visions of ourselves and our lives and our society.

Mothers Together

We are slowly coming together not only through our common bond of having children but also by sharing the experiences of pain and oppression we have known as mothers, as women. We are coming together too as we recognize that there are few women indeed who have not given of themselves in nurturing and in the life-giving capacity of mother, even if it has not been with one's own children but with one's sister's or friend's children. Perhaps it has been through the role of teacher or childcare worker or nurse or therapist or physician. Perhaps we have been called upon to mother our own aging parents, or to be there for another woman, "mothering" her as she tries to become whole again in a world that closes its eyes and ears to rape or battering or incest.

There are costs to such mothering. For some of us, mothering costs us our health or even our lives as we die in childbirth. For most of us, mothering costs us some or much of our freedom. For all of us, I hope, mothering has cost us our old, worn-out images. They are too small as we come to know what we and our husbands and children and families can be. We are giving birth to a new culture with new grasp of what is most real, the Ultimate Reality that enlivens and transforms our lives, our families, our world.

I hear and am moved by the new images a singer like Carolyn McDade uses to celebrate this dawning awareness among women of ourselves. When she sings of our "love blowing over the land" and of our "loyalty to life and freedom," she is singing to my heart. In her vision women have "neither a nation nor boundaries to extend," because of "the love of life we share." Her images of what it is to be a woman are fresh and new: "We are the forest of ten thousand seeds," ". . . the waters, each small drop of rain life-spawning ponds and seas," ". . . the hope in solidarity," ". . . struggling not for things that best be gone."

Sometimes when I am feeling the need for inspiration, I turn to the letter of Idania, a twenty-four year old woman who was also a Nicaraguan revolutionary. She wrote to her young daughter shortly before she was killed. "A mother isn't just someone who gives birth and cares for her child. A mother feels the pain of all children, of all peoples, as if they had been born from her womb."[7] I am strengthened by the idea that there are many of us who feel the pain of all children, of all peoples. For if there are many of us, can we not use this maternal knowing to work together for change in our world? We have the numbers. We have the instincts of self-preservation and the motherly instincts of protecting our young. If women everywhere could be mobilized, couldn't we put an end to poverty, hunger and wars? But already I know the answers, and I am easily discouraged. Tiredness, isolation, fear of retaliation, poverty, fragmentation, subjugation, little or no access to the tools of education, lack of networks, depression, childcare responsibilities. I know these answers because at last I am beginning to know myself and my own limitations. I am struggling to know the depths of my wellspring so that I will know better how and when to give to my children.

The Continuing Struggle

This struggle has almost been too difficult. I am not superwoman, and I don't have boundless energy and wonderful self-esteem. Sometimes I feel as if I don't even have my own self. But I am slowly learning to appreciate and accept the real "me" who underneath it all is very often just a needy child herself.

Because of my growing self-acceptance, I have a fledgling faith that the demonic will give rise to the graceful in myself. Someday I will be strong enough to trash the tape recorder in my closet and its false voices. On that day I will have claimed my own truth. And in looking back I shall recognize that I (and other women) were finding our own way to what is good and right and sacred—even if in raising the hard questions, it meant that we were to leave husbands, homes, church.

NOTES

1. See Mary Daly, *Beyond God the Father* (Boston: Beacon Press, 1973).

2. See Frances Moore Lappe, *World Hunger: Ten Myths* (San Francisco: Institute for Food and Development Policy, 1985) and Marie Augusta Neal, *The Just Demands of the Poor* (New York: Paulist Press, 1987).

3. See Penelope Washbourn, *Becoming Woman* (New York: Harper & Row, 1977).

4. The opening lines to one of the many songs about Mary the mother of Jesus.

5. See Adrienne Rich, *Of Woman Born* (New York: W. W. Norton, 1976).

6. See *Sisterhood Is Global,* ed. Robin Morgan (New York: Doubleday, Anchor Books, 1984).

7. Carol McDade's songs and Idania Fernandez' letter are available from Womancenter at Plainville, 76 Everett Skinner Road, Plainville, MA 02762.

Listening as the Language of Love: Caring for an Aging Parent

Marie L. Norton

MARIE L. NORTON *began her professional career in nursing. She then married and had three children and during this period she also returned to college. Her initial encounter with midlife was as a time of crises, questioning and searching. Drawn by her emerging philosopher/scholar/dreamer self to Harvard Divinity School, she spent four years earning a Master of Theological Studies degree. During this period Marie acted as a family facilitator to her sisters and brothers as they joined together to care devotedly for their mother in her prolonged illness and dying. Her search for more holistic methods of healing led her to Pastoral Counseling and Spiritual Direction based upon Jungian psychology and the Intensive Journal Method of psychological and spiritual growth created by Ira Progoff. Marie is presently a candidate for the Master of Divinity degree at Harvard Divinity School.*

The Aging of a Matriarch

My mother was a remarkable woman who for many decades enjoyed vigorous good health and an amazing capacity for meaningful activity. For almost thirty years after my father's death she remained actively involved with her matriarchal role of service to her eight children and many grandchildren. "I just want to help and be useful and above all do some good around here," she would say, "—until the good Lord takes me."

For her, helping out included responding to weekly invitations from her three daughters and five sons to come to their nearby homes. She was a gourmet cook and greatly enjoyed cooking favorite treats for her grandchildren. She was also an accomplished seamstress and she enjoyed sewing and mending for everyone. Above all she wanted to be kept busy, active and useful. In *The Dream Book: An Anthology of Writings by Italian American Women,* Helen Barolini describes the unique characteristics of women like my mother: "Family was the focal point of her duty and concern, and, by the same token, the source of her self-esteem and power, the means by which she measured her worth and was in turn measured, the reason for her being." [1]

But at the age of eighty-six my mother came into the saddest time in her life, a time in which she confronted an unexpected and devastating illness. She struggled now to complete tasks which once were a source of pride and creativity for her, and she began to discern the impairment of her mental functioning. She would often become angry and frustrated, considering herself "useless" now that she felt she was unable to make a contribution of her talents to anyone. Needless to say, she was filled with grief. Instead of visits to her children's homes, she now sought the sanctuary of her own home where everything seemed more familiar to her and where her confusion and disorientation also seemed much less. As she recognized the loss of her former lifestyle of independence and meaningful activity, she became depressed. As my two sisters and five brothers and I attempted to confront this family crisis, each of us (or so it seemed) was similarly plunged into our own grief over the loss of this vital and dear person, our mother.

A Family Crisis

A great deal of mutual trust, loyalty and caring always existed in our family relationships. Mother had always been a generously giving person. She was always there for support in times of our life-difficulties. It only seemed fair and just that we now reach out to her in this time of her illness as she had to each one of us—in love and care. But this reaching out on our part would not be simple or uncomplicated.

All of us had assumed other responsibilities and commitments. Each of us now were married with spouses, with children in college, and our lives already seemed to be overflowing with responsibilities. We were all well into midlife and beyond, and most of us were already dealing with our own illnesses, or our children's illnesses. Each of us clearly had different resources to draw upon to find this new capacity of caring for an aging parent.

Nevertheless we were able to respond together as a family with great concern for my mother's dilemma. Everyone made their own unique contribution of time, care and love. We were able to keep our mother in her home for four years. After she was hospitalized with pneumonia, she was transferred to a nursing home where she died nine months later. During this entire five-year period my mother suffered a great deal. We her children suffered with her. It was a difficult time for all of us.

We finally came to understand that my mother had Alzheimer's disease. Little was known then about the devastating effects of Alzheimer's disease on the patient and on the patient's family, and we were pioneers in our efforts to deal creatively and compassionately with this extremely demanding situation.

Midlife, the Unexpected

My mother's illness was becoming evident about the same time I was that completing my undergraduate studies. After ten years of marriage and three children I had returned to college on a part-time basis while still caring for my family. I graduated several years later, almost concurrent with the first signs of my mother's illness. I remember how at graduation I stood so proudly in celebration of myself and my academic accomplishments. I was poised to plunge into a full-time professional career. Like so many women influenced by the feminist movement of the 1960s and 1970s, I looked forward eagerly to a new kind of recognition and self-esteem as a wage earner.

So it was within this cultural context that I began to recognize my mother's increasing helplessness and dependence. I gradually realized that life in all its ironies and contradictions was presenting me with unexpected events. I was being called upon to be a caregiver again, this time to an aging parent, and this time within a more consciously aware society which valued even less the role of caregiver. I felt in conflict. Instead of reestablishing my competence in a full-time career, I was now being called upon to consider new choices.

Choices Opening to Life

I was reflecting upon the relationship my mother and I had shared these many years. I was also looking not only at her crisis but at my own needs, values and yearnings. Was there a way to find some balance? In my heart I knew that intertwined with the difficulties of my choice were the love and admiration I felt for this woman whose creative spirit had enhanced her own life and the lives of all with whom she shared her gifts.

In choosing to care for my mother, I felt open to a powerful movement of spirit, an almost magnetic pull, in which I knew that doing this was what I most wanted to do—and what I must do. As I chose this direction for my life as the most authentic one for me, I sensed that my life was unfolding in a way that I was not fully aware of. But gradually I became certain, not that I had made the "right choice" but that the choice I had made would not demean me and would enhance my full personhood in some way.

Somewhere in this process I came across Gregory Baum's words about becoming capable of transcending ourselves to care for others: "In so doing we sense that we are acting in accordance with what is deepest in us and thus opening ourselves to reality and to life as it is and as it is meant to be."[2] I repeated these words over and over again—"Opening ourselves to reality and to life as it is and as it is meant to be." The words seemed profound and to offer a wisdom I could only partially grasp.

Perhaps the fundamental issue was life. I realized that my own life had begun in a very close relationship with my mother in which—she had lovingly cared for me and sustained me in my early months and years. It seemed inherent in the whole process of life that there should be someone who would in turn continue that relationship of love and care for her at the end of her life.

As I became aware of this flow of life events, I came to see that our human lives are often mirrored in nature and that nature adjusts growth to the cycle of the seasons. My mother had cared for me in the early spring-like days of my new birth and dependence. We had gone through summer's growth and independence to autumn's maturity and interdependence. Now it was the winter of her life, a time of her vulnerability and dependence and, soon, death. It seemed natural, after all her care for me, that we should be so connected now, and that I should be caring for her in these last days.

Together Alone

I was alone with my mother a great deal on a daily basis in the early stages of my mother's illness. For the most part this involved alleviating some of the loneliness, fear, depression and grief she was experiencing as a result of her gradual recognition of her inability to perform her much-loved tasks. In the beginning she was agreeable to going out for car rides to the beach or to lunch or to shopping trips. But as her illness progressed, many days she refused to go anywhere, preferring now the safe surroundings of her home. This presented me with a more restricted set of circumstances that intensified our emotional proximity to each other.

Our relationship of the past had rarely included long conversations. This was not my mother's style. She was so involved in projects and doing for others that she was always too busy to sit down and just talk. Now was the first time we had ever been alone with each other on such an extended basis. There we were day after day in her living room, sitting across from each other, now in a face-to-face relationship with so much unexpected and unfilled time to spend together. The first few days spent like this seemed overwhelming to me, for I was totally unprepared for this new kind of togetherness.

It was a new experience for us both. I simply did not know how to be with my mother in this new way. Everything was different. We were in her home now, there were no grandchildren, no tasks, no work projects, no miscellaneous distractions to keep us preoccupied and apart. After the initial conversations about recent happenings in the family, the weather, and the like, the hours seemed endless. At times each moment seemed like an eternity.

Listening

Our voices were silent. Within this vast stillness, the hushed muteness of our voices seemed to echo within the walls of the quiet space we now shared. Even with the suppression of sound between us, I could sense that much of the uniqueness of our individual life-stories remained concealed deep within us. Each life-story as a buried treasure was waiting patiently to be discovered, yearning to be told, eager to reveal its wisdom. But immersed in my frustration, all I could hear were my whispers of harsh indignation and exasperation about our seeming incapacity to cope with this new situation we both faced.

It was within this revealing silence that I first heard—and then felt so deeply —my own anger at the unexpectedness and contradictions of these events. My long-range plans for my midlife had certainly not included caring for an aging parent. I continued in these moments to feel and acknowledge my feelings of anger, always in the hope of finding new strategies and new wisdom for coping. Only later was I to find meaning in Beverly Harrison's words that "Anger is not the opposite of love"; and "Anger is a mode of connectedness to others and it is always a vivid form of caring"; and also "Anger is a signal that change is called for, that transformation in relation is required." [3] But for now I felt the silence, the distance, the deep anger at my plight and our plight. In desperation I often prayed for direction.

Then gradually what I have come to call the philosopher in me awakened and began asking questions again. At first the questions were simple ones, such as "What can we do to fill the time?" and later, "How can I create something meaningful out of this seemingly difficult set of circumstances?" I was beginning to view our situation in a new way, as a challenge calling for some creative response. It was then that I happened upon Irene Burnside's words about the aged in the *American Journal of Nursing.*

In describing the wisdom that is available to those who take the time to listen to the aged, Burnside points out that the aged can teach us about life, death, courage, love and generosity. They are "a distinguished faculty without formal classrooms, tenure, sabbaticals. They teach not from books but from long experience in living."[4] Her article provided me with so many insights and helped me to understand how I might respond to my mother in a new creative way. I knew then what I could do with this new expanse of time together.

It was with some hesitation that I suggested to my mother that she might like to become involved in giving her life story as a living legacy to her family. I was surprised when she agreed, and soon I was listening to my mother and writing her words down in a notebook. In time I realized she was enjoying this attention, for her face would brighten when I would say, "Let's write in your book today." Sometimes she would hesitate momentarily and protest slightly by saying, "Oh who wants to hear about my life, it's no great story." But almost immediately she would proceed to tell me of another event and, to my great amazement, a part of her previously vital self would miraculously come alive again.

Hearing for the First Time a Different Voice

Over a period of two-and-a-half years my mother told me about her life, more frequently at the beginning and, as the months progressed, less frequently. All of the entries were about significant events in my mother's life. As you can imagine, they produced much back-and-forth dialogue between us. I often began by asking questions about her memories of her early years. She responded by telling me stories her mother (my grandmother) had told her about their life.

The stories began with my mother's crossing the Atlantic Ocean at the age of six, coming alone with her mother from Italy to the United States. Her stories of her growing-up years provided me a new dimension of her life with which I was not fully acquainted. They were my favorites. Intertwined with these mostly joyous occasions were other stories, especially of the later years when the continuing struggles of raising a large family, sicknesses, and the death of beloved friends and relatives combined to weave a colorful design. The tapestry of her life was a balance of joy and sorrow.

This process of listening to and writing down my mother's life story had a powerful effect on me. Often as we sat there together, engaged in much animated dialogue and discussion, I would think of how amazing it was for us to be just sitting together talking for such extended periods. It was such a contrast to our past relationship. Then gradually these times together began to feel almost miraculous.

I realized I was now hearing, perhaps for the first time, a different voice of my mother, a voice from some deeper part of her. As she spoke and I listened to her talk about "the good old days," I was now beginning to have a new feeling of connection to this deeper part of her life. There was for both of us an awareness of an inner sense of peace and harmony and connectedness. The anxiety and tension of my mother's situation had temporarily subsided, and these moments together now were deeply enjoyable for us both.

I knew now that I very much wanted to be there with her and that I was no longer just passing the time with her. These were very special times together for reasons that I could not totally explain. In these moments of deep harmony together as mother and daughter, I was slowly becoming aware of the healing presence of the sacred. I knew that this new experience, so ordinary and so simple, was simultaneously extraordinary, and that, in some soon to be discovered way, all this would become a memorable part of our unfolding life together.

My experience supports the thesis of Carol Gilligan's book *In a Different Voice*. She writes of how women's experience brings a new perspective to responsibility and care in relationships. "In the different voice of women lies the truth of an ethic of care, the tie between relationship and responsibility."[5]

Listening as the Language of Love

I feel very fortunate that I was able to gather so many of my mother's thoughts and feelings in written words before the all-encompassing clouds of memory loss and confusion enveloped her almost completely. My listening to my mother's life story, which began as a desperate attempt on my part to fill the time, had gradually evolved into learning to be with my mother in what was for us a totally new way.

Through this process of listening and hearing her tell me her life-story, I at first shared my presence with my mother, affirming her in the telling of her story and allowing her this much-needed time for reviewing her own life. But as our dialogue extended from hours to months and several years, I began to know my mother more fully in the creative depths of her person. Only when relationships go beyond the dimensions of role, status and position do we become truly related.

It seems necessary that we share these inner depths of ourselves so that a full relationship can come into being. One day my mother and I were reading magazines together. We came across a poem, "Fine Tuning" by Janet Petersen. The poem gave words to what we had been experiencing together:

> When I can hear you—what you be—
>> What lives most deeply in you—
> When your hearing speeds
>> the beating of life in me—
> then our meeting is a song,
>> and harmony invades our silences,
>> and all the language that we know
>> is love.
>>> In fact,
>>> loving is
>>> a language
>>> of the ear—
> not so much the words you use,
> not the thoughts I share,
>>> but
>>> how urgently
>>> we tune ourselves
>>> to the meaning
>>> of each other.[6]

Transformation within Relationships

Our interaction now included a meaningful dialogue in which we shared our lives. There was an openness between us that seemed to evolve from the connection each of us now had to the deepest parts of our own being. This connectedness to our individual depths appeared to be possible for us because we felt connected to something far greater than ourselves.

As my mother related the details and significant events of her life, she offered me the gift of herself as a whole person, a unique presence. And as I listened to her, I had received the empowerment of her indomitable spirit through her telling me of her life with its joys and its pains and struggles, with its hopes and dreams. All this was now visible to me within these new depths of meaning and connection. I now see a new thread of understanding about the transformation of relationships.

I became aware of a similar pattern of change and transformation in my relationship to God as I experienced this new dimension of my relationship to Mother. Within this period of my midlife I was also in a new dialogue with my own spiritual life as I was beginning to listen to the wisdom arising from my inner depths. I found I yearned for a more personal relationship to God. I was moving away from my earlier sense of God as an distant authoritarian who compelled from an external position of power, control and punishment. As my relationship to God became transformed, I began to image God as a dynamic movement of the Holy Spirit within myself, within all persons and within the world.

My experience with my mother in her last years helped me develop a theology in which all my relationships as well as my daily life-experiences are potential revelations of the divine. Listening has become for me not only the language of love but my pathway to an increasing consciousness of the sacred.

NOTES

1. Helen Barolini, ed., *The Dream Book: An Anthology of Writings by Italian American Women* (New York: Schocken Books, 1985), p. 9.

2. Gregory Baum in *Catholicism,* by Richard P. McBrien (Minneapolis: Winston Press, 1981), p. 191.

3. Beverly Wildung Harrison, "The Power of Anger in the Work of Love: Christian Ethics for Women and Other Strangers" in *Making the Connections: Essays in Feminist Social Ethics,* by Beverly Wildung Harrison, ed. Carol S. Robb (Boston: Beacon Press, 1985), pp. 14-15.

4. Irene M. Burnside, "Listen to the Aged," *American Journal of Nursing* (October 1975): 1801.

5. Carol Gilligan, *In a Different Voice* (Cambridge, Mass.: Harvard University Press, 1982), p. 173.

6. Janet Petersen, "Fine Tuning" in *A Book of Yes* (Niles, Ill.: Argus Communications, 1976).

SECTION 4.

CREATING SACRED SPACE

4. Creating Sacred Space

The Magic Circle

What is sacred space? It is a magic circle, a ring of sanctification. Circles include and exclude. Males and male rituals have always been inside the magic ring. Within the sacred circle drawn by men, male fertility and the shedding of male blood have been celebrated and honored. [1] In Judaism this was and is done by the marking of the covenant upon the male organ in circumcision (see Genesis 17:10–14). [2] In Holy Communion or the Eucharist Christianity commemorates Jesus' blood-sacrifice on the cross and on the altar.

Within that male magic circle, women's fertility and the shedding of female blood in menstruation and childbirth has been declared contaminating (see Leviticus 11–15, especially Lev. 12 and Lev. 15:31). Thus within the magic circle of male religion, male blood saves and female blood defiles. [3]

What hallows a space is what happens there. Jacob hallowed the spot where he struggled all night with the angel of God (Genesis 32). The voice from the burning bush said to Moses, "Take off your shoes, this spot on which you stand is holy ground" (Exodus 3:5). In male religion a hallowed spot seems always to be conceptualized as one where someone has experienced a fleeting power-surge of the transcendent. The surge, the energy, is always other-worldly and comes from *beyond* human life, from *above* human life.

Male theology has the right principle—what hallows a spot is what happens there—but males have looked only in one direction, namely above and beyond human life. When women direct attention differently, toward this world and to human interactions as sources of sacred energy, what happens to our sense of sacred space?

Hallowed by Caregiving

The bedroom I share with my husband of more than thirty years is a good example. I always felt this space was sanctified by the good lovemaking we do there. But for many years that feeling was always compromised for me by the guilt I felt about the unending paper and book clutter in the room, clutter I felt socialized to feel I should have dealt with successfully, and never could. My recent experience has changed all those feelings.

For three-and-a-half years I spent long hours in pain in that bedroom. My husband brought breakfasts and dinners to me in bed, meals he lovingly prepared. We ate many times together in that bedroom. The only respite I had from pain were the naps I took in that bed. Television was my frequent companion there and often helped me think of things other than my pain. That bedroom has become for me a truly sacred space, consecrated by the dailyness of the incredible nurturing care which sustained me through a long dark tunnel.

How Wide Is the Circle?

It will be interesting to see how wide the sacred circle will be drawn when women claim the power to define sacred space. The sacredness of family life will definitely be included. In "Women as Creators of Sacred Order" I suggest that women are doing holy work when they transform the empty space of a new apartment or house into a functioning home. "As women we order the shapes of furniture in the spaces of our home, and by that we create the order that brings life: what we create makes certain human interactions and feelings possible."

Terry Y. Goldstein in "Creating Sabbath Space" expresses the vision she as a homemaker has of making her house sacred in celebrating the Jewish Sabbath. "I step back and survey the masterpiece of how my house sparkles and how my table glows. Everything is truly fit to welcome the Sabbath Queen."

Speaking from within a Protestant Christian tradition, I write in "Painting the Seasons ''Sacred'" about our own family and our at-home celebrating of the natural and liturgical seasons. "What we experience here is a flow of rich images and deep rhythms which surround and undergird each day in its uniqueness and difference."

But this is not just the experience of white Western women. Elinor W. Gadon in her chapter takes us out of the United States into a broader international context of women's sacred work. She writes of her experience with the rituals of Bengali village women in India, which they use to celebrate the sacredness of the lives of their families.

In the very different culture of northeast Brazil Mikelli Smith-Omari tells of women descended from African slaves who have created a woman's religion that is complete with its own separate space apart. "Both women and men can be initiates, but the leadership and the power and general ascendancy belongs clearly to women because of women's power in giving birth and thus closeness to life itself."

Coming Home to Our Home on Earth

In women's hearts and minds there is emerging a sense that the sacred circle must be drawn to include our whole planet. A spirituality luminous with the sacredness of nature abounds in women's art, women's writing, and women's conversation today. An example of this is the water ceremony by Carolyn McDade and Lucile Schuck Longview, "Coming Home Like Rivers to the Sea." They created this ritual in 1981 for a Unitarian Universalist conference on Women and Religion. "We were beginning to reach for new and inclusive symbols and rituals that speak to us of our connectedness to one another, to the totality of life, and to our place on this planet. We moved in an intuitive response to the potential of water as a symbol of women's spirituality."

The idea of honoring the sacredness of water in our lives has been picked up and used ritually in many women's groups, UUA gatherings, and even later that year by the National Council of Churches of Christ at its third-decade celebration in Cleveland. In 1987 a water ceremony was used by Lutheran denominations for the ceremony establishing a merged church.

At the end of the ritual, Carolyn McDade in her song "Coming Home" sings about the sacred connections between human lives, and rivers, and the ebb and flow of tides, and the phases of the moon, and women's work and leadership toward a world of justice and of peace. Women know that life is connected to life, and that justice is connected to peace. We are now claiming our power to name those connections sacred. We are determined to draw the sacred circle so that it includes not just our own humankind but all that lives and supports life on this planet.

> So, dear humans,
> Come inside the circle of creation.
> Find your unique place,
> But give up your arrogance.
> Join hands with "Brother Moon" and "Sister Fire."
> Find your place,
> And at last be "at home" on the earth.[4]

—Elizabeth Dodson Gray

NOTES

1. Nancy Jay, *Throughout Your Generations Forever: A Sociology of Sacrificial Religions* (Chicago: University of Chicago Press, forthcoming).

2. See also Elizabeth Dodson Gray, *Patriarchy as a Conceptual Trap* (Wellesley, Mass.: Roundtable Press, 1982), pp. 25–26.

3. I am indebted to my husband for this insight. See David Dodson Gray, "Female Blood Defiles, Male Blood Saves" (Paper delivered at the Theological Opportunities Program, Harvard Divinity School, Cambridge, Mass., 1 November 1984).

4. Elizabeth Dodson Gray, *The Energy Oratorio* (New York: National Council of Churches of Christ, Energy Study Project, 1978), p. 18, adapted.

Women as Creators of Sacred Order

Elizabeth Dodson Gray

ELIZABETH DODSON GRAY is an unordained minister who in the mid-1950s earned her graduate professional degree in theology. For fifteen years she was both traditional wife and mother and also her husband's colleague in the Episcopal parish ministry. Since the early 1970s she has been a feminist theologian, futurist, lecturer, and since 1978 Coordinator of the Theological Opportunities Program at Harvard Divinity School. She is author of GREEN PARADISE LOST (1979) and PATRIARCHY AS A CONCEPTUAL TRAP (1982), and co-author of CHILDREN OF JOY: RAISING YOUR OWN HOME-GROWN CHRISTIANS (1975) and GROWTH AND ITS IMPLICATIONS FOR THE FUTURE (1974). A lover of color and change, she feels the touch of an erotic God in the sensual deliciousness of being alive. She aspires to embody her deeply-felt creation theology in the changing decor of their house which is both home and workplace.

Order Which Becomes Life

All women have had the experience, perhaps many times, of going into a newly rented or purchased house or apartment and looking around at the empty space between the four walls—and feeling keenly the emptiness, the void. This same experience is recorded in the beginning of Genesis in Hebrew scriptures when God confronted the emptiness and the void, and then began to create the order which became our world.

This is the experience of the woman who confronts the emptiness of a new house or apartment, and then begins to create for herself and perhaps for others the order which will become the world of her home. When the moving man asks, "Where does this go, lady?" it is she who decides.

Such an ordering of a world was sacred work when God did it, and it is sacred work when we do it. Establishing the order which becomes life *is* sacred work.

Color As Prism of the Nature of God

Like a painter the woman looks around and immediately asks herself, "What color?" Color is sacred in this world of ours. For me color is one of the largest clues I have to the nature of God. Color is a sensual "extra" in creation. I think that perhaps the world could have worked in black-and-white, but God with characteristic prodigality threw in color as an extra. The colors of flowers, the colors of birds, the colors of sunsets and sunrises, the color of photosynthesis and of autumn leaves—color gives us a large clue that God is incredibly sensual and erotic. (I am using the word *erotic* not in the genital arousing sense but in the overall and deeply sensual sense of generalized and heightened responsiveness and sensitivity.) I like the phrase I have heard attributed to Norman O. Brown, "the erotic sense of reality." Just suppose reality *is* at its heart truly erotic. Why else the symphonies of sight and sound and color and feeling which flesh out creation well beyond what is necessary or useful? [1]

Just think of it—colors for our eyes, sounds for our ears, smells for our noses, sensitivities of touch for our skins, tastes for our eating. What an incredible Creator! So, to use color is for me to respond to the sensual erotic nature of that Ultimate Reality many call God.

We are now discovering that different colors do to us different things. Pinks and rose colors feel nurturing to us. Bright colors warm us in winter, blues and greens cool us in summer. In the days before air conditioning we had a church in St. Louis and discovered that everyone we knew covered their winter upholstery in summer with cool white Bemis-bagging slipcovers and decorated with greens and blues to foster a sense of coolness. It worked.

Certain colors have always been almost magical for me. My earliest childhood memory is of golden sunshine and being a child small enough to play, sheltered among the massive white and blue hydrangea bushes in my yard. The sun is warm and I feel contented and companioned by all that is around me. I think this is where my religious feelings first joined my feelings for nature. I have always felt connected in some profound way with the ultimate transcendent dimension of my life whenever I have allowed myself to experience the mystery and majesty of the created world.

Perhaps this is why I have always felt bathed in God's presence when bathed in sunshine. I've always wanted my kitchens to be yellow—because, to me, sunshine is yellow. The kitchen in our house is a place I spend a lot of time, and I've always wanted it to be filled with the transcendent dimension which yellow brings to me.

Color Is Serious Business

When I think of color I think of my daughter Lisa when she was pre-school age. I saw her only once draw a stick figure. From then on she occupied herself only with arranging bands of color while other children were drawing all sorts of things. She would ask me with great seriousness and urgency in her voice, did I think this color was the right one to go next to that color? It was a matter of utmost gravity to her. Recalling this now, I find myself thinking of God when God made the first rainbow, perhaps asking Herself, Does this color go right next to that color?

Color, coming from the sensual and erotic prodigality of God, functions in my life as an invitation to worship that God. For me color is that trumpet which calls me into the presence of God, that melody which lifts my spirit into praise, that visual and golden pathway into the abundance of love which lies at the heart of the universe.

Color helps my heart to sing. It is not sacred in my life because it relates me to other people, but it is sacred in my life because it relates me to the majesty of God and the beauty of the creation. And since God must love beauty and color as much as I do, the bond between us is as deep as my soul's ability to resonate with the beauty of God's work in creation. In some mysterious way we are joined, God and I, in the color of yellow.

Shaping a World of Life

But we women do not just use color in ordering this sacred space we create, we also use shapes. Shapes also are sensual, and a delight to the eye. But the ordering of the shapes of furniture in the space of our homes is sacred because, like God's giving order to the shapes in the creation of the world, it is an ordering of things that brings life. As women we order the shapes of furniture in the spaces of our homes, and by that we create the order that evokes certain kinds of living. What we create makes certain human interactions and feelings possible.

Let me give you some examples of this. We all have experienced living rooms which were too big and in which no cozy conversation seems possible. Placing chairs and sofa to create easy human interaction is to create the order that brings life. We know too the feel of a family room which promotes rich and exuberant interaction in a family. Again, we know that there can be places which encourage and shelter special activities, such as sewing or crafts, places which provide for easy putting aside or putting away of those activities. Still again, we know that decorating and ordering can also create the wonderful gift in the home of a bedroom which is right for rest and refreshment and renewal. But beyond being restful, bedrooms need to be nurturing of the erotic in our lives. If our sensual and sexual lives are a gift from God given to us by the gift of our bodies and our lives and our love, then bedrooms should facilitate by scent (perfume, incense), by sound (music), and by sight a holy and satisfying erotic life.

We take so for granted what women do in ordering space that the power of that silent ordering is almost invisible to us. But the truth is that the ordering we do by our decorating makes possible—or changes—the life which is lived in that space.

One is invited to the joy of reading in a particular spot by a comfortable chair, good light, perhaps a view or the sight of flowers and the sound of gentle music. The good conversation that precedes an evening with guests is evoked and focused by a subtle placement of chairs around a coffee table. The ordering of furniture silently, subtly but very powerfully calls into being certain kinds of moments.

We create space when we build, and then we create it again in how we choose to use that space. Before our summer house was built we had spent many days on that beach. So we knew we wanted not only a large deck but also a roofed and screened porch for a refuge at midday from the sun which at other times of the day we so enjoyed. For us this porch was always preeminently a dining space, for we like to dine with a view. But for one tenant that same porch became an out-of-doors living room so that living-room life could be lived with a view, complete with all the comforts of reading lamps, easy chairs and wicker sofa.

Another friend in her home wanted to be a part of pre-dinner conversations as she prepared dinner in the kitchen. She made into a living-room area what (because of its proximity to the kitchen) most of us would have taken to be a dining room. And now the lovely bay window at the front of her apartment bathes in sunlight her dining room/office, and her dining room table doubles in the absence of guests as a very large desk-surface.

So the ordering of space shapes the life we live in that space. Any woman who decides upon the placement of furniture is creating sacred space for a certain kind of living. Any woman who chooses color to fill a space with its pervasive and mysterious magic, is creating space sacred to the feeling tones of that color.

Decorating Proclaims Our Sense of Life Itself

Beyond all this, our woman's decorating reflects our values, our sense of life, what we find important. It proclaims that visually to every guest. It resonates it every day to our family, our children, ourselves.

My spirits always lift when I enter the living room of one friend. Years ago she had started out with colonial furniture and a chocolate brown rug. But her son began to create contemporary paintings and sculpture, some of which he gave to his parents. When they moved to another house, her living room blossomed forth with a jonquil-yellow wall-to-wall carpet, a peach-pink corduroy sofa, springtime-green upholstered chairs, and one of her son's paintings prominently displayed over the fireplace. The rooms my friend created in house after house tracked the changes in her life and spirits as they unfolded decade by decade.

Our own front hall has been graced for many years by a three-foot tall wooden sculpture of a Norwegian fisherwoman holding out a large wooden fish. By placing her in our front hall, we meant to be a Christian household offering our guests the IXTHOS (fish-symbol) of the Christ. But for years no one noticed or understood. Then a young Unitarian Universalist minister came to our house for the first time, walked past, turned, took another look, and said, "She's offering the fish!" Delighted, we said, "Yes!—you understood."

The Sacred Choice of Icons for Living

In church when we construct stained-glass windows or we put up crosses or crucifixes or sculptures, we call them icons because we understand that they are to become for us focal points of meditation which gather up meaning over time. Such icons in a church summarize for us what we value. They focus for us our commitments.

In a similar way the art, the paintings, the sculpture we live with in our homes become objects of a sort of everyday and at-home devotion. At home we contemplate day after day the objects that surround us, and they reinforce our values and reinspire us in our commitments. Perhaps we're most aware of this in the Christmas season when a Christmas tree bright and sparkling with twinkling lights and fragrant with the aroma of fresh-cut evergreen, speaks powerfully to us of the magic and the wonder of the season. For those of us who are Christian, the Christmas creche centers our attention upon the birth of the Christ child—and whatever that means to us. We expect the Christmas tree and Christmas creche to be icons, symbols for us of larger meanings. But perhaps we do not notice the role that all of our art has as icons in our lives. We drink in and meditate on what we surround ourselves with. What we look at become the icons of our everyday living.

So the choosing and placement of these icons for living becomes sacred work. We are choosing how we and our family and our friends will reexperience our values and commitments. What will we contemplate? We decide. What will be reinforced and renewed in our hearts? We decide. What will be refocused and deepened? We decide.

We often have in our living room a wonderful deep-brown wooden abstract sculpture of a woman's body. My husband and I chose this because we wanted our children to grow up with a visual celebration of our incarnation as embodied selves, as people in bodies. For us as a minister's household it was a delicate thing to choose what would seem to us as well as to parishioners an appropriate nude! We have also enjoyed a pastel of a nude woman given to us by an older friend whose husband is an artist. That picture has spoken very powerfully to us over the years about the sacredness of a woman's body. We have another sculpture, of a mother playing with her small child, and in this we celebrate the deep yet playful commitments of parenthood.

We also use posters on our walls as icons, giving us "words to live by." They proclaim in vivid colors and images such slogans as "The Creator Has Made The World—Come and See It," "Celebrate Life—The Gift That Keeps On Giving," "Today Is The First Day of the Rest or Your Life," and "Vision Is The Art of Seeing Things Invisible."

When I was first groping my way through days and weeks of what came to be five years of recuperation after surgery, I put up on my bedroom wall a poster with these encouraging words, "That God is alive means that tomorrow will be different from today." That poster became an important focus of hope, an icon, as I struggled through a time of trauma and its emotional aftermath. Then one winter midway in this process, when I began to feel I really was healing, we found ourselves drawn to new kinds of pictures. First we bought a lovely serigraph of tulips in spring-bloom. A little later we fell in love with a Harold Altman poster of a brilliant summer-scene of sunlight beyond darkness. For the next years this Altman poster was our constant visual companion, first over the fireplace in our living/dining/work area and then in our kitchen. Its sunlight beckoning beyond darkness seemed always to be calling us to hope and healing.

Let us not think that this sacred work of "gracing the home" is only the work of affluent women, for it is not. An older black friend describes her childhood home in the South in which, despite their poverty, her mother insisted they eat every meal on ironed linens and best china. The novelist Alice Walker tells of her mother's gardens and her use of flowers to create beauty and sacred space among impoverished surroundings.

So whether we are rich or poor, whether we do it consciously or not, we women have done this as we have fashioned our homes.

Sacred Work

Decorating, you see, creates not just sacred space but also the rich fabric of meaning which is the context in which you and your family live and move and have your being. All home decorating facilitates the meaning-filled relationships which happen in that home—the birthdays, the anniversaries, the weddings, the funerals, the festivals, the daily exchanges of anger and love, of joy and tears, as well as all our conversations about hopes and dreams and futures as well as our processing of past failures, anxieties and now-broken dreams.

Carter Heyward, in her book *The Redemption of God*, says that "God is the power of relationships."[2] Relationships, she is suggesting, are a window into the nature of Ultimate Reality. That suggests to me that we tap into that sacred power of relating when by our decorating we put in place that whole meaning-filled context of color and shape and order which fosters the building and maintaining of relationships. As in Genesis, so now, establishing the order, the color, the shape and the flavor which becomes the life of relationship is sacred work.

NOTES

1. "Reality as erotic"—For a more complete treatment, see Elizabeth Dodson Gray, *Green Paradise Lost* (Wellesley, Mass.: Roundtable Press, 1979), pp. 93–95.

2. Carter Heyward, *The Redemption of God: A Theology of Mutual Relation* (Lanham, Maryland: University Press of America, 1982), p. 159.

Creating Sabbath Space

Terry Y. Goldstein

TERRY Y. GOLDSTEIN has lived all her life in New York City. Her father was an orthodox Jew, and for twenty-one years her professional career has been working with Reform Jewish youth, finally as director of the North American Federation of Temple Youth. "My professional duties were to instill in Jewish teenagers a pride in being Jewish, to suggest a moral and ethical code to live by, to teach them about their five-thousand-year heritage, and to encourage them to think about a professional Jewish career. My accomplishments in that goal are the numerous young men and women I have had in my charge through my career who have become rabbis, cantors, Jewish educators, presidents of congregations, and on the secular side righteously upstanding lawyers, doctors and business people." Terry is one of a growing number of Jewish mothers who can say with pride, "My daughter is a rabbi!"

Creating a Context for *Shabbat*

My home is the sanctuary of my heart. In it I create my sacred space all year round and every day. But I do this most especially one day a week, the day called *Shabbat* or the Sabbath. To me Shabbat is a spiritual and emotional experience which I lovingly share with my family. It is especially enhanced because my home is a kosher Jewish home. This is not because I am bound to follow the commandment to keep kosher but because I choose to do so. I am a Reform Jew and not bound by Halacha, the 613 commandments Orthodox and Conservative Jews observe. Nevertheless I do observe those commandments that are aesthetically meaningful to me and that I feel are culturally important in terms of the traditions of my Jewish heritage. So the commandment to keep the sabbath is another commandment I choose to observe.

The Sabbath is a time of blissful tranquility which only exists for the twenty-four hours between Friday sunset to Saturday sunset. But I prolong it by starting early Friday morning my preparations for the celebration of what is considered by all Jews to be the holiest day of the week. I awake Friday morning with the happy feeling that tonight is the night of nights. I am also a little more than proud of myself that in spite of my four-and-a-half-day job I have managed to shop in advance the previous evenings. Bless the twenty-four-hour supermarkets! This means that my refrigerator and freezer are already stacked with the ingredients to prepare the special delicacies for the Sabbath meals of that evening and the Sabbath Day. Throughout my career I have arranged to work no more than a half-day on Fridays so that I can devote my energies to creating in my home—and for my family—the beautiful atmosphere that I want the Sabbath to be.

Creating a Gift

I start by making the house shine. Carpets are vacuumed, floors are washed, and furniture and silverware are polished. This is no menial woman's job but a labor of love. Next comes the food preparation for what will turn out to be a small banquet of Jewish ethnic delights. Since it will be a kosher meal, the meat will be slaughtered according to the ritual humane method. There will be no pork (considered an unclean product) or shellfish (for they are scavengers), and there will be no mixing of milk and meat, according to the biblical injunction, "Thou shall not boil the kid in its mother's milk." Within hours there will be mouthwatering odors emanating from my home through the doors and windows, and I will feel a culinary kinship with my mother and grandmother who handed down these magical recipes.

The last piece of preparation is the setting of the table. A special cloth, reserved only for the Sabbath, covers the table. It is a creation of my own and embroidered by hand. Out comes the best china, the polished silver, the crystal glasses, the long-stemmed wine glasses, the cut-glass wine decanter filled to the top with sweet wine, and the silver goblet for whomever blesses the sacramental wine. In the center of the table are the brass candlesticks with two short candles and the challah (a twisted bread, soft in the middle with a brown crust) freshly baked in the morning and indescribably delicious. I step back and survey the masterpiece of how my house sparkles and how my table glows. Everything is truly fit to welcome the Sabbath Queen.

Now that the house has its glow, it is time to prepare and cleanse myself to greet Shabbat. I bathe, scent myself, fix my hair, and polish my nails. I put on my holiday clothes. Soon the family will arrive and do the same. It is said that a Jew receives an additional soul for the sabbath, the better to appreciate all the extra emotions this day will bring. I behold myself in the mirror and I not only feel, I see, this extra soul.

Blissful Tranquility

It is now about sundown. There is laughter and gaiety in the voices coming from every room. The warmth of the Sabbath has already spread and engulfed my family in it. The dark evening shadows fall and we all gather at the table. An awesome silence falls as if we are all holding our breath waiting for something wonderful to happen.

I rise and light the Sabbath candles and bring their glow closer to my heart by beckoning them with three waves of my hands. I cover my eyes not to see their holy light until I have blessed them. I then proceed to chant the blessing with the words both in Hebrew and English. "Praised are Thou the Eternal God, Creator of the Universe who has hallowed us by Thy commandments, and commanded us to light the Sabbath lights. May God bless us with Sabbath joy, may God bless us with Sabbath holiness, may God bless us with Sabbath peace. And I hear the Matriarchs of the Bible, Sarah, Rachel, Rebecca and Leah echo with my family, Amen."

Next there is the blessing over the wine: "Praised be Thou our God who createst the fruit of the vine." And we bless the challah, "Praised be Thou O God who bringest forth bread from the earth." We are ready to partake of the meal after one more prayer, a particular custom of our family but not necessarily in all households. Everyone around the table joins hands and offers God their own personal prayer for the week. My personal prayer starts by thanking God for all the good things that have been given me during that week. And then I ask God for good health, happiness, and the continued togetherness which we are blessed with as a family. We say our amens, wish each other a good Shabbat with a kiss, and dinner begins.

There is constant bustle back and forth from the kitchen to the dining room with everyone carrying something either in or out. Cold things, hot things, sweet, sour—the array of dishes and drinks never stops until the refrigerator which has been bulging, is emptied, and the stove which was perking, is shut off. The room is alive with conversation between the family and our Shabbat guests. What has happened in our individual lives during the week, what is happening in the headlines, what shows we have seen, what books we have read, and some Jewish thoughts are likely topics for us. It is the first time all week that with our busy lives we have the time to interact with each other in this way.

The empty dishes disappear, and in their place what looks like a Viennese table at a wedding appears. When the desserts and pastries are finished, it is time to thank God with a special prayer for the food we have eaten, and for sustaining us through another week so that we may once again celebrate Shabbat. Then each person chooses a favorite Hebrew hymn or song for all of us to sing. The walls of the dining room reverberate with the sounds of the music. You can feel the joy surrounding you.

Throughout the day's preparations and through the Shabbat meal, a theme keeps running through my mind. How special the things I am doing are. Most of all, they please me as well as others, and that makes me feel special. It must be the kind of feeling an artist has when she finishes a painting and steps back to look at it with a sense of pride at her accomplishment.

From Doing for Others to Doing for Myself

Now I have finished my physical part of Shabbat and doing for others. I can relax, sit back and enjoy the spiritual part for the remainder of the evening and for the next day. I begin to create more of my sacred space for doing for myself.

For the rest of Friday evening and on Saturday morning, our family will join the community of our Jewish friends at Sabbath Services at our synagogue. The rabbi's sermon, which I may or may not agree with, will nevertheless give me food for thought. The prayers that I say will give me comfort if anything is bothering me, and if all has been well for that week, it will give me another opportunity to thank God for good fortunes.

After the services the congregation will celebrate an Oneg Shabbat (the joy of the Sabbath) with a social collation. Over coffee and cake we will exchange family news with our friends and have the chance to wish each other Shabbat Shalom (Sabbath Peace). The family will return home tired but spiritually uplifted. Each of us will return to our rooms to read or listen to light music (English, Hebrew or Yiddish) until sleep overtakes us. The evening of Shabbat has ended and I look forward to tomorrow when I can experience the full rest and peace I have waited for all week.

The Sabbath's purpose is to lift the Jew out of the week's routine to a higher plane of existence. On Saturday morning I change the routine of dragging myself out of bed at 6:00 A.M. to make breakfast and also sandwiches for lunch. I sleep for two-and-a-half hours longer than ordinarily. Breakfast is waiting for me (courtesy of my husband), and lunch will be leftovers of last night's dinner. It is a time for me to feel free of all the weekly chores. It is time for me to reach a spiritual high and refresh my soul. I will go to morning services and through prayer renew my strength and peace of mind.

Once home again, after a light lunch, I will indulge in the rest I looked forward to all week. There are many things I do from week to week on Shabbat, some I vary each week and some remain the same. All of them fit into my sacred space. I might take a chair out and read, or just sun myself. I plug my Walkman into my ears and shut the world out while I enjoy favorite tapes of Frank Sinatra, Barbra Streisand, Willie Nelson, "Yentel" and "Fiddler on the Roof." There is for me no blast of rock and roll to spoil the quiet atmosphere I have chosen. I love to embroider and I am always embarked on a project. Right now I am in the process of making a very large tablecloth for my daughter to use for Shabbat dinner in her home. I try to do a piece of it each Saturday.

I block off two hours each Saturday to visit my mother who is in a nursing home. I bring her sweets, library books, and we have long talks while I take her in her wheelchair for a walk. My visits make her Sabbath a little happier and that adds to the joy of mine. I have fulfilled the commandment to honor thy mother and father, and also the edict that if you bring joy to someone on the Sabbath you bring joy to yourself.

Separating the Holy from the Mundane

Again the sun is sinking for the day. Too soon, too soon, Shabbat with my sacred space will disappear for another week. One more ritual is left. It is called the Havdalah Service. It is one of the most beautiful of all services in Judaism and it is my personal favorite. Havdalah means separation. The Havdalah Service separates the holy Sabbath from the mundane days of the rest of the week. The religious symbols used for this service are a candle with a double wick intertwined to remind us that all qualities are paired: light and darkness, male and female, laughter and tears. There is a cup of sacramental wine, because wine gladdens the heart and allows us to see beyond the ugliness and misery which sometimes stain our world. Our eyes open to blessings till now unseen, and to the promise of goodness we can bring. There is also a spice box with sweet spices. The bouquet of its fragrance will remind us of the sweetness of this Sabbath, and console us with the thought that when six days pass the Sabbath will return.

The room is dimly lit, the candle is kindled with the appropriate prayer. The flame illuminates the room and all those in it. The goblet of wine is blessed and passed from hand to hand, and we all taste its sweetness. The spice box is blessed and passed around the room, and each person smells deeply from its fragrance. The candle is held high so that everyone can see it shine. Then it is extinguished in a plate of wine, since wine is symbolic in all our ceremonies. We sing, "A good week, a week of Peace, may gladness reign and joy increase." We embrace and wish each other a good week. My emotions have reached an unbelievable peak from these past twenty-four hours.

Generations Past and Now

My children are older and living in other places in homes of their own. But they remember that even in their teenage days no dance or party enticed them from their home on Shabbat. And although most of our Sabbaths are spent with friends these days, whenever my children can make it home for the weekend, that same warm experience we had throughout their earlier days remains the same.

Our prayer book says, "The people of Israel shall keep the Sabbath, observing the Sabbath in every generation, as a covenant for all time. It is a sign between God and the people of Israel, for in six days the Eternal God made heaven and earth, and on the seventh day rested from all labor." The Sabbath and my extra soul have departed, but the portion of the prayerbook I have just quoted stays very much in my heart. I feel that the sacred space of my Shabbat binds me to all the generations of Jews before me, and strengthens the relationship between me and the generation of Jews today.

Something also happens to me over those twenty-four hours of Shabbat that extends over to Monday morning when I go back to work. For I am not the same person who left the office at the end of the week tired and bedraggled. Shabbat has renewed me, and Monday morning is the fresh start. It shows in the way I approach those I work with. I may start to drag a little and get rough around the edges by Thursday, but Friday comes and the whole process begins again.

And so Shabbat Shalom (Sabbath Peace) to you all whether your Sabbath is Friday, Saturday or Sunday. May it bring you joy and refresh your soul as it does mine.

Painting the Seasons "Sacred"

Elizabeth Dodson Gray

A Theology of Seasons

I have tried to have our home "speak out" visually in a theology of seasons. I began by wanting our children to experience a whole reality in which there was a continuity between what happened in church and what was happening in the world. How do I explain to my child that Advent or Lent are seasons in the church's year, but only happen in church? When Advent and Lent are celebrated with special color and activities, but only in church and not at home and not in the surrounding secular culture, the result is a splitting apart of reality. It seems to me akin to expecting a child to learn that two plus two equal four—but only in church; at home or elsewhere, two plus two equal five, or three. So my husband and I decided to bring the church's liturgical seasons of celebration home with us. We would make these seasons come alive and be real in our home space as well as in our church space.

But once I had asked myself what it was important for us to celebrate at home in our life with our children, I found I could not stop with Advent ("waiting for Christmas") or Lent ("preparing for Good Friday and Easter"). These church seasons celebrated the past and what God had done there. But I knew that God is also incredibly active and present right now. I saw it every day as I participated in our ever-changing New England seasons on this part of planet Earth. To my religious sensibility at least, God as that Ultimate Reality and Presence in all our lives is also fundamentally revealed in the day by day processes of creation. I saw (and see) God's "hand" in the processes of earth and soil and air and rain, the processes which maintain all life on this planet. It is these processes which make themselves partially visible to us in the changing all around us of the natural seasons of hot and cold, wet and dry.

So we began to celebrate God not only acting in history past and in Jesus Christ. We also celebrated God revealed day by day, particularly in the wonder of the turning seasons. [1]

Responding to the Wonder

Life on this earth is filled with wonder. In our New England setting that wonder changes from the flaming golds and reds of autumn leaves to the quiet soft white of snowfall to the born-again newness of springtime crocuses and flowering trees. We decided we wanted to celebrate this wonder of the ever-changing but ever-steady revelation of the creativity at the heart of the universe. We wanted to bring that wonder inside our home. We wanted to be in touch with its variety and its changing nature, and to have our lives resonate to its changing rhythms and colors. We would try to live and move and have our being within its pervasive power.

So we began changing the house with the changing natural as well as liturgical seasons. In mid-autumn, as the days began to shorten and the nights lengthened, we put down under our coffee table a cozy long-haired Greek rug in powerful deep orange tones. Over the years we made or acquired pillow covers in gold and orange, like gold and orange leaves of the season, to go on our black-and-brown tweed sofa. We also got similar colors for napkins, table mats and tablecloths. The deep orange of bittersweet was picked up not only on the dining room table but also in the candles over the piano. It seemed natural to decorate the dining room sideboard and the piano with fall leaves and flowers. In this season we bring out pictures that convey the mood and fruitfulness of the harvest. I recall particularly reproductions of Cezanne's apples and Millet's "Harvest of the Grain." One year I created a wreath of nuts and artificial fruits that each autumn adorns our front door. All this leads to and culminates in our celebration of Thanksgiving Day.

But after Thanksgiving there is a stark change of pace. We strip our house to its barest components and during Advent as we prepare for Christmas we only decorate with purples and blacks and whites. The liturgical color used in church for Advent and Lent is royal and penitential purple. So in Advent (and Lent) purple becomes the color of the accent pillows, the candles, the table mats and napkins. We have some etchings in black and white that go up on our walls in this season: faces, bare trees, drawings of children and parents by German artist Käthe Kollwitz. Our house seems hushed and expectant—waiting like Israel for Emmanuel to come.

Christmas and Deep Midwinter

Then on the day of Christmas Eve, all of the Advent things are put away, the house is thoroughly cleaned, and Christmas bursts forth in it. The house is adorned in the bright reds and greens of Christmas through the Twelve Days of Christmas until a party with a neighboring family on "Twelfth Night" ends the Christmas Season for us with charades acting out the story of the Three Kings as well as the dismantling of the tree.

In our part of the country in midwinter we see around us in the outside world a soft and muted wonder. Browned shrubs and barren black tree trunks stand in brilliant sunlit contrast against fields of white snow. It is subtle and very beautiful, and we try to bring that white and brown and black patterning inside in January. Bold brown/black/white patterns adorn tablecloth, and sofa cover, and sculptures of wooden birds stand out on the surface of a white formica coffee table as though it were a field of winter snow. The brilliant area rugs of autumn and Christmas are gone now, leaving only the basic understated gray-green rug beneath to continue the soft muted theme. In this understated season of warmth and chill we ponder the providence of God which hides underneath the cold blanket of snow the potentiality of seeds and spring and life-renewal. Midwinter is in many ways life pausing and waiting, waiting to begin again.

By the time we have gotten to February it is still very cold outside in New England but our spirits thirst for the strong colors and sentiments of Valentine's Day. David and I have created a new and passionate season of riotous red hearts around Valentine's Day. It is neither natural nor liturgical but something celebrated in our secular and commercial culture which we have recaptured and made to serve our own purposes. All the blacks and browns and whites of early midwinter are now replaced by masses of hot-pink and red in hangings, in pillows, in art work, in table coverings. This is the season when for many years we created homemade Valentines for our friends out of what in nursery school they call "glorious junk." We are down on our hands and knees on the floor, playing with rug remnants and scraps of fabric and bits of paper lace, fashioning with red construction paper and Elmer's Glue and odds and ends special messages of friendship and affirmation for those we know need such encouragement and companioning this year. When in late February we are finally ready to lay down our Valentine Season, we find ourselves filled with the warmth of the many relationships in which we nourish and sustain our life.

"Spring Training" for the Soul

Now, once again, we are ready to strip our souls down to the bare necessities of Lent. If Easter (and Ash Wednesday) are early, we informally postpone starting Lent at home until after we have had our Valentine time with our friends. Then we are back to the royal and penitential purples and more black-and-white drawings and etchings. For many years we have had two pieces of art which are so emotionally powerful that we do not want to live with them as icons in our lives for too long. One is a large etching of Jesus' head with crown of thorns, by George Rouault. The other is Käthe Kollwitz' "Mother searching the battlefield for her dead son." We fill the silence of the black-and-white house with Lenten music. It seems a time of more quiet and meditation, and in our dining area an enlargement of Fritz Eichenberg's "Christ of the Breadline" reminds us of our commitment to justice and bread for the poor, the hungry and for homeless "street people."

After the silence and darkness of Lent comes the bursting forth of Easter. The joy, the liberation, the triumph is all mirrored for us in the born-again quality of nature's resurrection in the coming of springtime. Inside I find it in the colors of yellow and orange. So these colors radiate from sofa pillows, table covers, and from our walls. A large serigraph by Corita Kent, "Yellow April," focuses the theme in our living area. Guests for Easter dinner bring yellow and orange tulips to fill the house with the rejoicing of flowers. Antonio Vivaldi's trumpet music sounds out the season for our ears. At sunrise on Easter Day a champagne festival-breakfast gathers friends and family to rejoice together in a liberation celebration. We join at Easter in celebrating newness of life in both our liturgical and our natural seasons.

Resonating to the Rhythms of Life

Our movement from season to season is a pondering of the presence of both change and stability in our lives. In the natural world we are savoring the changing moods and dimensions of the seasons, which all take place within the stability of God's care. And with our family we are celebrating the changing feelings of love, anger, fear, joy, and tears—all of which happen within the unchanging stability of our relationships and our being available for each other.

This celebrating is a way of life, a kind of sacred order repeated over and over in the sacred space we have created in our home. What we experience in our home is a flow of rich images and deep rhythms which surround and undergird each day in its uniqueness and difference. Such celebrating helps to open the eyes of the soul to look within the mysteries of the seasons not only of a particular year but within the mysteries of the seasons of our lives. What we are learning to find there is the deep and pervasive presence of God, the Pulse of Life. Then life begins to glow, to light up from within.

A Rich Fabric of Meaning

Finally I want to tell you about our rainbow wall. Out of the blizzard of paper that moves through our professional lives I found myself several years ago wanting to save and savor some of the expressions of feeling which from time to time friends, colleagues, relatives, our children send to us—especially those which use in their card-design the symbol of the rainbow which, about a decade ago, we chose as the logo of our Bolton Institute for a Sustainable Future. I began taping some of these letters and cards up on a wall in our living room. That wall now overflows with a visually-rich montage of rainbows and hearts and birds and butterflies and flowers and even faces of our friends.

Then one August, after a National Peace Day march in Concord, Massachusetts in which we had carried Crane Trees made of fifty multicolor origami paper birds, we decided the rainbows of cranes were too beautiful to stow away. Since then they have been cantilevered out over our rainbow wall in a cascade of moving, flowing, wind-shimmered, colored birds.

I find now that no matter what my mood, whether up or down, I look at our rainbow wall and I feel immediately woven about with relationships of love and caring. It has become a rich fabric of meaning which delights my eye, lifts my spirit, and nurtures my heart daily in my living/working space.

NOTES

1. For a book-length treatment of the "theology of seasons," see Elizabeth and David Dodson Gray, *Children of Joy: Raising Your Own Home-Grown Christians* (Wellesley, Mass.: Roundtable Press, 1975).

Sanctifying the Home:
The Ritual Art of the Women of Bengal

Elinor W. Gadon

ELINOR W. GADON today is a cultural historian; she has been an academic wife and mother of four. Her fields of interest are India, world religions, and women's culture and art. Her focus is on the analysis of visual images and symbols in their cultural context. Her approach is cross-cultural and inter-disciplinary, using the methodologies of art history, history of religions, and cultural anthropology. She has taught at Harvard, the New School of Social Research in New York City, and the University of California at Santa Barbara. She is the author of a forthcoming book, THE ONCE AND FUTURE GODDESS: A SYMBOL FOR OUR TIME (1989).

A Different World

Imagine what it must have been like for traditional village women in Bengal to have grown up in a culture in which those natural events in our lives as women that most profoundly affect our being—first menstruation, sexual initiation and childbirth—were ritually honored by other women, by our family and our community.

How would it have been for us if we had learned as small girls that our bodies were the source of sacred power, of the life force itself, and that in our growing up, in our physical maturation, we would develop the capacity to participate directly in the most sacred of all human activities, the creation and nurture of new life? What possibilities would it have opened up for us if as young daughters all of us had learned from our mothers how to create sacred space in our own homes, a space where we could invoke the powers of divinity for help in the inevitable and ongoing problems of marriage and childrearing—and that divinity was female like us?

How reassuring it would have been to have known that the divine presence would enter our very beings, empowering us so that we could enhance our own lives as well as those of our loved ones. What an affirmation of our womanhood it is, and what delights are promised, when this divinity affirms our whole selves, not just our caring, nurturing selves but also our erotic, sexual natures.

So it was in traditional India. For thousands of years the women of India have performed their own domestic worship, the *vrata*, to secure the happiness and well-being of their families. This practice was at home and separate, outside the domain of the male priesthood who serve in the temples and control the public sacred world. The priests officiate at family events like weddings and the initiation of young boys. But *vrata* is exclusively a women's ritual. Tradition has it that this was not always so, and that in prehistoric times, before the coming of the Aryan invaders and their patriarchal sky gods, men and women both performed *vratas* to the Goddess. Within memory *vrata* is exclusively a women's sphere, a women's concern.

Village Life

Westerners are often confused about the realities of ordinary Indians' lives. We tend to see India as a country of extremes and contradictions: wealthy Rajas and starving beggars, profoundly spiritual asceticism as well as enormous eroticism and sexual licentiousness, a country that is deeply religious and wracked by partisan religious strife, a rich and ancient tradition that is hopelessly backward.

Reality in India is often much less dramatic. Eighty percent of Indians still live in villages. Even with such modern innovations as radios, television, bicycles and tractors, for many the round of daily life still goes on in traditional ways. Our concern is with village life in Bengal in easternmost India, adjacent to Bangladesh, environs of Calcutta.

There are ninety million Bengalis. They are a physically beautiful, golden-skinned people, delicate and small boned, of quiet bearing or presence. They have a natural grace in work and in repose. They are a gifted, poetic people. Theirs is a very ancient culture with their own language, folklore, music, literature, foods and customs. The landscape of Bengal is varied but much of it is fertile rice-growing fields watered by the life-giving rains of the monsoon and the annual flooding of the Ganges River. Much of Bengal borders on the sea; the Bay of Bengal is its heartland and the Bengalis are fishermen as well as farmers.

Most people are poor despite the bounty of the land. Nature can be generous but also cruel and capricious. The monsoons can fail, and there have always been devastating famines followed by raging epidemics. At other times the typhoon winds can drive sea waters across the flat farmlands, destroying crops and killing cattle.

As in most Indian villages, the Bengalis live in straw-roofed one- or two-room mud houses within an extended family compound in which three generations share a common courtyard that teems with animals and small children. Life is mostly lived out-of-doors. Women cook while squatting over a simple stove on the ground. All water for cooking, bathing and washing is brought from village wells. As women wait for their turn by the well, they gossip with other women about children, husbands, and mothers-in-law who often rule like cruel tyrants over households.

The sight of the women carrying the water back to their homes in large brass pots on their heads, their graceful bodies gently swaying under their heavy burden, is one of the indelible impressions of village life. Despite the hardship of their lives, the women sing as they work, they laugh with their children and they take comfort from the strong bonding with other women. They would sometimes ask me to sing to them the songs I sang to my children, and I would have to reply that I didn't know any, that it was not our custom.

Vrata, or Women's Domestic Religious Rituals

Bengali women, like their sisters world-wide, would like some control over their lives and security for their loved ones. They seek protection from the malignant forces of nature, disease and society, and they observe the *vrata* to satisfy the natural forces of divine powers.

The word *vrata* means vow, and the usual preparation for the ritual is a solemn contract between the devotee and the Goddess, a promise to fast or do some other austerity in return for her favors. The ritual is later performed in the company of other women of the extended family and neighbors. Central to every *vrata* is the ritual drawing made by the women on the floors, on the walls, and in the courtyards of their homes, whereby they create the sacred space in which they will invoke the Goddess and establish her beneficent presence in the household.

The girl or woman making the *vrata* draws the ritual diagram. She will include the symbols and images of things she is asking for, the forces of nature whose goodwill she is seeking, and the divine power she is invoking. The diagram is believed to be magical and the channel through which the energy of nature can be trapped and used for transformation.

Transformation is the goal of all ritual activity. The origin of the *vrata* tradition lies in the belief that when desires are visualized in symbolic language, made concrete through the sacred diagram, and then activated through ritual, these desires will generate an energy that makes them come true. The woman herself is empowered through her creative act.

A Women's Religious Tradition

This ritual art has always been a woman's prerogative. It is known by various names and styles in different regions of India. In Bengal it is called *alpana*. The *alpana* is essentially nonfigurative, its motifs organized into designs which are traditional. The magical function of the *alpana* is vested both in the patterns themselves, patterns evolved by women over millennia of time, and in the primary material used to make the drawings, a rice paste. The paste is made from rice powder, which is believed to scare away evil.

In the *vrata,* the ritual art itself is the means of communication between the devotee and the Goddess. The act of making the sacred diagram is always referred to as "writing," not painting. It is an oral tradition handed down from mother to daughter. The visual elements of the *alpana,* like the disparate threads of myth spun together in oral tradition to tell a story, preserve memories of thousands of years of women's cultural history. The young girl's training begins at the age of five or six, so that she will have mastered it by the age of twelve when, at the onset of puberty, she will perform her first ritual.

The *alpana* is traditionally made from rice paste. Rice is the staple food, the symbol of life, and hence an essential part of the religious ceremony. A handful of powdered rice and a piece of cloth are all that are required. The rice is moistened with water and made into a thick paste. The piece of cloth is first immersed in the paste, then held in the lower part of the palm. The paste is released slowly and allowed life.

The Thursday *Vrata* and Seasonal *Vrata*

Every Thursday throughout the year Bengali women invoke Lakshmi, the Goddess of Abundance, Wealth and Beauty. Married women are identified with

Lakshmi, for like the Goddess they bring wealth to their husbands and his family through dowry and sons.

The motifs used in the Lakshmi *alpana* are those essential to personal and family prosperity. The first group is associated with rice, and symbolized by the paddy, the rice measure used in daily food preparation, the plough used for planting, the sun for growth, and the sickle for harvesting. A second group represents the Goddess herself: the circular spirals are her icon without her form, and the owl is her animal stand-in. A third group of motifs is associated with objects for the beauty and adornment of the married woman: her personal ornaments—the nose ring, bangles and necklace—and the vermillion box into which she dips daily to make the red dot on her forehead which signifies her married status.

Bengali women also "write" the Lakshmi *alpana* at the seasonal festivals, invoking the Goddess' bounty for an abundant harvest. For the Lakshmi *alpana* the rice paste which is ordinarily used in its natural white, is colored according to the time of the year. It is tender green before the sowing in the spring; vibrant yellow in the autumn when the earth and the Goddess have been awakened by monsoon rains, and deep gold at the winter harvest.

Vrata for the Major Events of a Woman's Life

In the Mithila region of the neighboring state of Bihar, the *alpanas* made for the woman's life-cycle rituals focus on passion, sex, and her own fertility. The puberty ritual begins at the onset of first menstruation with the young girl's seclusion in a small shelter made from the shoots of bamboo and banana trees. The bamboo is likened to family life which, like a clump of bamboo trees, grows up around an ancestor.

On the fourth day, the girl draws the Shasthi *alpana* on the earthen floor of her hut, calling on the goddess of fertility and childbirth, the divine power appropriate to her new status as a potential mother. Shasthi is represented by her footprints on the vermillion circle at the heart of the six-petaled lotus. Red is the color of the goddess as well as of the life-giving blood of menstruation and childbirth. The circle is the *bindhu*, the mark of the goddess. Tiny dots, the seed and sperm of life, are placed along the outline of the lotus. Within float small lotus buds, symbol of the female generative organ. Above the flower is drawn the tautly drawn bow of Kama (the god of desire, the Hindu cupid), its arrow ready to spring forth. "The young virgin, awakening to desire, love and procreation, is likened to the strong flash of young lightning."

After the girl has taken a cleansing ritual bath, the family gathers round to perform the rites. They anoint her forehead with a drawing of bamboo shoots and they paint her sari (dress) with the favorable astrological signs of the sun, the moon, and the nine planets; the symbols of the goddess and of the female and male principles (the lotus and the bamboo). Then the family members place the foodstuffs used for daily meals—the threshed unmilled rice, tumeric, betel nut, banana leaves and coconut—within the folds of her sari and place clay images of a cow and her calf (representing motherhood) on the *alpana*. In India the cow is sacred, the exemplar of the nurturer. Through the symbolic language of the ritual performed within the hallowed space created by the *alpana*, the young girl has been introduced to her future social role as wife and mother in which her religious and moral responsibilities will be to bear sons and to nurture her family.

The *alpana* of marriage is "written" large on the walls of the auspicious room of marriage and birth. The bold forms of the bamboo and the lotus represent the male and female principles. The archaic symbolism of the lotus links it to the primordial waters out of which all life emerges. The bamboo shaft pierces the lotus; their meeting symbolizes the sexual encounter and union. Surrounding the primal pair are whirling lotus spheres, potent with *shakti,* female cosmic energy, the activating force of nature.

Sacralizing a Different Home-Life

Later the women of the extended family write another *alpana* in the bridal chamber. In traditional India, falling in love comes after marriage, not before. The falling-in-love diagram, the *mohaka,* is intended to break down the barriers between the young couple who may well be total strangers to each other, and to awaken their sexual desire. The *mohaka* is written on the fourth day when the boy and girl are alone for the first time. The female symbol, two fully opened lotus blossoms with two unopened lotus pods are joined by the male, a heavy bamboo shaft. The bride and groom sit before the diagram and feed each other rice and curds. Husband and wife anoint each other's eyes and repeat the sacred words of the ancient Vedic hymn. First the bridegroom says "Put thou me within thy heart, may our minds verily be together." The bride, covering the groom's head with the end of her sari, replies citing Manu, the venerable sage who first codified Hindu law, whose word has the sanctity of scripture: "I bridle thee with my Manuborn garment, that thou may be wholly mine, and may not make mention of other women."

Newly married Bengali women have a similar ritual, which like the *mohaka,* is performed when the bride sees the face of her husband for the first time. In traditional India marriages are still arranged by the parents. Today the boy and girl may meet ahead of time but only in the company of family members. The ceremony, held at the home of the grandmother, is very emotional because it is after these rites that the beloved daughter leaves her childhood home and enters a new life among strangers. Because marriages are arranged along strict kinship lines, girls are married out, that is, outside their extended family, to another village which is often far away.

The leave-taking of the bride is compared to that of the baby bird who must leave the nest. In the ritual drawing, seventeen birds with outstretched wings fly toward an open lotus flower. The *katha,* the accompanying story, identifies the birds as ducks flying toward the mother duck, Subhasini, who is none other than the Goddess. In the related ritual, pairs of ducks and drakes are drawn all around a small water hole that has been dug in the courtyard. The hole is then filled with milk, the nurturer *par excellence,* and the married women of the family anoint the bridal couple in hope that they will soon be blessed with a child. The purpose of the *vrata* is the bride's desire for a fruitful marriage which alone will ensure the stability of married life.

Life as Ritual Process in Sacred Space

The symbolic language of the women's ritual art is straightforward, clearly identifying key elements from both the sacred and profane worlds. In traditional India there is no separation; all of life is sacred. The ritual process incorporates the symbolic into the women's life; the whole—ritual diagram, ritual act, ritual story—is a tightly knit and interrelated and self-reinforcing system.

Their participation in *vrata* has a significant influence on the lives of the women who perform them. In addition to invoking the transformative powers of nature and divinity, *vrata* provides a fundamental social code around which women's whole life is structured and which integrates the women's role into the life of the community.

That women's religious experience is different from men's has never been an issue in India. Traditional Indian culture (which does not value individualism) is unlikely to provide a model for the modern Western woman. In Hinduism, moral responsibility (*dharma*) is to family, not to personal needs and self-fulfillment.

However it might well be useful for Western women, at this juncture in our own culture when we are seeking to resacralize our lives, to reflect upon how ritual and art have provided for the Indian woman a structure through which she integrates her emotional needs and moral responsibility and her sexual/biological self within the sacred dimension of her experience. This integration is a great source of inner strength for the ordinary Indian woman, enabling her to develop an identity and a grounding rarely known by Western women.

What can we as Western women of the late 20th century take from this age-old Indian tradition? Despite our vast cultural and geographical distances, there are some essential human needs we and they share as women. Even more important, there is the need to acknowledge and honor those biological changes in our bodies which are unique to us as women and which constitute our rites of passage. We need to honor our body changes of menstruation, sexual initiation, and menopause.

Sexual initiation today for most women is no longer tied to marriage. But this sexual revolution has not always been liberating for women. Too often the glorification of sex, divorced from emotional relationship, has been brutalizing for women. On the other hand, menopause, euphemistically called "the change of life," may now be just that—a time of freedom from childraising, a time of personal growth and new career choices. As some of us will surely live to be a hundred, menopause may only mark the midpoint of our lives.

But we also have great need to honor those life passages which are so violating to our sense of the sacred: divorce, abortion, sexual abuse, and the loss of a child through death, addiction or estrangement. From Indian women we can learn to create the sacred space and take the sacred time to be together as women in community—for the affirmation of our womanhood and for support in times of joy and also in times of pain. [1]

NOTES

1. For further information, see Pupul Jayakar, *The Earthen Drum: An Introduction to the Ritual Arts of Rural India* (New Delhi: National Museum, 1980); Sudhansu Kumar Ray, *The Ritual Art of the Bratas of Bengal* (Calcutta: Firma K. L. Mukhopadhyay, 1961); and Guiseppi Tucci, *The Theory and Practice of the Mandala, with special reference to the modern psychology of the subconscious*, tr. Alan Houghton Brodrick (London: Rider, 1961), pp. 49–84.

Sacred Solutions: Afro-Brazilian Women, Ritual Power, and Art

Mikelle Smith-Omari

Dr. MIKELLE SMITH-OMARI is both an artist and an art historian of African and Afro-American arts. She has her M.F.A. in painting and print-making as well as her M.A. and Ph.D. in Art History. This gives her a dual vision—a studio approach to her material as well as a vision that is critical and historical. She has published a monograph that is widely respected in her field. She has also been a Fulbright scholar. In her volunteer work she has been a Big Sister and she is a single parent of a ten-year-old daughter. Her professional work led her to a women's religion from Africa that flourishes in Northeast Brazil. She has been initiated into ISIN Yoruba and writes in this chapter from an insider's perspective as an active practitioner of the religion and participant in the culture.

A Religious Alternative to Women's Lack of Power

In Salvador, the capital city of the impoverished state of Bahia in northeast Brazil, women of African descent are relegated to social roles and occupations outside the home that are essentially powerless. As far as their being able to control or influence others outside the family circle, their position has not changed significantly since slavery.

It is generally acknowledged that these women wield a great deal of power both directly and indirectly in their homes. I was in their midst from 1980 to 1983 doing anthropological field work. What I saw was that only in the religious sphere have these women attained any significant degree of power. What came to be the focus of my work was how the Afro-Brazilian women have created for themselves in the religious sphere a way of attaining power. They then use that power and maintain themselves in that power by their ritual use of art—in the form of liturgical costumes made by and for Afro-Brazilian women themselves.

The Outer World

These women live in a modern bustling metropolis distinguished by constant crowds of people, beautiful beaches and dazzling sun. It is easy for the tourist to focus upon the more positive images for which Bahia (also known as Salvador) is famous: bright, exotic clothing, pervasive music and dance, and the exotic aroma of African-derived foods, usually sold by these Afro-Brazilian women wearing "traditional" dress that is very similar to their religious ritual garb.

It is only closer scrutiny that makes it clear to you that Bahia is also distinguished by traffic jams and other forms of intense competition for space. Bahia is characterized by vivid contrasts between the modern luxurious homes and apartments of the rich and the slum settlements of the poor. A brief experience of the city as a tourist does not reveal the extensive urban poverty that is Bahia's most salient negative characteristic.

The slum settlements in which these Afro-Brazilian women live are built of "found" materials—corrugated cardboard, tin, wood, sticks, plasterboard, and mud. The poorest neighborhoods are those built over water and those built on steep hillsides. None of the dwellings has sanitation, electricity, running water, or trash disposal; everything that enters or leaves must be carried. Most energies are directed toward the most basic daily survival.

Most households have a female head, usually with numerous children. The occupations of these Afro-Brazilian women are either domestic in nature (maids, cooks, seamstresses, babysitters, laundresses) or are connected with street vending of cooked foods, fresh fruits, candies, and almost every conceivable item, including individual cigarettes. Most of the sellers I interviewed were initiates of the women's religion I will describe later. Many of them wore white secular versions of their sacred liturgical vestments. Their average salary during the period of my research was the equivalent of US$25. monthly.

To Be Last and Excluded from Power

To be an Afro-Brazilian was to be excluded from power and prestige in the society. There was a pervasive preference for lightness of skin color, straightness of nose and hair, thinness of lips, and European heritage. Family background, educational accomplishment, and economic status also mattered, and all this was visibly expressed in a preference for Western-style clothes and residences.

As an Afro-American who spoke Portuguese fluently at the time, I was frequently mistaken for an Afro-Brazilian. I performed a number of experiments and found that depending upon how I was dressed, whether or not I spoke English, and whether I wore my Gucci bag and straight-haired wig or a cheap Bahian cotton dress and plastic shoes, I could experience a variety of treatments ranging from solicitous to rough and brutal. I confirmed that the vast majority of Afro-Brazilians—and in particular women who are Afro-Brazilian—cannot hope to attain social mobility or power within that system. They simply do not possess the necessary biological, educational and economic qualifications. Hence they and those like them must remain (with *very* few exceptions) on the periphery of mainstream society.

The religious institutions known as *Candomblés* are the only significant opportunity for social mobility and power that is open to the Afro-Brazilian woman and to the overwhelming majority of Brazilians of African descent.

A World Apart

While I was still in the United States I became an initiate and devotee of *isin orisa,* the traditional religion of the Yoruba-speaking peoples of Nigeria and the People's Republic of Benin in West Africa. I still actively maintain that initiate status, and it facilitated my entry into and participation in the religious life created by Afro-Brazilians. What consistently impressed me was the great number of women actively involved in the religion. Women had the leading roles in preserving the tradition and in creating a sphere of power for themselves, even though they had little or no access to power outside their religion.

Candomblé is the Portuguese term most commonly used in Bahia to describe Afro-Brazilian religion. As the term is currently used it describes the physical locality where deities are enshrined and ceremonies are held, as well as the ideological content of the religion, its myths, rituals, values, ethics—in short, its "world."

The religion is first of all a place apart, a physical site of the Candomblé known as the *terreiro*. It usually encompasses many acres of land and it must include an area of virgin forest and one or more brooks or streams. The land is owned in common and is dispensed by the head priestess to those who need it to build houses. The *terreiro* constitutes a sacred space or microcosm. In the temple Axe Opo Afonja in São Gonçalo do Retiro where I stayed and did most of my work, the sacred space is physically set apart from the outside "profane" world by means of a tall fence of cement or stucco which entirely surrounds and protects the religious world within its bounds. Each initiate who enters the *terreiro* grounds must immediately change her Western street-clothing for a daily ritual uniform. Women who live there permanently must wear this special uniform daily. Initiates usually refer to the physical site as the *roça*, Portuguese term suggesting being in a rural or country region or a backwoods plantation or ranch. There is a sense of leaving the profane urban openness for a rural, cloistered, sacred physical and spiritual space where different rules apply.

Through a Looking Glass

The sphere of the Candomblé religion is in many ways a reversal of the dominant "outside" world of Brazilians of European descent. My own observations, participation and research in the field confirm this inversion. Here value is placed on direct descent from Africans. Black skin confers prestige. I observed that the highest officials in the spiritual organization were very dark in skin color. Other important values include mastery of African languages used in chants, songs and esoteric rituals. Some of the criteria for speeding one's upward mobility in the cult hierarchy involve acquiring familiarity with medicinal and spiritual properties and uses of leaves and herbs, the ability to dance well, and use of African dress.

The preservation of "pure" African behavior and ideas is important to Candomblé as are the meticulous maintenance of esoteric religious ritual processes of African origin. It is clear from my work that minor alterations have occurred during the transatlantic migration and under the oppressive conditions of slavery. But a considerable amount of control and continuity has been possible because ritual activity is guided by a continuous oral tradition passed on in secret by word of mouth. What is consistently honored and celebrated is the African memory and heritage. Candomblé is a West African Yoruba-derived religion alive and well today in Bahia.

An Alternative Identity and Family

Candomblé is a series of extended family units with descent traced through religious initiations rather than through blood lines. Allegiances are formed which frequently even supercede biological family ties. Initiation is conceived ideally as a rebirth, a creation of a new being. The officiating priestess is considered to function in a creative capacity which has been compared to the biological state of giving birth. During my participation in initiation rituals I frequently overheard congratulations on the successful *parto* or birth, much in the manner as would be extended to a woman who had recently completed a successful physical birthing.

Because of the nature of initiation, one who is initiated even a few minutes earlier than another is like an elder child and entitled to special privilege or behavior which acknowledges this position. Likewise only women are allowed to perform the funeral rituals, whether the deceased is male or female. This is because women are believed to have greater power in spiritual matters concerning death as well as life (as in the rebirth of initiation). All this is because of women's close connection with life and death in the birthing context. Both women and men can be initiates, but the leadership and the power and general ascendancy belongs clearly to women because of women's power in giving birth and thus closeness to life itself.

Art and Costume as Expressions of Power

Candomblé Nago functions as a microcosm, a subculture that is an entire universe within the broader white Brazilian society. Here white European values are reversed. The overwhelming majority of members and devotees are women and Candomblé offers the Afro-Bahian woman a significant channel through which she can achieve a measure of self-esteem, prestige, power and social mobility.

Social mobility in Candomblé is based upon mastery of esoteric African ritual and religious procedures. What especially interests me is the manner in which a strict socio-religious hierarchy is codified by the use of liturgical costumes. These costumes not only signal the degree of power the wearer possesses but communicate her prerogatives and also the appropriate behavior expected of others lower on the hierarchical scale. Costumes are also made for the gods. Costumes of the gods serve simultaneously as offerings to the gods, aesthetic displays, and a means of perpetuating the religion. By extension the costumes of the gods also serve to sustain the power of the Afro-Brazilian women who are the caretakers of this religion as well as the rulers of its sacred space. [1]

In short, Candomblé as a religious microcosm and universe offers a religious solution to the Afro-Brazilian woman's lack of power in the larger secular world, and their art powerfully reinforces these solutions.

NOTES

1. For a more complete treatment of ritual costuming in Candomblè Nago, see Mikelle Smith-Omari, "Cultural Confluence in Candomblè Nago: A Socio-historical Study of Art and Aesthetics in an Afro-Brazilian Religion" (Ph.D. diss., University of Southern California, 1984). See also Mikelle Smith-Omari, *From the Inside to the Outside: The Art and Ritual of Bahian Candomblè* (Los Angeles: UC Regents, UCLA Museum of Cultural History Monograph Series #24, 1984).

Coming Home Like Rivers to the Sea: A Women's Ritual

Carolyn McDade and Lucile Schuck Longview

CAROLYN MCDADE *is a composer and singer, feminist and social-justice activist. Mother of three grown daughters, formerly a homemaker and teacher, she has used her music to explore and express the deep connections between women. In 1982–83 she spent a full year traveling to 70 (mostly Unitarian Universalist) churches around the U.S., doing services and concerts, reflecting with women on their lives and values. In 1981 she went to Central America and is an active worker in the Sanctuary movement · and lives in solidarity with the people of Central America. She is co-creator of Womancenter at Plainville, Massachusetts, a small conference and gathering center for the evolving of women's perspectives on justice. "As a singer and songwriter, I believe in the power of women's voices and lives in creating the new society, one that is beautiful, limber, compassionate and just. My music is committed to creating the long-term feminist liberation movement that will birth this transformative change."*

LUCILE SCHUCK LONGVIEW *is a seventy-seven-year-old grandmother and liberation feminist. Formerly, as Lucile Schuck, she was a traditional corporate wife and mother. "I think of myself now as "Crone Longview,' named "Longview' by my unconscious nine years ago surprisingly but appropriately (because I consider myself a futurist). The term "Crone' claims the wisdom gained from experience in a long life. Each day I enjoy knowing the person I am becoming in this latest sense-of-self. I am caught up in the sacred task of undermining patriarchy. This involves taking apart and examining the threads of the intellectual cocoon into which I have been acculturated and then constructing a more life-giving and life-sustaining world view, a new consciousness that includes a revised sense of the sacred."*

Beginnings

We were beginning to reach for new and inclusive symbols and rituals that speak to us of our connectedness to one another, to the totality of life, and to our place on this planet. We moved in an intuitive response to the potential of water as a symbol of women's spirituality.

We were working together to create a worship service for the November 1980 "Women and Religion" continental convocation of Unitarian Universalists, to be held in East Lansing, Michigan. The universality of water as a symbol emerged as we worked on what became the service now known a "Coming Home Like Rivers to the Sea." As we worked to shape the service our awareness increased of water's presence and deep meaning in all our lives.

The water ceremony became the central part of a religious service that broke with tradition in significant ways. It was created by lay women, women who had long been silent in the pews. The ritual space was also made sacred by the women themselves. We gathered to worship in a way authentic and liberating to us, not as in a church but in a semicircle around a large common earthen bowl. It was a ritual of women's being connected by a universal symbol, water, a ritual of women being connected to the totality of life.

The vital parts of the ceremony are the bringing of the waters, the sharing of their meaning, the experiencing of the intermingled waters by the group, and the taking of the waters from the ritual. The ceremony flows from what the participants bring to it. Each brings a container of water that has special meaning to her. She shares with the group why this water is significant to her and what it symbolizes in her life. The water ceremony names water as a symbol close to us as women that is reflective of and enabling to our daily lives. The ceremony releases from us an expression in words of what is vital, rooted and connected to us. In small gatherings each woman can bring water and speak of its meaning to her. In large groups such as the one at East Lansing a number of women are invited in advance to bring water and participate in the ritual on behalf of us all.

When the water has been mingled, it is then experienced in some way by the women gathered together. We have subsequently been in small groups who circled the bowl, putting our hands in it; we have witnessed the water passed around the circle as women used it to heal one another. We have seen ceremonies spontaneously shaped in the moment or carefully planned, each portion reflected upon. During or after the service there should be an opportunity for those gathered to take a small portion of the water to be carried away. The collected and mingled water thus journeys on into individual lives and often flows into a common bowl at other water ceremonies. As the ritual is continued, water deepens in meaning for us, just as water deepens during its long and winding journey to the sea.

"Sometimes I Feel Like a Motherless Child"

Sometimes I feel like a motherless child . . .
a long way from home, a long way from home.

Sometimes I feel like I've never been heard . . .
a long way from home, a long way from home.

Sometimes I feel I like I've never been seen . . .
a long way from home, a long way from home.

Sometimes I feel like the day has come . . .
and I am coming home, and I am coming home.

—traditional spiritual, adapted

The Centering

Religions in recent times have been about the empowerment of men. Women have been lost-unseen and unheard. We gather to lift up our woman identity, our self-understanding. We come with our yearning to find her who acknowledges our birth and our presence, who nurtures life and spirit. It is she who is ourselves —she who, upon meeting, we recognize and need no introduction. It is she who gives birth to all we are and can be—to ideas, thoughts, words and songs—to foggy shaped longings and to fiery rage and to all-encompassing love. She is the center inside ourselves which is our truest truth, our primary honesty—that being, tender, insistent, and passionate toward survival and wholeness. We give birth to her as she gives birth to us, as we give birth to one another.

Making our way like rivers from places distant and near, we come together to give shape to a new spirituality. For there is no theology that calls women to strength rather than to support the strength of others; that calls women to action rather than to passivity; that calls women to full expression rather than to meek acceptance.

Recognizing that, we see we must question every box, every definition, every assignment from an authority outside our own be-ings so that we can create and re-create *for ourselves* the rituals and symbols that give meaning to us. So we come together to question. To hear. To share. To speak. To inspire. And to celebrate through new rituals, knowing that our energy and our love are trans-forming.

Celebrating now our connectedness, we choose water as our symbol of our empowerment. As rivers in cycle release their waters and regain new beginnings, so do we cycle. For us as women these beginnings are powerful, but not easy. But still we come to create and to celebrate and to live by the only spirituality worthy of our devotion—a spirituality that uplifts, empowers and connects.

The Meaning of the Waters: "Water Song"*

Listen, Sister, listen,
Listen to the waters
calling us like rivers
to run our truest paths to sea—
from high hill and lowland valley,
and remote areas of our inner be-ings,
in rushing fury, white-foamed and swift,
at times quieting
to hold the colored leaf,
settling in cracks and breaking dams,
tides waxing and waning to answer
the moon,
blood running,
rain falling,

tears
dropping,
the heart beating upstream,
the earth pulling down,
rising in vapor,
falling
in rain,
soaking the roots.

Birth waters holding the babe,
wetting the canal,
signaling the birth.
Water—the mirror giving us back
to ourselves,
our images, our beauty,
our strength,
bodies and faces double-lined
with waves and years.

Water, you fall—there is poetry,
you run, there is music,
you rise, there is dance,
sweeping, swirling, spinning, running,
settling, rushing,
quieting,
rising,
misting,
fog-thick and ice-formed,
thawing, dripping, enlivening
the dry root,
juice of the flower, wine of the fruit,
drop by drop and ocean full,
one water around one earth,
dashing the shore,
soothing the sand,
leaving, returning, together,
apart,
distinct
collective,
Source of Life,
the great recycler,
carver of rocks, writer of canyons, shaper of earth.

Water, you come from the early whispers of my beginnings,
on and on,
intimate of every generation and all to come.

The great equalizer,
morning tea, evening broth,
I know you waters.
We've met some time before.
Why do I know you so well?
You run over my body and I am at home,
you fall on my naked face and I feel
welcomed
from a long journey.
You of a thousand stories, a million
years,
spiraling through formless time,
you of the endless flow,
blood rhythmic, red, mindful
of the moon.

O, but waters, I know,
how I know
and will never forget
you are blood spilled,
blood of the girl-child terrorized
who never had a chance
against the man
entrusted with
her care;
blood of the victor's rape,
and rape
and rape again,
he the returning hero,
honored, medaled,
showered with paper
rain;
blood of the back rooms,
women anguished, near death,
in a world too moral to share the front.
Yes, you are like me, waters,
time upon time caught, channeled, used,
without rights or consultation,
receptacle,
receiver of wastes,
assigned to clean the mess,
or hide it, or
hold it,
exploited, bearer of life they call their own,
confined, owned, fought over,
lost, won,
feared, disregarded, unseen,
unheard,

motherless
in a world that milks the breast,
shuns the blood and terrorizes
the womb,
damming the creative flow for its own sake
while calling itself humane.

Water, I yearn for you in some place
deeper than hope,
surer than faith,
some place I only know must be
the source of love.
I strain my ears to hear you, Beloved Sister,
beloved one of my earth,
you in my veins.

As I hear, I shall never lose
your call
from rising cloud to running stream,
from feather frost to the deep
and holding sea.
I hear you call—
you call to me gently,
strongly,
clear-depthed, you say
"O, Sister, Beloved One,
      come home,
      come
      home."

The Bringing of the Waters

At the first water ceremony in East Lansing we asked women coming from distant points to bring water. From a stream near East Lansing Linda Pinti came with water, saying: "I took my bucket and went out to the Grand River. As I gathered water I watched the river: moving, flowing, changing. I was reminded of an image in depth-psychology which tells us that each of us, each of our beings, is like a well; if you dig down deep enough into the well of our beings, you will hit the ground water that we all share. The ground water which flows between and among us connects us to each other and to the ''All That Is.'

"For me the gathering of water is a symbol of the essence and meaning of [women's gathering.] It is a tapping into the collective ground water that flows among us; the collective energy of the goddess, the liberating, transforming power which is in each of our sisters and in the sister within our brothers."

There was water from the Rio Grande River in the desert near Albuquerque that another woman brought, but her words were for that moment only and never written down. Edith Fletcher came with water from a mountain lake in New York State. She said: "This water comes from a spring-fed pond on the summit of a foothill of the Taconic Range in upstate New York. To me it symbolizes the essence of the place where I find renewal—renewal of my physical well-being by swimming in it, canoeing, rowing, sailing on it, exploring fish and insect and plant life in it; renewal of intimacy with my children, grandchildren, and friends who share my love of this place; renewal of my pleasure and wonder in the natural world of forest and fields. This water symbolizes the sustenance and replenishing of those qualities I find good in myself."

Jean Bramadet from Winnipeg, Manitoba said: "I bring water from Canada, from the north, from the prairies. This water comes from the Assiniboine River which ultimately flows into Hudson Bay. The water from this river is very important to me because I live on the banks of this river; it is almost an extension of my living room and I constantly observe its changes. Sometimes it flows fast and sometimes slowly, quite a bit like my own moods and my own life. I have listened at night to the boom and crack of the ice flows breaking as winter turns into spring. I have watched helplessly as a man drowned in the fast-moving waters before me. I have observed with pleasure the blue herons receiving sustenance from its banks. I have enjoyed the river in all its seasons, skating in the winter, canoeing in the summer. But most of all the river is a symbol of the lasting power of life. The physical part of me may die but, like the river, my spirit will live on."

Jean Zoerheide, bringing rain from Maryland, said: "These drops of rain fell in Maryland a few days ago. While I held my pan to catch them, dripping from the roof, I could see rain almost filling a slight depression in the driveway where city starlings came to bathe. Cleansing is the property of rain, not purity. From what ocean, stream or field were these molecules drawn upward by the sun? With what other drops did they join to form the cloud that released them to rain upon my state? As I return them to their eternal cycle, I wonder whose distant thirst they will quench in some other land and some other year. Interaction, not purity, is the property of rain: cleansing, refreshing, life-giving, transforming rain!" Another woman whose words were not recorded brought water from the mouth of the Mississippi River.

Of water from the Atlantic Ocean Pat Simon said:

> Water, deep source,
>   embracing the earth,
>   rushing, confronting,
>   transforming this shore;
>
> Water, dear source,
>   cradling haven,
>   crystalline beauty,
>   rain on parched land;
>
> Water, sweet sources,
>   linking the eons,
>   stirring our memories
>   roots for our growth;

Water, warm cauldron
    of our revolution,
    for love of life that
    brings a sea-change;

Water, sweet message,
    nourish our spirit,
    christen and bless
    the new air we breathe.

Rosemary Matson said: "I bring this water from the Pacific Ocean, from a white sandy beach in Carmel, California. For me, water has been a sustainer, and a teacher. Whether from a pump in the backyard where we drew our water from a well, a task of mine as the oldest girl in a large family. Or our Saturday night baths, when water was heated on the woodstovand poured into a tub on the kitchen floor. The same water bathed us all, my brothers first. I never knew why. Or my job, as the eldest daughter, carrying out, emptying and cleaning the potty, the slop-jar, the night urinal, each morning when the cycle of water intake and discharge was completed. I accepted that role unquestioningly, but grudgingly. There was the happy splashing around in the old swimming hole in the gravel pit. I was resentful that my brothers could go into the water naked. I and the other girls wore bathing suits. There were angry, frustrating, painful times, as when my bully brothers would push my head under the water and I thought I would surely drown. It taught me a fear of water and a hatred of brothers. Surely water was teaching.

She continued: "This summer, water was teacher again to me, and all those early lessons came into focus. Crossing the Atlantic Ocean in July brought me to the United Nation's Women's Conference in Copenhagen. I was in touch with many women who had crossed many different bodies of water to be there too. These women talked about water and their relationship to it.

"Around the world, women are the traditional 'drawers' and 'carriers' of water: for household and animal use, for agriculture, for sanitation. It takes an enormous amount of time, and it is a strenuous physical burden. Thirty-two trips a week, forty in the dry season, of six kilometers, for fetching water in the Sudan.

"Low priority is given to improving village water systems, perhaps because few men carry water the long distance day after day. Women were asking to be included in the decision-making process that sought to reduce the distance and frequency of the collection of water. They know it will bring improved hygiene and better health. They have visions of time and energy for themselves, for socializing, sleeping, resting and caring for their children.

"What if some of this same water, from that beach in Carmel, has come from a river in East Africa where women have washed their clothes on a bright sunny day, and found itself mingled with other waters from other rivers and streams, running down to the sea, and into the ocean, and carried by the tides and waves, connecting me with my sisters and with all of us everywhere."

Coming Home to Our Women's Identity

As our ears become attuned to hearing our inner voices, and the voices of one another, so also do we hear the call of our sisters from far beyond. What spirals in, also spirals out, and beyond space and time. Thus we hear the anguished words and the more anguished silences of women around the earth and through time. We know that our sisterhood extends beyond our land and that we must reach beyond clans and nationalism, beyond languages and cultures, beyond institutions, beyond religions—to our sisters, living hand to living hand, eye to eye, thought to thought, with our compassion for one another, our love of this earth, our very love of life itself, creating bonds between us.

We must lift up in our culture women's significant strengths, insights and understanding, our ways of coping and thinking. We must enter now and shape our world toward one of compassion and a new justice that dares to see and to feel and to respond, toward human concern for life and affirmation of life, toward joyfulness and celebration, toward relationships of love, respect and mutual concern—toward cooperation, connectedness and responsiveness. We bring the inclusiveness of the cycles and the spheres. In our way of understanding life, we name a new meaning.

Such a promise demands that we keep our identity as women.

We cannot fall back to the false assumptions of the faiths of the past, to the biased assumptions that have failed our half, the female half, of the world. We can no longer embrace the patriarchal assumptions underlying traditional faiths. All religions keep women invisible, hide our issues, turn our energy and our loyalty toward concerns which, though labelled "human concerns," consistently lift the priorities of males above all else.

No vision, no world view, has the ability to sustain a just and caring society without a feminist perspective—a perspective that seeks the empowerment of women as well as men. Women must be the ones to promote that perspective, for we are the unbounded ones in crucial ways. We have an outsider understanding and we need to draw on that knowledge. We do not have the investment in the patriarchy that men may have. We do not have the bonds with the power of domination that men have been acculturated to hold and to cherish.

Ours can be an enabling power.

We must *come home*—come home to our self-understanding.

Let us embrace our woman-identity!

Taking the Waters for Women's Empowerment

We take these birthing waters *to name our empowerment*, to name our strength to be ourselves, and to name our ability to rise up and to move forth.

We take these birthing waters *to call forth our power of questioning*, our powers to doubt, our powers to examine every definition and every authority outside ourselves.

We take these amniotic waters *to name our imagination and creativity*, our power to unveil our thinking and to create new visions.

We take these waters, symbolic of our becoming, *to name the reclaiming of our energy and loyalty,* to signify that we put ourselves—the thoughts of our minds and the work of our hands—to what we most deeply value.

We take these waters, symbolic of a new genesis, *to name our love:* of this earth, of our connectedness with people everywhere, and of our devotion to life itself.

At East Lansing five women took of the waters in a symbolic way for all of us, because we were so many. Then we were told that, if we wished to take some of the waters home with us, we should find a way to do so. "Look among the items you brought," we were told, "the lotions, the creams, the perfumes. Those containers carry the veils we wear—the reminders of our inadequacies. Empty one of those containers. Take with you this symbol of our becoming. Take some of the birthing waters."

We must lift up life-giving symbols and keep them before us as symbols of our woman's identity, symbols of our empowerment, our questioning, our imagination and creativity, our energy and loyalty, our nurturing and love. We must have our own reminders that we have put aside those other symbols of exclusion and domination, those symbols which have diminished us and now lead to the destruction of our planet.

"Coming Home"*

> *We're coming home to the spirit in our soul,*
> *We're coming home and the healing makes us whole;*
> *Like rivers running to the sea,*
> *We're coming home, we're coming home.*

> As the day is woven into night,
> As the darkness lives within the light,
>   As we open vision to new sight,
> We're coming home, we're coming home,

> *We're coming home to the spirit in our soul . . .*

> Bearing words born new unto each day,
> Speaking bold where only silence lay
>   As we dare to rise and lead the way,
> We're coming home, we're coming home,

> *We're coming home to the spirit in our soul . . .*

As the full moon waxes into wane,
Changing, yielding all that she did gain,
   As from death she dares be born again,
We're coming home, we're coming home,

We're coming home to the spirit in our soul . . .

To reclaim the thinking of our mind,
Leaving shackles lying far behind,
   Bearing hope for every soul confined,
We're coming home, we're coming home,

We're coming home to the spirit in our soul . . .

To create a world of joy and peace,
Where the power of justice does release
   Love abounding, wars forever cease,
We're coming home, we're coming home,

We're coming home to the spirit in our soul . . .

Sharing of the Waters

As water changes form and moves in a life-giving cycle, so this water
ceremony must move, be in process, change, be in motion. It needs always to be
reflective of and integral to the time and place of the people creating it.

In reading or using this service we think it is important to notice that the
water ceremony was woven into a worship service. Creating that service has had
its own value for us in what it gave to us. It brought us together for many hours
of sharing and conversation, analyzing, planning, creating, clarifying. It called us
to articulation, to pulling foggy-shaped thoughts into words. We each spoke and
listened. We wrote down one another's words. We spoke them back with added
meaning. It was a bonding and empowering experience for us, and we commend
this sort of experience to you.

We hope our sisters continue to reach for the depth and inclusiveness of
symbols that speak to women and that draw upon our daily experiences. We
need symbols with enabling power that connect us with what we most deeply
value and which empower our expression of this in our lives.

SECTION 5.

Thomas Höpker/Woodfin Camp

DOING HOUSEWORK

5. Doing Housework

Sweeping the Hearth

What are we to make of the extremes of prestige, status and function that women experience? We can be "righteous women," presiding at the Sabbath table, lighting the candles and conducting the family ritual. Yet we also function as a household servant who removes the dirt and does the laundry. Every woman knows that the moments of high liturgical drama in her life are few and far between, while the removal of dust and soil is a daily occurrence. Most of the time Cinderella is not in her ball gown but sweeping the hearth.

Male cultures have never hallowed removing dirt, probably because men so seldom do it. The anthropologist Margaret Mead observed in her travels that whatever males did in a particular culture was valued and of high prestige, and whatever women did was of little or no prestige. [1] Doing housework has always been a lowly task. Unless women are employed by a stranger to do housework in someone else's house, we are never paid for all the straightening, sorting, scrubbing, washing, sweeping, dusting, shaking, and related tasks that keep up the usefulness and appearance of our household space. In our culture the comparative value of different kinds of work is indicated by the wages paid. To receive nothing at all for what we do is an indication of how little our work, when it is being done, is noticed or valued.

A Labor for Love Alone

Women have always done housework in their homes "for nothing." Yet in discussions about economics or legislation, men constantly ask me with incredulity in their voices, "How can we ever expect *anyone* to "do something for nothing'?" Their implied answer is "No," because they cannot imagine *themselves* doing something for nothing. They base public policy upon a mental picture of Economic Man [sic] who responds largely or even exclusively to dollar incentives and rewards. Within this construct no human would ever have any reason to perform work without the economic reward and psychological validation of wages.

Yet women have always been expected to do housework in their homes "for nothing." Society works hard socializing women to feel that our God-given role in life is to do housework "for nothing." Within a family, such work is deemed "a labor of love." Housework is almost an invisible "labor" since, oddly enough, our common language usage refuses even to recognize it as work. A re-entry wife-and-mother is always asked, "When did you start working?"

Most women have very mixed feelings about housework. For many of us it lacks the creativity of cooking or decorating. It seems dull and repetitive and—yes—boring. Doing housework, more than almost anything else we women do, is related to the status and functioning of servants and slaves.

There are currents of male theology which emphasize "becoming a suffering servant." But those theologians never consider embodying that ministry by actually doing the lowly work of servanthood. Generations of male theologians and ministers, priests and popes, have seemed perfectly content to write learnedly about "servanthood," while having their homes cleaned and their personal laundry washed by women.

Women in Sharp Debate

Many of us detest housework and are appalled at the thought of anyone, much less other women, declaring it sacred. It feels like a prison closing back over us again. As the prison door is clanging shut, a stentorian voice proclaims, "All who are ordained by gender to do housework—which no one else wants to do—enter here, and be content!"

These women fear that to call everything women do sacred is bad news for women. "It is a part of how men have controlled us," some say. "If it is so sacred, then let's make sure men do it too!"

We also fear the revelation of ourselves which an evaluation of a woman's housework brings. Women have so long been judged by our homes, as though they were presentations of ourselves, that housework is a woman's form of performance anxiety. Have we done it right? Have we been good enough at it? Are our floors clean enough, our colors bright enough, our spaces neat enough? Does inspection of our homes reveal us to be careless, or lazy, or, on the other hand, too compulsive?

Do we accept these imputed judgments upon our housekeeping? A major component of television advertising certainly reinforces these self-assessments, but are they really saying something crucial about our real identity as women? Or do we reject the whole idea? There is a motto circulating among my non-housekeeping friends which says, "A well-kept house is a sign of a misspent life." But whatever a woman chooses here, she *feels* she loses.

If you ask those of us who feel our housework is meaningful, we say things like this:

"It is a part of giving care to my family." "It is my gift to other people: clean sheets, clean rooms, the smell of clothes dried out-of-doors."

"I empower my family into certain kinds of living. For example, I select the books on the coffee table, and these books start certain kinds of conversations."

"I put fresh flowers into every room. It is my way of welcoming family and friends. I create sacred space with that flower welcome."

Creating Order

One housewife told me, "It is my way of creating order." Earlier in "Creating Sacred Space" we discussed the woman's role in bringing the order of color and form into the empty space of each house or apartment she moves into. Now we are talking again about the daily role the housewife plays in reordering life again and again against the tides of dirt, dust, clutter and randomness which sweep through a home as it is lived in.

A recurrent theme in male religion is that of bringing order out of chaos. Male gods often do this in creation myths. Men clearly conceptualize their hierarchical political structures as providing "order." They perceive a world which is fundamentally threatened with disintegration and chaos. The cause of chaos in male myths is often seen as female, as with Eve, Pandora, and others.

Thus in male religion, order is clearly sacred. The word "hierarchy" itself means "sacred order." To have things in place, in order, is definitely a prized value in all our lives. If order is so sacred, then women's constant work on a daily basis to maintain order *should* be highly valued. But when it is women who are doing this vital work, it is devalued by the culture. This is a blatant example of men denigrating women, so that even a work connected to sacredness is devalued when women do it. It is a struggle, even for women, to value our own contribution to life when it is seen by us as "doing housework" rather than "bringing order into life."

Cleanliness and Godliness

From childhood we have been exposed to the aphorism that "Cleanliness is next to Godliness." The aphorism is conveniently vague about whether it means "*being* clean" or "*making* clean." In the past male priests have been only concerned about ritual cleanliness. The janitor washes the church floors and the women of the altar guild wash and iron the altar linens. Priests ritually cleanse the communion chalice at the altar, but it will be sanitized—washed with soap and hot water—in the sacristy by others. Men have acted as though they are in charge of godliness, while women and other menials provide the nitty-gritty cleanliness.

Still, there *is* satisfaction in restoring cleanliness. The shine on polished silver or polished furniture, the smell of fresh laundry, the feel of clean sheets, are delicious sensual experiences. To feel the power of having brought these into your life and then given them as a gift to your family and friends can be very meaningful.

A Sense of Ultimate Value

What hope moves through a woman's being while she does housework? What sense of ultimate reality graces our daily round of unrecognized and unrecompensed activities while we keep our households operating as spaces potentially sacred for our families and ourselves? Is there sacred meaning to caring for one's family's space?

Phyllis W. Harlow was a home-economics major in college, and for more than thirty years she has viewed her household management as a sacred work that makes family life possible. She describes this in "Housework as Homemaking." "As I write this today, I am keenly aware of the date: it is the anniversary of my mother's death, now very nearly half a century in the past. My conception of what a home should be was formed in the home she made until her death, and then in the home of her mother where I lived after I started high school."

Kathryn Allen Rabuzzi in "Women's Work and the Sense of Time in Women's Lives" has a fascinating thesis: the repetitive nature of housework can open out to "the demonic realm of the Boring or the divine space of the Mystical." Finally Marlane van Hall, in "The Zen of Housework," tells of how at a time of disruption in her life she discovered in following the "way" of Zen that "eventually our heart is set free completely, we are united with the ground of our being and finally we know who we really are."

—Elizabeth Dodson Gray

Notes

1. Margaret Mead, *Male and Female: A Study of the Sexes in a Changing World* (New York: Morrow Paperback, William Morrow, 1975), pp. 159–160.

Housework as Homemaking

Phyllis W. Harlow

Phyllis W. Harlow is a homemaker by profession and choice. She was born in Bloomfield, N. J. and graduated from Douglas College. She has taught home economics. Being the mother of five children is one of the personal accomplishments of which she is most proud. She says, "I have spent thirty-three years creating and maintaining a home. It is the major prop, along with the family, for what I do for others and for myself." She does a lot for others: running fundraising campaigns for the retarded in her hometown (she has a retarded son), teaching sewing at the Plymouth County House of Corrections, sponsoring two Cambodian teenagers as refugees, working for twenty-two years to improve a state school for the retarded, singing in the choir and teaching church school in her local community church.

A Wonderful Place Called Home

Feeling at home has always been a very important part of my life as an adult. As I write this today I am keenly aware of the date: it is the anniversary of my mother's death, now very nearly half a century in the past. My conception of what a home should be was formed in the home she made until her death, and then in the home of her mother where I lived after I started high school. In both places I was wanted, and any homecomings were anticipated with enthusiasm. In each there were spaces for me to enjoy my hobbies without interference and there was great freedom of action. Furnishings served their purpose without pretensions, rugs provided warmth and quiet, clutter was cleared as it accumulated, and routine work was accomplished cheerfully. No one counted the number of glasses of milk consumed at a meal. My father was always proud that my mother did not have to work outside the home to help support the family, as so many women were forced to do during the Depression.

I still remember vividly little details of home life from those early years. Curtains drying in the spring on the stretcher on the porch with tiny pleats carefully folded over the pins. Grape and quince jelly being poured from steaming pots into glasses. The vacuum cleaner that was turned off in the middle of the living room rug being cleaned because my mother felt like playing the piano for a while. Frequently there were dresses being cut out on the dining room table, and I remember the whir of a treadle sewing machine and the handsome smocking and the beautifully hand-sewn buttonholes. Flowers carefully tended in the yard: tulips, lily of the valley, lilacs, roses, the snowball bush and a small blue spruce under which a favorite dog was buried. All are meaningful memories of love.

When that life and so much more ended, I am sure I yearned to replace the loss with my own home and the activities in it which I remembered so happily. It seemed like a natural fulfillment, a challenge to create a wonderful place called home.

Merging Two Styles of Being the Local Household of God

The haven of security I lost before I was twelve was a small six-room suburban house on a small lot in a middle-class neighborhood across the street from a park. What my mother fastidiously cared for was of much smaller scale than the very large old eight-room Victorian house, filled with old furniture, with two attics, three sets of stairs, three halls and more than twenty acres of land which George and I ended up buying. My parents had started out with a fairly new house and furnished it completely before my brother and I were born. They planned and prepared and lived in an orderly way. Part of my security depended on a maintained household; it was not that way after my mother died and the contrast disturbed me. Perhaps "mother" seemed present in a clean orderly house and especially absent in the presence of neglect. It is only recently that I discovered these feelings, but I am sure that part of the energy to create a home I could care for came from this early experience.

George, on the other hand, did not equate his security with any conscious need to hurry up with repairs on our large old house that were "mainly cosmetic." Once the utilities were in good working order, the bathrooms and kitchen were usable, and all the debris was cleaned up, one might have thought he considered the job done. It was to take him seven years to finish the library, and it took us a long time to acquire the curtains, rugs, and the furniture I had in mind.

Learning My Part in God's Work of Creation

Once rooms are in good condition and complete, I cannot say I mind routine vacuuming and dusting. But there were times when the children were growing when I often had different feelings. There is so much repetition clearing away meals, putting toys away and cleaning up spills. "Who left the pile of peanut shells on the rug I just vacuumed?" A polished coffee table has fresh sets of tiny hand prints. And somebody dropped the full container of orange juice on the kitchen floor after a fresh wash and wax job.

After my third child in as many years was born, I can remember trying in the morning to get all of us fed and dressed, dishes washed, beds made, trash disposed of, and laundry on the line. It was often more than I could manage by lunch time. Occasionally I catch myself mumbling "dishes, beds, trash" as I work around the house in the morning. Long ago it was hard to accomplish that little bit with three little ones.

It seemed as though I washed floors constantly when I had few rugs and the kitchen floor was their play space. Sometimes the job was especially difficult. For twelve and a half years I washed diapers for five children, and Clif, severely retarded, wore them for nine. It was important he spend some time outdoors, but it was hard to get two pails of dirty diapers rinsed and readied for the washing machine and also watch him. In need of assistance, I asked God to help me remember to look for Clif as I worked, and in that trusting I discovered God's trustworthiness for myself. It was a thrilling discovery.

However, comparing my life with others, I realized how hard I worked and how fruitless much of the effort seemed. Oh, to find a peaceful interlude in which to regain some serenity and a restored sense of beauty and order. Then one night after supper my husband laid down on the dining room rug with all five children playing and crawling over him, crowing with delight. Their giggles and excitement were contagious. Immediately I remembered my earlier feelings and thought to myself, "You are far richer and more favored than you realize." My envy of others' lives evaporated in joy and I was restored.

The Community of God

It may seem absurd to some for a homemaker to believe her or his job is important. When I was twenty-one I prepared a complete turkey dinner for 150 adults and children in a camp and did it almost alone, managing to coordinate everything by keeping to a careful order of work. When some saw my plan, they thought it was amusing. It was not, and I plan most of my days just as carefully in order to see to the details of a very busy household. Sandra Day O'Connor who today is a justice of the United States Supreme Court recently credited her years at home as a homemaker and mother as the best school for administrative efficiency!

It requires constant careful planning and replanning to have a large family, a busy professional husband with long hours, and also have meaningful civic and personal pursuits that are important. Sickness, special occasions and holidays, travel and occasionally wartime put added pressure and responsibility on home-makers. So do endless school activities, which make the simple act of regularly eating dinner together in a civilized fashion a constant Herculean effort. I was recently admonished that family meals were out of date, and that now each person heated up their individual meal in a microwave. How does one cultivate conversation and table manners, not to mention relationships with one another in a large and busy family? Is not the evening meal the high point of the day? I question the spineless surrender of this important event.

What I find meaningful to me as a homemaker is the mutuality of helping each other and, as our various talents become apparent, using them for one another's benefit. I like teamwork and the sharing of skills. My younger daughter can make bread as good as mine—and she can change the oil in her car as well. My oldest son, an auto mechanic who is now living in his own home, compares recipes with me, and we chose his curtains together.

Housework amid Homemaking

In my life housework has been secondary to homemaking. Caring for the seven of us and whoever else happened to be living at home was the most important work. Keeping telephone calls straight, planning expenditures, doing the necessary driving and tutoring and nursing and cooking and mediating and correspondence and shopping, and a lot of painting—all this required far more time than mopping and washing dishes. When one is around a houseful of housebound children, a good cleaning job is actually a refuge; it cannot argue. It also keeps us humble, "in case we are feeling too important," as my grandmother used to say.

Another aspect of housework that is therapeutic is getting rid of unneeded clothing, papers and items in which children or their elders have lost interest. Reworking domestic items is a favorite effort. For years my children believed that all single sheets came with a seam down the center because theirs were made out of the sides of worn full sheets. (One simply brought the side edges together to form a center seam and hemmed the new side edges.) Most of our pillowcases were sewn from the stronger sections of old sheets as well. Certainly God always reworks the materials of the natural world.

"Good" old coats with new linings, music books carefully cloth-taped, a freshly painted old high chair with an amusing decal, a new room arrangement or a chair carefully recovered with a remnant—all these are small victories over wear and tear, and are accomplished with little or no expenditure of money. The same creativity can be practiced on fresh refrigerator leftovers and in gardening and carpentry. There is always something new, a surprise perhaps, a fresh idea, a turnaround. The biblical words of God, "Behold, I make all things new," say nothing about a purchase at the nearest mall, do they!

Giving Shelter

Right now there are two elderly guests at home with us for a week of vacation. Because of their physical constraints, I must walk ever so slowly, listen far longer than I can barely endure, and prepare and clean up after three meals a day which suit their poor teeth and diabetic requirements. I am hopeful that this respite will brighten their lives and renew their zest for living. Will it revitalize my own gratitude for unappreciated blessings—a better education, healthier body, more opportunities, a wider horizon of experience? Will it also warn my children that their now active mother with all her faculties may someday be even more exasperating than I am now? Being able to provide space in our homes and lives for those who need us, and being willing to do the work required, is holy helping. I am humble before those who spend lifetimes caring for others.

Caring for others also includes party preparations and celebrations, which are frequent here. The one I am planning now for the Labor Day weekend will celebrate a college graduation, a fresh master's degree, a new job, a daughter's return from India, a birthday, and the end of summer. A boyfriend and a girl-friend will be included and I pray for the stamina to endure the confusion as well as the sense to enjoy the rare moment when we can be together and literally count our blessings. When so much happens at once, it helps to have "all systems go" in the housekeeping department so all can help cook and enjoy themselves. When all are gone, I hope to savor the pleasure as I sweep up the sand, fold all the sheets, and wonder how so much food could disappear. Will there be some late summer sun shining on the deck for a pleasant snooze on the chaise?

As we get older, get the children educated, and replace worn furniture, appliances and decorations, it is easy to feel proud. But what we tend to feel proud of is "stuff" and things. What we should feel proud of is our children who are decent people doing work that is useful; proud of having skills that are well-honed by years of use and are productive. Whether we work in a carpenter shop (as Jesus did) and have to sweep up after a day's work, or work in the kitchen after a day of cooking, pride in good work and a cheerful cooperation with others in the family are worthy and wholesome things to have nurtured over the years in ourselves and in our children. Our parenting, like our homemaking, is a giving of shelter. It is a worthwhile effort, and if it allows others to gather in an hospitable atmosphere, if it gives each person in the home a space to grow and find loving warmth and security and encouragement and peace, then certainly our housework has helped create here the community of God.

The Zen of Housework

Marlane van Hall

MARLANE VAN HALL comes from an old political family in Amsterdam. She was a young teenager when the Germans invaded her country on May 10, 1940. Overnight the fabric of daily life was completely destroyed and her family moved into the Resistance movement. Ever since, this clear action in a moment of truth has been a deep inspiration in her life. After the war she participated for many years in the Dutch Reformed Church's dialogue with Eastern European Christians and Marxists and peace organizations. She studied art history and was actively involved in avant-garde music, theatre and radio-TV productions. She married and became the mother of two; her husband became dean of a new department of architecture, later moving to the United States to head a similar department at MIT. She has since studied Zen and was recently ordained a priest.

A Radical Journey

How did it happen that ordinary tasks in my house took on new meaning and were seen in a completely new light? The word "radical" means literally "examining the roots," and in that sense I chose to make a radical journey. The process started with culture-shock fourteen years ago. I moved with our family from tiny Holland to a vast continent, America, and the result was a complete breakdown of our ordinary routines. We discovered the great power of absence when the daily fabric of our lives was no longer supported by regular interactions with family, friends and colleagues, something we had always taken completely for granted. Suddenly we found ourselves without our familiar environment. The sounds, smells, the light, the skies—everything was different.

We learned to communicate in a new language, verbal and nonverbal, finding out about the multitude of social conventions in this incredibly diverse society. Gradually another rhythm and lifestyle evolved as we were forced to clarify for ourselves what we wanted to keep or change of our former Dutch way of life.

Life became very bare. I found out this was a good opportunity to ask myself some basic questions. The stage was set in my life for a transformation of consciousness, although of course there were some points of continuity.

I was a survivor of World War II. The slogan "Never More War!" touches me deeply, and early on I made up my mind that the only way to deal with my traumatic war experiences and my fear for the future was to begin a search for what "peace" really means—how to be at peace in the world and with myself, living and acting peacefully from the ground of my being.

I had been one of the three hundred women who had come together in Amsterdam in the summer of 1967 to launch the women's movement. For many years we were indefatigable, engaged in grass roots activities to build the movement. I combined this with work in a wide range of political and cultural organizations and committees and was for some years a member of the school board of a large city in the Roman Catholic south of Holland. In those years of great change in the country this meant we had to deal with endless conflicts. These issues and the ongoing experience of struggle and social conflict pushed me to deeper levels, challenging my own attitudes toward life and society. Why, I asked myself, do we spend so much of our time struggling with the past? Why not invest more energy in imagining the future, searching for new ways to express and embody our own values and dreams? Increasingly I longed to live my life in my own terms, and, to my great surprise, my doing housework became an unexpected tool for discovering a new approach to reality.

Another theme I brought with me from Holland was my lifelong struggle with a severe physical condition, spina bifida. I was always in pain. I spent a good part of my life in hospitals or at home recovering from one or another treatment or operation. From early on I began to question our society's attitudes toward sickness and health. In a very personal way I came to see the limits of Western civilization's dualism between body and mind. As a young girl and then later as a wife and young mother, I asked myself whether housework could ever become healing-work for me. Little did I dream that I would gradually discover in the simplicity and concreteness of housework a healing factor in my life.

A final theme in my life came out of a decade of study and intense involvement in the visual arts, electronic music, radio and the theatre of the absurd in Paris and Holland. All this trained me to be open and sensitive to new ways of perceiving time and space, light and sound. More and more I began to experience my daily environment as a multidimensional reality with physical, emotional, aesthetic, and transcendental components. My home was being transformed for me into a laboratory and training ground, a place where all the parts of my life interpenetrated. It was becoming a mirror in which to see myself and the world, a window which was open to me, free and spacious. Doing housework now meant acting in that space.

I was beginning a radical new journey. Here I was, whatever I was—and also a wife, mother, and now a homemaker in charge of a complex household. I was experiencing chronic distress in my body which the medical professionals were unable to help. I simply had no other recourse than actively seek my own way to survive my pain and be healed. And here I was in the United States as an outsider, who was having to create all over again a way of life which would sustain and, I hoped, enhance my being myself and really my own person. I was determined to be self-defined and to be living my experience "in my own name." As I saw it, the bottom line was that I was living out my commitments to work, citizenship and social justice as well as my caring concerns for my family and my friends. I was busily balancing these many quite heterogenous concerns all within one life, my own.

Discovering the "Way" of Zen

I looked up suddenly and was shocked. Ripples of laughter burst out of me, seeing myself and countless other women making perfect machines out of ourselves and our daily lives, controlled by our accomplishments known as "hard work," many of us "trying to beat the system" and thereby prove to ourselves that we can do it all. This is hysterically funny, I thought, crazy, admirable, impressive, both hilarious and ridiculous, frustrating, stupid, sick, unbelievably utterly sad. A sardonic smile came to my face as I asked myself, Women, where ever are we headed?

The essence of Zen practice is to free the mind and make it its own master through an insight into its proper nature, the very reason for its existence. Zen centers on the great mystery of the fact of our actually living our lives. The Zen practitioner seeks to attain the original freedom of the spirit and simply experience reality. Zen is a practical and creative method for training the mind to see this mystery as it is daily performed and created by ourselves and by everyone else. It has no need for doctrines. It simply asserts in a most direct way the truth that lies in our inner being.

The meditative state is the creation of a space in which, by "doing nothing," we allow our problems to come to the surface rather than ignoring them, leaving them at the bottom of our unconscious minds. The meditative state is a precise awareness of our physical situation and our breath, of our being present here-and-now and conscious of who we are—our emotions and life-situations and the space in which they occur—and relating to our daily life all the time. Gradually this opens up to a larger awareness of ourselves in the world. A compassionate attitude, a warmth, develops as we come to a fundamental acceptance of ourselves and our world, including the painful as well as joyful aspects. [1]

The Zen schools developed in the seventh century of the Common Era in China, after its contact with Buddhist thought and teachings from India. Compared with the elaborately metaphysical systems of Indian thought, the Chinese are very practical, worldly, and attached to the earth. Although the Taoist thinkers of China were profoundly influenced by India's Buddhism, the Chinese never lost touch with the practical side of daily life. This is why they developed a new form of monasticism which was democratic, self-governing, and actively involved in service to the outside world. Most of the day the Zen master and his students were at work together in manual labor on the land or engaged in their various other tasks. Cleaning, cooking, harvesting, the teacher guided the students by living the day-to-day reality of spiritual practice directly before their eyes. Learning took the form of quick dialogues in which humorous or cryptic questions and answers were exchanged during the work.

Zen experience and expression are one. There is no conceptualizing but in an intimate and lived experience there is instead a pointing directly to the heart of that experience, the ultimate. Zen master Dogen (1200–1250) said, "Zen is our everyday life as we experience it in the moment—washing our dishes, drinking a cup of tea—this is the essence of our spiritual practice." [2]

Ascetic training or yoga is a technique for unifying body and spirit by gradually opening the *chakras* or energy centers of the body. In the great Hindu, Buddhist and Islamic cultures of the East yoga has always been an essential part of religious practice as well as important for training in the arts and professions. All aspects of life were seen as simultaneously interpenetrating—the ultimate and the mundane, as well as the physical, mental and spiritual. In Japan especially a further development took place in which housework and its embodiment in a spiritual practice were brought together in a new concept: "the way," which is a blending of Zen with the Japanese sense of simplicity, love of nature, and artistic expression.

Zen came to Japan from China in 653 A.D., but its real growth began in the thirteenth century. Contrary to Zen's rural character in China, many of the main Japanese temples were built in or near cities, where they were associated with political elites and the warrior *samurai* class. Later on Zen penetrated to the heart and intimate life of the common people. Gradually the tradition developed that Zen could be practiced through various "ways." There were the "ways" for the literary arts of calligraphy, poetry and painting. There were "ways" for the performing arts as well as the martial arts. There was also a "way" for the household arts of flower arranging, cooking, the tea ceremony, and gardening, among others.

Originally the term "way" meant simply the "how" or a description of the skills and techniques used for professional training. But later the term came to include general principles, truths and teachings which could benefit ordinary people as well. In time the various "ways" became an educational tool for developing one's character, for bringing one's inner self to maturity through teaching these skills along with the meditative way of life.

The Way of Tea

The teaching style of a famous Zen or Tea master is always uniquely his own. Its foundation is a longtime intimate and hearty teacher-student relationship in which the student is challenged during rock-bottom confrontations: "Let go of all your stuff and be your true self, totally present in this moment!"

The masters of the "ways" teach by concrete action. The student learns intuitively, primarily by practicing the traditional "bodymind" movements in a silent dance. Gradually one learns to attune one's being to a state of meditative clarity and mobility, realizing that even one's smallest actions reflect the way of tea, because "Tea drinking is not just drinking tea; it comes directly from and goes deeply down into the roots of existence."[3]

Cha-no-yu, or the Ceremony of Drinking Tea, also involves the activities leading to it. The master and the student are involved with the utensils and food used, the physical environment, the entire atmosphere surrounding the procedure, and most important the frame of mind or spirit which mysteriously grows out of the combination of all these factors.

Tea drinking is the art of being truly present with each other and the situation, sensitive to the sacred quality of everything. It is the realization of a spirit of absolute poverty, nonattachment or emptiness (*sunyata*) beyond any dichotomies of body and spirit, subject and object, good and evil. Out of this no-whereness and no-timeness the practitioners of the tea ceremony drink their cup of tea together, eat, talk, and work together, all the time experiencing *sunyata* or emptiness, the heart of Zen, as the fountain of infinite freedom.[4]

Breathing deeply, a state of prayer, a rhythm of moving hands that are polishing, sweeping, washing dishes, cooking—and amid dazzling colors and ordinary movements a new connection happens. Cleaning the house becomes a metaphor for opening the heart; I am literally cleansed when I am working with the right intention. As I move back and forth between different modes of being, day by day I become more at one with my true self. I am delighted to be alive! The sun shines, the flowers bloom, I am in everything and everything is in me.

No Escape but a Total Response

When I boil tea water, cook a dinner or am busy with other housework, what kind of mindset do I have? Am I bored, hurried, absent-minded? Am I yearning to be somewhere else doing things that seem more interesting or rewarding? This desire to be somewhere else or wanting things to be some other way which they are not—this is neither bad nor good. It is just my life-energy expressing itself as desire.

When this basic life-energy arises in the moment and we become aware of it, we can choose not to go along with it. Instead we can bring "what is" and "what we want" into closer harmony in ourselves. Paying close attention in this way to our inner states is neither to indulge them or to judge them. On the contrary, we become intimate with ourself, not separate from who we are in our life-situation. Transcending duality means allowing both the feeling of the moment and its opposite to exist within us at the same time.

The "way" of meditative action ceases picking and choosing. It experiences events without subjective judgment. It is not a special consciousness reserved for prayer or meditation but it fully experiences pain as pain and pleasure as pleasure, without adding a thought or anything. By becoming nothing but pain—or anger, grief, joy, boredom—paradoxically we free ourselves from attachment to them.

This "way" is no escape but instead a total response to all the aspects of our life, in our home and in the world. It makes no distinction between the ordinary and the extraordinary, between spiritual practice or nonpractice. This meditative work immerses you ever deeper into the flow of your worldly existence, affirming and transforming it in rejecting any leaving the world somehow behind by one or another escape into dualism. The key is bare attention to all the elements of daily life, one breath at a time. This practice changes the quality of our reflective consciousness, and slowly an intuitive awareness begins to work.

Our actions and way of life become more and more spontaneous and direct, not centered anymore around attachments or self-concern.

Eventually our heart is set free completely, we are united with the ground of our being and finally we know who we really are.

We enter the realm of paradox, the Unthinkable. AWARE in the moment, our life has become breathtakingly, unbelievably playful.

At the end, everything is simple and straightforward. We do what we have to do in our life, and drink our tea together, inspired by the source of infinite freedom.

NOTES

1. See Chogyam Trungpa Rinpoche, *The Myth of Freedom* (Boulder, Col.: Shambhala, 1976).

2. See Francis Cook, *How to Raise an Ox: Dogen's Shobogenzo* (Los Angeles: Zen Center Publications, 1978).

3. See Daisetz Susuki, *Zen and Japanese Culture* (Princeton, N.J.: Princeton University Press, 1979).

4. See Soshitsu Sen, XV, *Tea Life, Tea Mind* (New York: John Weatherhill, 1983).

Women's Work and the Sense of Time in Women's Lives

Kathryn Allen Rabuzzi

KATHRYN ALLEN RABUZZI comes from a two-career marriage of long duration. She and her husband have raised three sons while she has taught English literature at Syracuse University. She earned her Ph.D. in Humanities with an interdisciplinary concentration in Religion and English at Syracuse University. She is a member of NOW and has been a supporter of the symphony and chamber music in her city. She was founding editor of the journal LITERATURE AND MEDICINE (Johns Hopkins University Press). The author of THE SACRED AND THE FEMININE: TOWARD A THEOLOGY OF HOUSEWORK (1982) and MOTHERSELF: A MYTHIC ANALYSIS OF MOTHERHOOD (1988), she is currently working on a book about the hermeneutics of childbirth.

Traditional Women's Experience of Time

"If you could be anyone in the world, living or dead, actual or fictional, who would you choose to be?" I was asked this question once and I answered without hesitation, "Teiresias." My answer reflected my desire to know, from inside, what life is like from the perspective of both female and male. In a certain sense, however, I now know that I am Teiresias, for I too have experienced both modes of existence. In what was once almost exclusively a male mode, I have been student and then teacher; in the now almost obsolete female mode, I have been full-time housewife and mother. What then, is the major difference between the two?

Above all, the difference is not anatomical but temporal. In the traditional Western male mode of existence, time is experienced as it is typically understood in the Western world. Time is linear, historic and moving. By contrast, in what used to be a traditional female mode, time is circular, boring, and repetitive. Typically, the kind of time experience usual for a male in the Western world takes place within a pattern of questing. In myth, fairy tale, and story, the quest is usually presented in adventure form, the hero setting off from home in search of riches, love, salvation, or some magic talisman. In so-called "real life" the quest, while more prosaic, still involves a daily setting off from home, usually to office or factory, a pattern also traditionally shared by children and nowadays by most women as well.

The corresponding life pattern associated with circular time is radically different. This is a pattern of waiting. It is epitomized not by the generic hero but by Penelope, wife of Odysseus, who spent most of her adulthood awaiting his return. Whereas questing is active, goal-oriented, and storied, waiting is reactive, nongoal-oriented, and seldom told about. Often waiting is thought of pejoratively as "empty" time, which must somehow be "filled." Yet waiting, the mode of traditional women's lives, very much deserves to be looked at as a legitimate time pattern in its own right.

Waiting

In its more commonly recognized negative form, waiting is unquestionably demonic. In this form time in its circularity becomes the famous "vicious circle." For a housewife most chores seem to fall readily into this pattern. Who, having once dusted, can ever forget the feeling of frustration at watching the tiny dust motes fall right back down onto the surface from which they have just been removed? Or who, having just washed the dishes, only to have her children and half the neighborhood troop in for snacks and Kool-Aid, can ignore the repressed anger that flickers when the same work immediately piles up again. The same can be said of ironing, washing, picking up, and cooking. No matter what the chore, a woman's work, as the rhyme so pithily states, "is never done." The satisfaction of a goal visibly and finally accomplished does not seem to exist for a traditional woman. Instead she might as well be Sisyphus, endlessly rolling and re-rolling his rock up the hill, only to have it come tumbling right back down again, no progress ever to be made.

But there is another side to this nonstory of waiting. Sometimes instead of being experienced negatively as endlessly repetitive, boring, imprisoning time, waiting feels positive.

When it happens that waiting feels positive, the viciousness of the circle recedes as it metamorphoses into the divine circle of myth. Then, when the endless return takes the participant back to her starting point, she no longer feels doomed like Sisyphus but favored like the goddesses and gods. That is because in archaic thought, time ideally is circular, not progressive, for in the beginning when all things first come into existence, they are perfect, having just been created by their divine makers. The longer things remain in the world, the more they degenerate, just as women know our houses do. Periodically things must be renewed; hence human agents must act in such a way as to return the world to its time of origin. Such time is by definition sacred.

Connecting with a Long Line of Female Ancestors

For a woman (or a man) enacting the traditional housewife role, this mythic dimension of waiting may well be less evident than its demonic counterpart. Nonetheless, the ritual enactment of housework typically connects a woman back to a long line of female ancestors before her. Such linking back to origins is a frequent and important element of most religious ritual. Just as family stories or memorabilia may be handed down within families, so may traditional ways of doing certain tasks. As religionist Mircea Eliade says, "To do the rite again is to join with the ancestors and regenerate the ideality of their lives. . . ." [1] Thus one benefit ritual behavior confers is to convey special knowledge nonverbally from one time period to the next.

To do a task precisely as you observed or were taught by your mother or grandmother is to experience a portion of what they each once did. Two kinds of knowledge are thus imparted: knowledge of what it is to be a housewife and knowledge of what it was to have been Grandma X in her homemaking aspect. For example, at times I catch myself in what was presumably a characteristic gesture or attitude of my mother, and I have the eerie feeling that I *am* my mother.

The ritual enactment of housework thus helps provide continuity from one generation of women to another. Consequently, although housework as it is generally practiced is a solitary occupation, some sense of community is provided by the *method* of doing, when that method reflects the performance of earlier women. Obviously for women who hire their work done or those who have rejected the methods and attitudes of their mothers, this connection will have been severed.

Homemakers in general are the largest group in the post-industrial world still to connect back in this particular fashion to their forebears. In the days when sons more frequently followed the occupations of their fathers, most men also engaged in handed-down ritual enactment. Now, however, except for those who are farmers or those who apprentice in skilled trades, even individuals who do pursue a parental career are apt to be trained outside the family in professional or trade schools. Furthermore, relatively few children nowadays grow up fully aware of the day-to-day activities which fill their working parents' lives. Not many share even a few hours a week with a parent at her/his place of work outside the home. Therefore, the experience of learning to enact a task precisely as your mother or father did it, even if you follow the same trade or profession, is increasingly rare except for avocational pursuits such as woodworking or sports. In that regard homemakers and peasants, like tribespeople, appear to be beneficiaries of a mode of knowledge now essentially lost to most people in our post-industrial age.

The linking back in time provided by this kind of knowledge is one of the major benefits that ritual enactment bestows on its participants. It is one of the major ways that women (whose lives have typically been isolated from the public sphere dominated by men) have been able to share in the entire community of women. In such enactment women celebrate the unstoried pattern of Hestia, goddess of the hearth.

The Boring and the Mystical

In addition to such sharing in the community of women which housewifery traditionally provides for a woman, now and then something special happens in the course of her habitual round, making what is ordinarily demonic suddenly assume a distinctly different quality for her. She may perhaps be dusting, and like the poet Rilke (admittedly an unlikely example), experience an epiphany:

Under my zealous dustcloth, [the piano] suddenly started to purr mechanically . . . and its fine, deep black surface became more and more beautiful. When you've been through this there's little you don't know! . . . Politeness tinged with mischief was my reaction to the friendliness of these objects, which seemed happy to be so well treated, so meticulously renovated. And even today, I must confess that while everything about me grew brighter and the immense black surface of my work table, which dominated its surroundings . . . became newly aware, somehow, of the size of the room, reflecting it more and more clearly: pale gray and almost square . . .

well, yes, I felt moved, as though something were happening, something, to tell the truth, which was not purely superficial but immense, and which touched my very soul: I was an emperor washing the feet of the poor, or Saint Bonaventure, washing dishes in his convent. [2]

Unquestionably what Rilke describes is a mystical experience occasioned by his dusting of the piano in the absence of his maid. While it is by no means the norm for a housewife to be transported into a mystical state, it is certainly true that precisely the kinds of repetitive chores she must engage in are those most likely to effect just such a result. Such chores may strike the doer in one of two ways: either they seem boring or they lead into a mystical state.

Boringness and mysticism each name a dominant quality of women's waiting mode. A number of qualities characterize both: monotony, abstraction, plotlessness, minimalness, repetitiveness, incompleteness, to name a few. Many of these phenomena occur too in certain traditional religions through chanting, drum beats, ingestion of various drugs, twirling, fasting, engaging in lengthy vigils. All are used to induce a trance-like, mystical state in which consciousness is altered and rationality put in abeyance. Similarly when you are bored without being turned away from the source of the boredom-producing stimulus, you are thrown into such a state.

In art and literature as well as traditional women's lives, a mystical state may be produced by manipulating these "boring" qualities in varying ways. *Monotony,* for example, occurs in numerous contemporary paintings in its most literal sense, as a single tone or color. You need only recall an Ad Reinhardt all-black or all-navy blue canvas in this respect. Closely related is *lack of variation.* Too close a focus on a single theme frequently occurs in many of Andy Warhol's works. How different can one Campbell's soup can be from another? Similarly think of the monotony and lack of variation involved in such household tasks as drying dishes or ironing one white shirt after another after another. Is monotony of this sort any different from that produced by countless repetitions of the word *om?* In all these instances an individual's sensitivity to stimuli is being abnormally manipulated.

There are two characteristics of the Boring and the Mystical which are slightly more difficult to evaluate: elements *devoid of interest* and elements *conducive to tedium.* Both are inherently subjective. Thus while you can objectively call an Ad Reinhardt black canvas monotonous, one viewer might nonetheless consider it interesting while another sees it as devoid of interest and hence conducive to tedium. Similarly, one woman may consider ironing interesting while another does not. In this respect the Boring and the Mystical, like the Ugly and the Beautiful, are only partially amenable to objective analysis.

Besides analyzing the objective and subjective elements of the Boring and the Mystical you can examine different types of each as well. One type is caused by *surfeit.* Too much of anything overwhelms a percipient. Such excess can result from too many stimuli on the one hand, or too great an expanse on the other. For this reason, a picture crammed full of various elements can be as boring as one too little filled. In contrast to surfeit, the latter kind of boringness results from *deprivation.* Here you might compare the overstuffed house full of antimacassars and objets d'art to its blank-walled, nearly furnitureless counterpart.

Leading to the Breakup of Illusions

Both surfeit and deprivation occur in what might be called *the Boring of the large,* such as you experience when confronted with vast stretches of space or time. Either temporally or spatially, such vastness seems infinite, tending to overwhelm you. Opposed to this overwhelming type of the Boring there is *the Boring of the small* in which there is too little to occupy your mind. Hence you are bored for exactly the opposite reason. Whereas story tends to *create* illusions, either of reality or of make-believe, elements of the Boring or the Mystical reverse the process, *breaking apart* illusions instead. Generally we tend to see disillusionment as undesirable and negative. Actually, however, if we think of it as dis-illusionment, separating the prefix from the root, its opposing, positive meaning is more apparent.

Almost any fairy tale involving metamorphosis deals with disillusionment in this sense. The familiar stories of swan men or maidens are all illustrative. In the Grimms' story of "The Six Swans," for example, an archetypally evil queen-stepmother enchants her six stepsons by witchcraft, giving the illusion to the world at large that they are swans. To dis-enchant them their sister must neither speak nor laugh for six years. The task nearly costs her her life, and deludes her husband into thinking she is evil. When she is falsely accused of killing their own children, unable to speak in her own defense, her silence does create the illusion that she is the evil woman he mistakes her for.

Nonetheless, she completes the task, dis-enchanting her brothers at the appropriate time: "The swans came close up to her, with rushing wings and swooped round her, so that she could throw the shirts over them. And when that had been done the swan skins fell off them, and her brothers stood before her quite safe and sound." [3] And with her brothers' dis-enchantment comes the dis-illusionment of her husband. Now, as she talks for the first time in six years, the illusion that she is an evil woman shatters for good.

As a means of helping us see through images that hold us in thrall, dis-illusionment though painful is a vital source of growth. What is revealed through such shattering of images is mystical knowledge, which is characteristically difficult to put into words because it has broken through to a realm beyond words or named images.

Liberation from Enthralling Images

As agents of dis-illusionment, elements of the Boring and the Mystical similarly help counter enthralling images. Take any Andy Warhol sequence of Marilyn Monroes. Monroe is an obviously enthralling image, at least for most males. Yet Warhol's endless repetitions with minimal variation change their original fascination. By multiplication he creates surfeit. One Marilyn Monroe is a fascinating image. Twenty Marilyn Monroes first appear tedious, then somewhat frightening. As we look at them we begin to stare uneasily, questioning what we see. Why should there be so many look-alikes? What does that mean? What has become of individuality? With only one we are far less likely to think consciously that it is an image. With twenty we can hardly do otherwise. And yet these images do not seem to exist as images ordinarily do. If we are looking at an image, what is it an image of? Is there anything behind it? The ontological questions are insistent; hence our fear.

Such dis-illusionment or breaking of images is typical of any initiation rite that seeks to reach the sacred. To reach the sacred an initiate must die. That way he may return to the absolute beginning, to chaos. Only then can his or her rebirth on a new, spiritual plane take place. An artist purposely working with the Boring strives to disengage attention, scatter it, and force the viewer back upon herself. This effect closely resembles what happens to a novice enduring his initiation ordeals. Typically he will be left in a special hut or even by himself in the forest. Given no food, he will be instructed not to sleep. In such a setting he will inevitably enter a trance after periods of restlessness and sleepiness.

Mircea Eliade describes this initiatory, mystical process of dis-illusionment in the rites of Tantrism known as *tchoed* in which

> the novice submits himself to an initiatory ordeal by stimulating his imagi-
> nation to conjure up a terrifying vision, which, however, he masters by the
> power of his thought. He knows that what is before him is a creation of his
> own mind; that the Goddess and the demons are as unreal as his own body
> and with it, the entire cosmos. . . . This initiatory meditation is at the same
> time a post-mortem experience, hence a descent to Hell—but through it the
> novice realizes the emptiness of all posthumous experience, so that he will
> feel no more fear at the moment of death and will thus escape being reborn
> on earth. The traditional experience of bodily dismemberment . . . serves as
> an instrument of knowledge; by virtue of it the novice understands what is
> meant by the universal void, and thereby draws closer to final deliverance. [4]

As with the novice, so frequently with the housewife. Particularly during the years when she is also mother to young children, she must endure prolonged periods of sleep deprivation in response to her children's often nightly demands. Such deprivation, combined with the repetitiveness of her daily chores, is apt to make her as restless, sleepy, and bored as any initiate. Once she passes beyond these surface responses however, she too is likely to enter into a trancelike state in which seemingly negative conditions alter into their positive counterparts. Whether responding to art, initiation, or housework, the body of the viewer or participant inevitably reacts to this situation which is so radically unlike more traditional artistic attempts to focus attention on an intense situation and thereby force viewer/reader identification with an appealing character.

Bertold Brecht's alienation effect—which purposely introduces illusion-shattering devices at appropriate intervals—obviously works this way to prevent viewers from over-identifying with characters. Yet if alienation from the situation at hand is too great, the reader, viewer, initiate, or housewife will become so thoroughly disengaged that the potentially mystical stimulus loses its effective-ness. When that happens he or she will turn away completely, severing the potential connection between viewer and performance, initiate and rite, or housewife and task.

Conversely, when there is no alienation separating a viewer from a story or an initiate from an ordeal, dis-illusionment is unlikely to occur. Then an individual remains so caught up in the image or story that she remains hooked at the state of idolatry, rather than gaining sufficient distance to move into the nothingness beyond.

Mirroring Infinite Nothingness

Those who tout story as the *sine qua non* of human existence frequently view this nothingness as bad. Michael Novak says: "Not to have any story to live out is to experience nothingness: the primal formlessness of human life below the threshold of narrative structuring. Why become anything at all? Does anything make any difference? Why not simply die?" [5]

Or instead of demonizing nothingness, story advocates may simply try to encapsulate it within another, more encompassing story. In that case the nothingness is framed on either side by content as is promised, for example, in the play *Harvey* when Elwood P. Dowd explains that Harvey has the ability to stop time for as long as he wants. That time-stoppage, in which normal life abates, is another way of naming what we otherwise variously call "death," "eternity," "a mystical state," or "nothingness." But in that context, or any of many fairy-tale versions of it, story frames and controls it. But if that "nothingness" is valued for its own sake, the need for such framing disappears; this is the situation which is frequently exploited by practitioners of the minimalist art.

In addition to the minimal aspects of art that lead into the Boring and the Mystical, there is often associated with both an altered attitude towards humanness that has great bearing on the way women might possibly come to be perceived. Usually when we think of stories, we think of humanity. In fact, one of the traditional characteristics of stories is character. Even in stories about machines or animals, the "protagonists" assume human characteristics. Ray Bradbury's "There Will Come Soft Rains" comes to mind, but even there the house has humanoid qualities. By contrast, many contemporary works of fiction deemphasize human roles. Absurdists like Ionesco and Beckett create characters who approach some outer limit of humanity (as is particularly evident with Beckett's Unnameable).

Surely this shifting of humanity out of center stage means something. And surely it is no accident that we tend to equate the Boring with things we cannot identify with, thus suggesting that the Boring in part alienates percipients because it is in some way "beyond" them. Frequently we even use that metaphor to describe how we feel when a work bores us: "It's beyond me" or "That's nothing," we may say with a shrug of dismissal.

It is precisely this nothingness or beyondness that is important. Contrasted with Story, which stands for and/or creates a finite something, the Boring is an artistic mode which mirrors infinite nothingness.

Storyless Stories

In sharp contrast to the (largely masculine) artistic tradition in which story and image dominate, one strain of twentieth-century art, the minimal, is so devoid of either story or image as to occasion cries of "Nothing is there, " or "What happens?" Where traditional storytellers create narrative continuity, "storyless"

story tellers deliberately destroy it. Consider, for instance, this small segment
from Samuel Beckett's *Waiting for Godot*. In Act II Vladimir sings this song:

> A dog came in the kitchen
> And stole a crust of bread.
> Then cook up with a ladle
> And beat him till he was dead.
>
> Then all the dogs came running
> and dug the dog a tomb—
> Then all the dogs came running
> And dug the dog a tomb
> And wrote upon the tombstone
> For the eyes of dogs to come:
>
> A dog came in the kitchen
> And stole a crust of bread.
> Then cook up with a ladle
> And beat him till he was dead.
>
> Then all the dogs came running
> And dug the dog a tomb—
> Then all the dogs came running
> And dug the dog a tomb.[6]

Is this story? Or is this something else? Clearly it has some of the characteristics
of story: a rudimentary plot, a character of sorts in the form of the dog; action;
and a climax. Yet despite all these qualities, it lacks the *sine qua non* of story: a
clearly articulated beginning, middle, and end.

What then has Beckett created instead? In this song which Vladimir sings,
Beckett has abridged an endless series, abstracting from it its actual length while
giving us in part the feeling of the whole. By its form he indicates eternal
progress, making this an "endless story." Hence it is no story at all in the
Aristotelian sense. In other words, he has used a *pars pro toto* technique to
present an image of the infinite in finite form.

By having only the single repetition he has minimized the physical time span
for the percipient at the same time that he expresses the *essence* of the greatest
possible time span. To borrow from Suzanne Langer's terminology, what Beckett
has created is "virtual" rather than actual boredom.[7] Thus while we may feel the
boredom presented in his compressed presentation of the boring nature of
infinity, because this is such a carefully abridged, and therefore delimited,
version of the whole, there exists a strong enough counteractant to the boredom
to carry us on through without making us turn away.

A similar phenomenon occurs visually when an artist like Nassos Daphnis
chooses to cover an entire canvas in black with only two white stripes to relieve
its sameness. And Brecht deliberately destroys the continuity of his plays every
time he obtrudes one of his editorial comments upon the scene, reminding his
audience that this is indeed a play, not an illusion of life.

What I. A. Richards says of poetic metre in his *Principles of Literary Criticism* suggests a possible analogy. He says: "metre adds to all the variously fated expectancies which make up rhythm, a definite temporal pattern, and its effect is not due to our perceiving a pattern in something outside us, but to our becoming patterned ourselves." [8] A poet who uses too highly regular metre will inadvertently create a monotonous effect, thus lulling his reader into an almost hypnotic state. Likewise, an artist may deliberately choose to use elements of the Boring to so pattern his audience.

The Boring as Altering Space-Time

It is here that we see just how strongly the Boring, whether in art or housework mimics mystical states. As opposed to story and image, the Boring does not offer the reader a vicarious experience of some virtual space-time. Instead the Boring alters space-time. It is this same characteristic which transforms some enactments of housework and sacred rituals.

To understand the significance of this distinction between virtual and altered space-time, consider what Aristotle says of the aesthetic aspects of tragedy: ". . . a beautiful object, whether it be a living organism or any whole composed of parts, must not only have an orderly arrangement of parts, but must also be of a certain magnitude and order. Hence a very small animal organism cannot be beautiful; for the view of it is confused, the object being seen in an almost imperceptible moment of time. Nor, again, can one of vast size be beautiful; for as the eye cannot take it all in at once, the unity and sense of the whole is lost for the spectator." [9]

Obviously the unspoken measure here is human. Now while such an anthropocentric view appears to be the only logical one, you could argue that its implied fixity makes it a somewhat static measure—that humanity could indeed learn to expand and contract its powers of attention in accordance with altered space/time intervals. It is just such stretching and manipulating of human response that appears to be part of the rationale for minimalist art.

Thus Andy Warhol presents the public with a movie showing a single face and nothing else for a period of two hours. Here is the Boring in art; indeed, it is art that would bore most people. But if you contrast the amount of time given to a single entity in the movie with the amount given to a face in "normal" time, it is obvious that something once unconsidered is occurring here. The dislocation of the normal time sense has been exploited in such a way that the viewer's whole space/time perception is put into question.

What we ordinarily accept tacitly has here been made glaringly explicit. While writers from Swift on have exploited such qualities as variations in size vis-à-vis our human scale, it is not until this century that such experience has been presented directly, minus the framing device of a story about it. And it is just such unframed experience that traditional women have enacted through their lives for centuries.

Being Stretched Aesthetically

Much as the old Euclidean notion of space/time has been altered significantly in favor of complex non-Euclidean models, our human sensibility to that continuum appears to be undergoing a similar artistic re-creation. On the one hand, there is a surfeit of stimuli in certain multimedia works of art. On the other, there is minimal artistic input. It would seem that humanity is being stretched aesthetically beyond its old mean, in two directions at once.

Story and image once were taken for granted in art. For part of the twentieth century, however, art pushed both aside. Usurping their place were elements of the Mystical and the Boring. Whereas story, as Aristotle defined it, was made to human measure, the Mystical and the Boring extend beyond us. And whereas story and image are artistic modes which reveal some*thing,* the Boring is a mode which reveals *Nothing.* Story and image both *fill* space, but conversely the Boring and the Mystical lead into the *emptiness* of space itself.

As vehicles of revelation, these two modes are therefore radically different from both story and image. To say of anything boring, as we commonly do, "That's nothing," is therefore highly appropriate. But also to turn away from it, as if *nothing* were equivalent to *meaningless,* is to ignore the significance of that nothingness.

If we take the view that all art and literature, not just so-called sacred texts, are revelations of the divine, then the repeated emergence of the Boring in so much mid-twentieth century work has to be revealing something to us with great insistence. Anything that insistent surely demands our serious attention.

Rather than deplore these tendencies, which have already abated greatly as other modes of painting and writing in turn have developed, it makes more sense to ask what they mean. From a feminist perspective, such seeming absence of images and stories, instead of signifying a horrifying emptiness, suggests that women's traditional mode of experiencing life was, at least momentarily, given shape artistically. Whether women or artists choose to retain this mode or not is beyond the scope of this chapter.

The Discontinuity We Feel

Furthermore, the emergence of this waiting mode from obscurity into art indicates that we may be engaged in a second Copernican revolution. But the Copernican crisis of our time is not between our expectations of where the earth should be relative to the sun and the planets. Ours is the discontinuity we feel between the spot human males have traditionally occupied in human thought relative to women, children, animals, plants, and inanimate objects, and the place women are beginning to assume ourselves.

The so-called Death of God theologians of the 1960s foreshadowed this crisis. To the extent that the ultimate term humans can conceive—*God* in the Judeo-Christian tradition—has been envisioned as masculine, the term has revealed more about human minds than about anything truly ultimate. This situation has been equally true, of course, in cultures whose symbols of ultimacy have been feminine or theriomorphic (in the shape of animals), and multiple as well as monotheistic.

When a number of theologians such as Gabriel Vahanian, Thomas Altizer, William Hamilton, and Richard Rubenstein took up Nietzsche's statement that God is dead, they spoke of this death in various ways. In Vahanian's view this death of God reflects the demise of a certain way of thinking. For Vahanian, if that particular mode of envisioning and speaking about ultimacy dies, that in no way means that the ultimate itself dies. Rather it means that a certain conventionally accepted human way of constructing ultimacy no longer works for an entire community of believers, even though it may linger indefinitely for many.

Following Vahanian's thought, when that long-accepted symbol begins to lose its potency for enough people that it "dies," that indicates that something significant is occurring within a number of human minds. Much emphasis has been laid on numerous negative affiliates of this death: the loss of a sense of human purpose, coupled with scientific theories of indeterminacy, pluralism, leveling of transcendence into immanentism, and estrangement from ancestral Christendom. But few thinkers have pointed out that concurrent with this Death of God theorizing is another important cultural phenomenon: toward the beginning of the period often referred to now as the *post mortem dei* era, feminist theology began.

Not from Adam's Rib but from Eve's Womb

Simply to replace the old masculine God with a feminist variant called the Goddess is to ignore the implications of the Death of God theologies. Similarly, to retain the biblical God and His Son but to repristinate the meanings of both terms, as others would do, is also to ignore those theologies. But to see in feminist theologizing a correlation to Death of God theologizing is to move closer to understanding what is happening to *homo* [sic] *religiosus* at the present time.

For woman, the silent partner in the term *homo,* what is happening is discontinuous with a whole previous history. A traditional woman's life was once so fully bound up with waiting that she was merely an egg's way of ensuring another egg.[10] Nowadays that view, which implicitly values the life *process* above all else, with no concern for *quality* of life, is being questioned and disavowed by thousands of women. Many flee it in horror.

At this point relatively few have yet discovered how to be whoever they think they are without polarizing their lives into either/or choices. Many find themselves caught. Either they can exist primarily in the familiar mode of waiting with its day-to-day emphasis on housework, or they can adopt an alternative (masculine) quest pattern. Relatively few of us have learned to cope with the ambiguities inherent in both patterns. Until we do, it is unlikely that many will be able to create genuinely new modes of being forged from the best of both traditions.

This predicament shared by so many women is cogently expressed in Martin Buber's parable, "The Query of Queries." "Before his death, Rabbi Zusya said, 'In the coming world, they will not ask me: "Why were you not Moses?" They will ask me: "Why were you not Zusya?" ' "[11] For most women the first task now is to stop being "Moses," whether a Moses locked into the home or one aspiring to be a man in a "man's world." The second is to discover, acknowledge, and then create a Zusya born, not from Adam's rib but from Eve's womb.

A Past Neither Worthless Nor Glorious

Only when women can accomplish both tasks will we legitimate ourselves as full human beings in female form. Such self-legitimation will free us from accepting internalized masculine conceptions of who and what we should be. That legitimation depends on carefully examining the ambiguities of our past, a past neither worthless nor glorious.

It is a past spent for the most part living out an ambiguous Hestian pattern of enactment characterized by waiting. From one perspective this pattern is profane, experienced primarily with despair as meaningless. From another, however, it is felt as sacred, opening out alternatively into the demonic realm of the Boring or the divine space of the Mystical. To ensure the birth of a Zusya, it makes sense for women to ponder both poles of that sacred dimension.

NOTES

1. Mircea Eliade, *The Sacred and the Profane: The Nature of Religion* (New York: Harcourt, Brace World/Harvest, 1959), p. 74.

2. Rainer Maria Rilke, *Lettres d'une Musicienne,* quoted in Gaston Bachelard, *The Poetics of Space,* trans. Maria Jolas (Boston: Beacon Press, 1969), pp. 70–71.

3. The Brothers Grimm, "Six Swans," in *Grimms Fairy Tales,* trans. Mrs. E. V. Lucas, Lucy Crane and Marian Edwardes (New York: Grossett & Dunlap, 1945), p. 113.

4. Mircea Eliade, *Rites and Symbols of Initiation: The Mysteries of Birth and Rebirth,* trans. Willard R. Trask (New York: Harper & Row/Torchbooks, 1958), pp. 105–106.

5. Michael Novak, *Ascent of the Mountain, Flight of the Dove: An Invitation to Religious Studies* (New York: Harper & Row, 1971), p. 52.

6. Samuel Beckett, *Waiting for Godot* (New York: Grove Press, 1954), p. 37.

7. For a discussion of the difference between *virtual* and *actual,* see Suzanne K. Langer, *Feeling and Form: A Theory of Art* (New York: Charles Scribner's Sons, 1953), particularly chapters 5, 6, 11 and 15.

8. I. A. Richards, *Principles of Literary Criticism* (New York: Harcourt, Brace & World, 1925), p. 139.

9. Aristotle, "On the Art of Poetry," in *On Poetry and Music,* trans. by S. H. Butcher (New York: The Bobbs-Merrill Co., 1956), p. 11.

10. A paraphrase of a comment in John Langdon-Davies, *A Short History of Women* (New York: Literary Guild of America, 1927), p. 48. The original reads, " . . . a hen is merely an egg's way of laying another egg."

11. Martin Buber, "The Query of Queries," from *Tales of the Hasiddim—The Early Masters,* reprinted in *The Norton Reader: An Anthology of Expository Prose,* 4th ed. (New York: W. W. Norton, 1965), p. 1136.

SECTION 6.

FEEDING AS SACRED RITUAL

6. Feeding as Sacred Ritual

I Remember the Mothers

When I think of family holiday feasts I recall that *Saturday Evening Post* cover by Norman Rockwell in which the mother is proudly bearing the beautifully browned turkey to the table while the faces of the assembled family beam in anticipation of the Thanksgiving meal they are about to enjoy.

I remember such festival meals when I was growing up. The women of my family gathered in the kitchen, talking and laughing as they cooked together for hours before the actual meal. The delicious odors of baking turkey and vegetables permeated the house. I was allowed to turn the tiny key in the lock and open the large glass doors of the china cupboard in our dining room to get out the most elegant glassware. My mother's best white damask linen cloth already covered the large oval dining room table. This was the cloth she had carefully monogrammed during her eight-year engagement. By each place I put one of the large white linen dinner napkins, also monogrammed. I set the table with delicate long-stemmed glasses for water and wine. My family was Southern Baptist and wine was served only on very special occasions. The best china and silver were already on the table, and I put out the cut-glass serving pieces used for the condiments—cranberry sauce, freshly chilled and crisped carrot sticks and celery, and homemade pickles from our country relatives.

I worked slowly and carefully so I would not break anything. But the women in the kitchen were working quickly and purposively to finish the food preparation. The large square table in the kitchen (where we usually ate) was covered with serving pieces ready for the hot food: the soup tureen for the mashed potatoes, a flat dish for the candied sweet potatoes hot from the broiler, a large platter for the huge turkey wonderfully brown from the oven, a graceful gravy boat with ladle, covered vegetable dishes for the sauerkraut and the stewed tomatoes (a Baltimore German element had joined my family's Tidewater Virginia cooking).

Suddenly everything was ready, the food flowed from stove to waiting serving pieces which were carried triumphantly in to the dining room where the men and children waited. My father raised his wine glass in a toast, we bowed our heads for the blessing, and another family feast had begun.

After the main course the women and children cleared the table and brought in several kinds of pies for dessert. At the end of the meal the men retired to the living room for cigars and conversation. Sometimes they took a walk together while the women once again gathered in the kitchen to do the dishes.

We had an old-fashioned hot water heater beside our sink which had to be lit a half hour before you could get any hot water from the faucet. The heater was lit and, while the water warmed up, all the leftovers were stored away in the refrigerator. This was long before Tupperware so my mother superintended the filling of assorted containers and saucers. Each in its turn was covered with wax paper held in place by a rubber band. By the time the water was hot, my mother was washing the fragile glasses, the silver and the china in hot soapy suds in the washtub in our sink. She then rinsed them with more hot clear water, and the women and children lined up with fresh white tea towels to dry them. When everything was all laid out neatly on the kitchen table, my mother put each item back in its proper place. Thanksgiving (or Christmas or Easter) was over for another year.

There was a wonderful woman-camaraderie during this whole process. My mother, my grandmother and my aunt were the core of the group, plus whatever women guests were invited that year. I remember a strong sense of purpose and identity (long before I ever knew such words) in the shared woman-experience of preparing and cleaning up after our festival meals. These women knew that they and their work were the center of the festival. They planned the meals, made the shopping lists, bought the groceries. They were the ones who knew in their heads and in their hands the old Southern recipes. They set and cleared the tables, washed the dishes. They *were* the feast; they knew that in their bones and in their souls.

Sharon Parks in "The Meaning of Eating and the Home as Ritual Space" is eloquent about the larger meanings and ritual significance of meals, both festival and daily, which families and friends share. "Food by its very nature readily lends itself to symbolic use; and a home where people share meals together easily becomes ritual space."

Kathryn Allen Rabuzzi, when she wrote in Section 5. about housework, observed how the "ritual enactment of housework connects a woman back to a long line of female ancestors before her." Marcia Zimmerman tells of this in "Learning to Make Grandmother's Strudel," a poignant account of an oral tradition transmitted between generations of women in her family. "I remember sitting around my grandmother's kitchen table helping her bake her famous strudel." The recipes and the motions for cooking that are learned from mothers and grandmothers make a sacred tie between generations of women parallel to the long silver line of all birthing mothers envisioned earlier by Sidney Morris (Section 2).

In God's Image

Alongside the festivals, there is the daily work of feeding a family. Does the routine of this "ordinary" feeding, repeated several times a day, obscure for us its meaning? Sarah Hall Maney in her chapter "Cooking: Divine and Destructive" recognizes that "the profound lives within the ordinary. The profound evolves out of the most ordinary of our day-by-day life experiences. Our women's work of cooking and feeding, *most* ordinary and *most* profound, provides us as women the opportunity for sacramental experience."

Women tend to feel good about cooking and feeding. Cooking smells good, tastes good, feels creative. Our culture rewards "good" cooks with praise, and prizes are awarded at state fairs and Pillsbury bake-offs for "best recipes." One woman says, "I have an earth-mother feeling about feeding." Another says, "I feel close to God when I feed my family." So much of our gratitude to God is expressed in thanks for food and the daily blessing of physical sustenance. Women are a daily, but often unrecognized, channel of that flow of life-giving nourishment.

One table blessing says, "Thou openest thy hand, and all are fed" (Psa. 145:15–16). Before women in the Christian tradition could claim as our sacred role any part of the work of that Feeding Hand, males rushed in to construct an imitation of the feeding women do, and called it holy communion. They declared this "shadow-feeding" to be ultimately important. Being fed at home is no big deal, Christianity has said; the real meal, the real food, is the communion bread and wine. What is important is the spiritual life, and that is sustained by the sacred ritual in church. In another patriarchal reversal, that food which actually sustains physical daily life at home and at work is not even mentioned.

None of women's life-sustaining roles in connection with human feeding are declared by male religion to be a manifestation of the sacred Feeding Hand of the universe. Yet in developed or industrialized countries women plan the meals, shop for them and prepare and cook them. In developing countries of Africa, Asia and Latin America women in addition actually grow the food and harvest it so their families can eat.

We also often forget that the vast majority of us worldwide were breastfed by women during the first year or more of our lives. Breastfeeding is a routine part of the everyday feeding many women do. Dana Raphael has devoted her professional life as an anthropologist to the cross-cultural understanding and support of women's work of lactation. In "The Tender Gift of Breastfeeding" she speaks from her own experience on behalf of millions of women around the world when she says: "When else do I, in my own flesh, have such power of producing food without effort, filling another, growing a future woman or man. I give my essence; the baby grasps at life."

None of this is a theme for male religion's theological meditation. If it were, we would all be forced to recognize the sacred ministry of all the women who "make" the bread of life at home and in their bodies, and we would have to honor this fully as much as we honor those who "break" the bread of life in church.

"New Earth Demands New Bread"[1]

We cannot think about feeding without also thinking about all those around the world and in our cities who are dying from hunger and malnutrition. Large-scale economic structures permit people to starve at the same time that huge agricultural surpluses are being produced. Such structures need to be questioned. Why are there government subsidies for those who overproduce food but not for those who underconsume it? Why does the modern industrialized agribusiness system lay waste the soils and fill our streams and groundwater with herbicides, biocides and the runoff of agricultural fertilizers? Food is no longer largely a local or even a regional commodity, and agricultural commodity prices are set in global financial and commodity markets. The rising sales of "Whopper" hamburgers at the Burger King restaurants were a factor that encouraged the destruction of tropical rain forests to make way for cattle ranching in Costa Rica.

Beyond our traditional roles in feeding, women must somehow break open the bread of life in a new way for all upon the planet. We must *knead* the present system until it changes into something more life-giving, which sustains nature and humans alike. We have seen meaning in feeding our immediate families.

Therefore it is possible for us to join with other women who also have families they need to feed, and together fashion a world food system that feeds all.

There is on my wall a poster: "Woman is as common as a loaf of bread, and like a loaf of bread, will rise."[2] We as women have always had on our minds feeding and hunger. Now our consciousness as women *is* rising. Who knows what we can do when we claim our power to change the world according to *our* concerns, as men previously have done for their male concerns. New earth does indeed demand new bread, and we women must now make sure that *every mother worldwide* has bread for her family.

—Elizabeth Dodson Gray

NOTES

1. Poster by Deirdre, "New earth demands new bread. Women must break the bread of life." (Boston Collective on Women and Religion).

2. The text is a paraphrase of a poem by Judy Grahn, *The Work of a Common Woman: Collected Poetry 1964–1977* (Freedom, Calif.: The Crossing Press, 1984), p. 73.

Cooking: Divine and Destructive

Sarah Hall Maney

SARAH HALL MANEY *says that the major premise of her chapter "is that the profound lives within the ordinary. The opportunities for sacred experience, God-experience, are to be found not only in elaborate ritual and grand occasions but in the everydayness of our ordinary lives. I believe I personify what I speak of. I, an ordinary woman born into an unremarkable family, raised in a traditional manner, living out a traditional and common role of wife, mother and homemaker, have experienced the great mystery of God in my person and my everyday experience. That I, a woman with no distinguishing educational background, can experience in the deepest part of myself the importance of my own sacred work of feeding, or nurturing, or comforting, or speaking, or writing, is an honor to the God who created me and destined me for greatness within a very ordinary framework. I truly believe the words of one of my poems, "On the day I was born, God danced."*

Years Together at Our Dinner Table

My most enduring happy memory of childhood is of our family gathered around the dinner table. I remember laughing and storytelling. I also recall my brothers teasing me, and their trying to stab the last pork chop with their forks, thus discarding the good table manners my mother insisted upon. In those days we all came to our table hungry. Snack foods had not yet become a habit, so our mouths watered and our stomachs growled when we stepped in the front door to smell what Mother was cooking for supper.

I don't know if my mother liked to prepare meals for our family; I never asked her. I do know she gave much time and attention to meal planning and preparation. My father was diabetic and able to control his disease through diet alone. But that placed a heavy responsibility on my mother. In the first years of his disease all of his food was weighed and the combinations of foods for each meal carefully planned. I remember Mother creating a lemon meringue pie (my father's favorite), using honey in place of the forbidden sugar, so he could enjoy a bit of the dessert he so loved.

In later years my father was sick and dying. That very same dinner table, covered with similar meals still carefully and lovingly prepared, became the center of our pain and disconnection as we sat in numbed silence and watched our father alternately brood and rage. At those times there was no pleasure in eating, no matter how hungry I was. The food had a hard time moving down past the lump of emotion I felt in my throat. Even though my mother's work of cooking may have been sacred and life-sustaining, there were no sacred moments at the dinner table in those days.

Out of a Woman's Love and Creative Energies

I don't think my mother had any conscious notion that she was doing sacred work as she prepared our meals. Or if she did have a sense of the importance of her work, I doubt she would have attached the words "sacred" and "sacrament" to any part of the process. Except for things at church, those words and concepts were not part of our conscious understanding or our vocabulary.

In looking back on that time from the accumulation of my fifty-two years, it seems clear to me now that my mother did very sacred work in her kitchen. She presided over our dinner table and offered us a sustaining and life-giving sacrament, the product of her love and her creative energy. Such work becomes sacred, I now think, when we focus creative energy into doing something, or making something, that contributes to the health and healing, to the well-being and wholeness, of ourselves or others. So food, a meal carefully prepared, becomes a sacrament to me when I enjoy, I am nourished, I am comforted, or I am connected with others in the sharing.

As my mother's daughter, I carry on this sacred work. Like my mother, I was not aware through most of the growing-up years of our children that cooking, baking, meal planning, had any sacred dimensions. I did know I enjoyed cooking and meal planning. While the meals around our dinner table have not been as rollicking or as devastating as the family dinners of my childhood, our mealtimes have usually been the focus of our most joyous and our most painful times. We have celebrated here the special moments. We have also struggled at meals to find words to make connection with teen-agers who believed we couldn't possibly understand them. When my husband and I have felt distanced from one another, it has been at mealtimes together that we too have tried to reconnect.

With a certainty in my bones and a consciousness in my mind I know now that cooking, meal preparation, can be sacred work, holy stuff. Perhaps in the deep-down part of me I always knew this, and perhaps my mother's deep-down part knew it too. If it is only just in these last years that I have been able to name it, then I honor the work by naming it sacred not only for myself but for my mother and grandmothers, my children and grandchildren.

The Satisfactions of Feeding Others

I need time and leisure for my work, if I am to be aware that something holy is going on in my kitchen. I like nothing better than the luxury of a whole afternoon or morning behind my apron, experimenting with a new recipe or baking something for guests that can be hidden in the freezer until needed. I often set my tables several days before a party, so I can have time to fiddle with the napkins, arrange and rearrange the flowers, add and subtract candle holders, or change the color scheme until it is just right, until it all delights my eye and I can enjoy for a time the setting for the sacrament.

I remember clearly how dumb I thought my grandmother was because she always set her table for Sunday dinner on Friday. After our son walked through the house last week and observed the tables all set for a party several days hence, he went home and told his wife, "Mother is so *organized*, she even has her tables set for the party." There was much laughter about that, and I am sure my grandmother's spirit was laughing with them. Why do we come to our wisdom so late? The set tables have much less to do with organization than with the pleasure of creating. I am making ready the tables for the sacrament that they will hold, creating the atmosphere for the sacred moment when friends will come together for communion with one another.

I think I have always had a sense that the setting in which a meal is presented is as important as the food itself, and that the care and attention given to this work is also sacred work. It matters little whether silver and china and flowers are used. Something beautiful can be created with the simplest of utensils.

I also know that sacred work has gone on when our daughter-in-law brings our granddaughter to me to baby-sit. She hands me Meghan's lunch box and I know that carefully wrapped inside are Meggie's favorite peanut-butter sandwiches, with the hated crusts cut off, the little sandwiches cut to two-year-old sizes, the apple cut into two-year-old bites, and a tiny box of raisins in the corner to satisfy a small sweet tooth. A friend of mine tucks a note into her daughter's brown-bag school lunch, often nothing more than a smiling face and a "Love, Mom," but a sign of sacred work nonetheless.

Perhaps it is important to note that food and food preparation are integral to our most profound experiences, life and death. The birthday cake has become the central symbol that marks the anniversary of our arrival on earth. When someone in a family dies, the most natural response of friends and neighbors is to come bearing food, some sacred work of their hands, in order to nourish and comfort.

The Dark Side of Food in Some Women's Lives

There is a great paradox around the whole issue of food for me and for many women. I have spoken of my sacred work with food and of the possibility of sacrament. Now I need to look at the other side, the dark destructive encounters with food that I and others in my family have struggled with. There have been recurring moments through my whole life when I have been obsessed with food, eating compulsively and being addicted to sugar and alcohol.

Perhaps at these times I am seeking the sacrament, seeking nourishment, comfort, pleasure, all the things I somehow feel bereft of. So I seek to fill the empty place in myself with food, more and more food. There is no sense of "enough" at these times. As I stand at the open refrigerator door and fill my mouth to overflowing with whatever I have been denying myself all day, there is no sense then that I am doing sacred work. The self-loathing that inevitably follows an eating binge fills me with despair and with longing for some way out of the clutches of food and its destructive power over me.

So food, which holds out to me the possibility of life, of sacrament, of nourishment and health and pleasure and well-being and wholeness, also holds out the possibility of destruction and death—death to my self-esteem, death to my body, death to my well-being by my becoming fat. I have struggled to learn, as my father learned with his disease of diabetes, that when we become addicted to something—when we can't control what we take into our bodies, when our consumption of a substance turns it from a good thing into a bad thing by the amount we ingest—then the path to good health and wholeness leads by the way of choosing to "give up" rather than "give in." It becomes sacred work to *refrain* from eating.

This past year I entered a weight-reduction program that was an almost entirely liquid diet. This is a radical program and I undertook it with some anxiety. But it has been a good program for me because it freed me from the necessity of making food choices about kinds of foods or amounts. At first I chose not to do any cooking at all for my family or guests. I had a strong sense during this time that I was doing sacred work by *not* focusing on food in any way, for myself or others. So for me the paradox is the knowledge that I can experience the same sense of doing sacred work in the preparation and consumption of food as I can in the non-preparation and non-consumption. Perhaps the link to the sacredness is in the knowledge of which choice leads me to health and wholeness. I continue to struggle with those choices. A choice to enjoy the pleasures of cooking can—and has—led me to compulsive overeating.

It is important to me that I remain conscious that I have choices about cooking, meal preparation, and my own food intake. If I ever perceive that I am cooking and preparing meals because it is expected, because cooking is "woman's work," then I will have given my power of choice away and my work would not be sacred because it would not be life-giving for me. I do claim the power to choose.

Women's Sacramental Experience

When sacrament happens around our dinner table with friends or family, I, a woman, have done the sacred work and I preside at that sacred moment. By contrast, the Eucharistic celebration I attend at church, with its circles of Styrofoam bread and the one plate and one cup on the bare table and no conversation, seems a pale, bleak imitation of the rich and profound sacramental experience that happens at home. But by removing the sacrament of feeding from the home, away from the hands of women, men can pretend that they are in charge, that they preside and make magic out of the sacrament of Eucharist.

I see not magic but a great mystery in the sacred. There is in our feeding the mystery of paradox. There is also the mystery of life being sustained, renewed, transformed, deepened. These are mysteries that are profound. But the profound lives within the ordinary. The profound evolves out of the most ordinary of our day by day life experiences. Our women's work of cooking and feeding, *most* ordinary and *most* profound, provides us as women the opportunity for sacramental experience.

Learning to Make Grandmother's Strudel[*]

Marcia Zimmerman

MARCIA ZIMMERMAN is married and an assistant rabbi at Temple Israel in Minneapolis. She is a graduate of Macalester College and Hebrew Union College—Jewish Institute of Religion. She was ordained rabbi in May 1988. She has been a rape crisis counselor and a crisis counselor for battered women. "As a Jewish woman I believe it is my obligation to carry on the traditions of my foremothers. I am working toward widening the Jewish heritage to accept women as equals. In order to facilitate this process, I believe we must include our grandmothers' and mother's stories as a part of our collective history, to weave our women's stories into ancient Jewish texts."

Modern Exodus

She was fifteen when she boarded the ship leaving Russia bound for America. America for her was the land of opportunity. She carried all of her earthly possessions safely hidden under her overcoat. My grandmother Lena, her mother, and her two brothers traveled across the ocean to meet Papa. She could not wait to be reunited with her father. She believed he would protect her. She had faith that he would enroll her in school. Over and over again during my childhood, my grandmother told me her story. I loved listening to her journey to America and her account of the hardships she and her family overcame upon their arrival.

I remember sitting around my grandmother's kitchen table helping her bake her famous strudel. I would sit on my knees so I could reach the top of the table. My job was to fix the filling. I would slowly stir together the pineapple, cherries, apples, jellies, coconut and spices. My grandmother stood right next to me, instructing me to stir a little more or to add more of this or that. After the filling was finished it was time to roll out the dough. It was my grandmother's thin and flaky dough that was the secret to her world-famous strudel. She would sprinkle the flour onto her mother's wooden board, the one they had brought over from the old country, gently rolling the strudel dough with a rolling pin. Next we would fill the dough with the fruit mixture and roll it tightly, tucking in the ends so that it would not come unraveled in the oven. The last touch was to sprinkle cinnamon on the top of the logs and put them in the oven. The smell of strudel would permeate my grandmother's apartment and spill over into the halls of her apartment house.

---

[*] Portions of this chapter were published in a different form in *Journal of Aging in Judaism*, 2:2 (1987).

Dream of a Promised Land

During these afternoons my grandmother told me her dreams as a young immigrant girl from Russia. She grew excited, her voice defiant and strong, as she told me how the Russian soldiers courted her, asking for her hand in marriage. For of course Lena Schneider was the most beautiful Russian girl for miles around. Lena enjoyed their compliments, but she had great plans for herself. She was going to America to learn how to read and write. She wanted to write novels, short stories, and also poetry. It was a dream she had nurtured ever since her Papa left Russia for America. In America she would be given the opportunity to break out of the role of maintaining her family. She could stop picking up after her brothers, washing dishes and cooking meals. These were tasks she was required to do since she was the only girl in the family. She was going to leave this drudgery behind. She was going to be a famous writer one day. These were the dreams of a young girl.

But on her voyage to America Lena's mother told her of her arranged marriage to her Yiddish teacher, Max Pasternak. He was waiting for Grandma in St. Louis, Missouri. There they would settle down and have a family. They would live off of the income from his job as a tailor. From this point on Lena's destiny was that of wife and mother, a life she lived to its fullest. These roles became the center of her world, even though this was not the life she once dreamed for herself.

What Women Teach Their Granddaughters

Lena never let go of her dreams. She never lost the sparkle in her eyes that grew brighter when she told me, her granddaughter, of her great hopes of becoming a writer. She always taught me that no one can take away your dreams, for they are sacred.

Sitting around her kitchen table, watching each turn of her spoon, I was an apprentice to this artist. My grandmother never wrote down her famous strudel recipe. She passed it down to me as an oral tradition. It was a recipe filled with the Jewish heritage of our foremothers. It was part of a tradition passed down from grandmother to daughter to granddaughter along with her stories and dreams. It was a heritage based upon women's experiences and upon a knowledge of the world and its ways that stems from our women's physical uniqueness combined with our women's experiences of what society asks of us, makes of us, and makes us do.

My grandmother believed that a book would liberate her from the drudgery of her biological and social destiny. Through my own rabbinical studies I have learned to find nourishment not only from my kitchen but also from my study table. I bring the knowledge of my grandmother's recipes to my study of the *Sefer Torah*. I treasure the heritage of my foremothers. My grandmother's recipes are as much a part of Judaism as our sacred texts, for her recipes hold the untold stories of women throughout the ages.

I am proud of the care and love with which my grandmother prepared her food and the enjoyment she experienced teaching me her ancient art. My grandmother's greatest joy was to feed her family, to nourish us with the food she so lovingly prepared.

Dinners at my grandmother's apartment were an all-day ritual. She began her preparations in the early hours of the morning, long before we were to arrive for her feast. Lena would rise at five in the morning to begin chopping onions, cutting potatoes, seasoning the meat, and combining the ingredients to create her various tantalizing dishes. Her culinary art was a tapestry of different Eastern European specialties: brisket, chopped liver, gefilte fish, matzo balls, and noodle kugle. She made certain that each member of her family would leave her table fully satisfied.

When the sun came up and the nearby markets opened, Lena took her shopping cart and made her way through the neighborhood streets to inspect and purchase the freshest produce available. The corner fruitman saved her the sweetest melons, the ripest peaches, the greenest string beans. My grandmother demanded the highest quality; she took pride in the food she fed her family. Returning home, Lena's basket was always overflowing.

My grandmother spent the rest of the day occupied with her labor of love. I often found her bent over her wooden bowl, the one with a crack in it, chopping and seasoning, adding and stirring. She worked furiously at preparing food to feed the ones she loved, her children and her grandchildren.

Upon our arrival my grandmother greeted us wrapped in the luscious layers of aromas from her long hours spent in the kitchen. We breathed deeply of these wonderful anticipations of dinner as we were warmed with her loving smile, hugs and kisses. She lived in a small one-bedroom apartment, and during these family dinners my grandmother performed a ritual dance as she brought freshly filled platters heaping with the delicacies of her affection. With every piece of kugle [pudding] she spooned out comfort; she ladled out care and cures along with her chicken soup. Lena never sat down to eat during a family meal. She was deeply satisfied keeping a watchful eye over every one of us, making sure we had enough to eat, and that we had received enough of her devotion. Lena's just reward for her efforts was our gratitude and appreciation, and a clean plate.

She listened eagerly to our moans of ecstasy with every mouth-watering bite. We gathered as a family around grandmother's table for support and comfort. She knew this, and her love for feeding us became for us a refuge, a place away from our daily worries and concerns. We knew her food would heal and rejuvenate us. Being at my grandmother's table was to be at a sacred place.

Preserving Women's Sacred Past

I am proud of the care and love with which my grandmother prepared her food and the enjoyment she experienced teaching me her ancient art. My grandmother and her experiences and her story and her recipes continue to be an inspiration in my life. It is my hope that as women we will acknowledge women's realms as sacred. My experience with my grandmother in her kitchen epitomizes for me women's need for a place where women come together, a place that is safe for us and where we can clarify our needs as we recall and transmit our women's experience as Jews.

Preserving the past is an obligation of all Jews. When we participate in the Passover seder we are commanded to relive the exodus from Egypt. When we recite the Sh'ma we cover our eyes to remember the revelation at Sinai. It is the unique way I as a woman experience the exodus and the revelation that brings me to the sacred place where the human and the Divine meet. If it is my relationship to the Holy One that mirrors my relationship to humans, then I as a woman bring my female experiences to my understanding of the Divine Being.

It is through this unique relationship with God that women approach Torah. The Torah constantly unfolds with new meaning. It is through my personal experiences, knowledge and needs that the words of Torah take on significant meaning for me or for anyone. For me, opening the Torah to the story of the exodus from Egypt is like looking into a mirror. I see in the account of the exodus the story of the lives of women like my grandmother.

Until now women's experience and the stories of women like my grandmother have not been valued. I believe it is my responsibility to pass on her heritage by telling her stories. When I relay her tradition, I find the strength to reclaim Judaism as my own heritage. It is time to include female insights into all aspects of Jewish life. Women are bringing a new understanding of Jewish theology by asking for themselves the fundamental religious questions. Women's voices and women's experiences need to be included in the creative process of redefining Judaism. Women are demanding that Judaism sanctify our women's physical and emotional experiences and be a tradition which grounds itself in both female experiences and in our Jewish past.

Dreaming My Own Dream

I was weaned on my grandmother's recipes and nourished by her love as well as by her food and her stories. My grandmother died two years ago. Her legacy lives on through the tradition she passed down to me around her kitchen table. It is an authentic Jewish tradition, and I bring it with me when I learn Torah and when as a rabbi I teach it. I will continue my grandmother's heritage and in many ways I will fulfill her dreams when I sanctify both women's and men's experiences in a Jewish context.

I have a vision too, a dream of my own. I am in my own home. My granddaughter sits on her knees to reach the open book laying on top of the table. I am standing by her side and engaging her in a discussion about the story of the Israelites' exodus from slavery in Egypt. She sees a kernel of her own truth in the stories of Miriam, Shiphrah and Puah, and Tzipporah. I sit by smiling, seeing the vitality of my grandmother's dreams four generations earlier. This comforts me, for I feel the warmth I felt at my grandmother's kitchen table as I pass down an oral history, a recipe filled not only with pineapple, cherries, coconut, and jellies but filled also with the heritage and experience of our foremothers.

William Irons, courtesy of The Human Lactation Center Ltd.

The Tender Gift of Breastfeeding

Dana Raphael

DANA RAPHAEL *has her Ph.D. from Columbia University in anthropology. Margaret Mead called her "a pioneer, the first woman anthropologist in this generation, after the long desert of the postwar years, to go courageously into her own chosen problems, in spite of discouragement." She turned a personal experience early in her career—her inability to breastfeed her first child—into the first serious research on breastfeeding. She continues a thirty-year investigation into the nature of mother/infant interaction and feeding behavior as Director of The Human Lactation Center in Westport, Conn. She is the author of* THE TENDER GIFT: BREASTFEEDING *(1973) and* ONLY MOTHERS KNOW: PATTERNS OF INFANT FEEDING IN TRADITIONAL CULTURES *(1985).*

In My Own Flesh

Special, peaceful, important, gorgeous, filled up full, no longer lonely, powerful, so full of love, closer to The Light: that's what I think of breastfeeding. When else are two beings so integral? When else do I, in my own flesh, have such power of producing food without effort, filling another,
growing a future woman or man. I give my essence; the baby grasps at life.

But it is not all one-way. Miserable with my breasts bloated, about to burst, I waken my son. I exhale in exquisite relief as he clamps onto the nipple, suckles, relieving the pressure. Thank you, dear child.

I know all about the letting down of the milk, the nervous-system pathways, the hormones, the ducts in the mammary gland, the cells, the ejection reflex. But what I cannot explain is how come my body is designed to feed another. How come a day or so after childbirth my body is transformed and, as if from nowhere, fluid issues forth. And how come each time the infant sucks, within a minute my breasts swell miraculously with fluid. That is a holiness, a big holiness.

As an anthropologist, I have asked women in dozens of cultures, the so-called uneducated ones, where they think the milk comes from. "The shoulders," some say. Most others say from the blood, and that is so. Unlike me, however, many say "What nonsense, it's just there." Like me, others whisper, "It is a special gift from the heavens."

Magic That Works

In Jordan, women collect white stones from the Grotto of Milk in Bethlehem, because, according to legend, some drops of Mary's breast milk sanctified the area, giving the pebbles special powers to enhance lactation.

Japanese women buy facsimiles of breasts and present them as offerings in special temples, hoping their prayers for abundant breast milk will be answered.

I had my version too. I believed that if I breastfed five minutes on one side and twenty on the other, all would be well. I thought I had to stomach three glasses of milk—yuk!—each day or I would dry up. My doctor told me that if I had intercourse before my six-week checkup, the baby would throw up!

Mothers know this sacred act often needs intervention. I'm lucky, affluent and Western. When I failed to breastfeed my first child, I was crushed, so upset that I am still going on about it thirty-three years later. And I had alternatives. Most moms, pour souls, don't have options. No breastfeeding and the baby will likely die.

What's sacred is, after all, magical, and lactation is magical. What is sacred after all is indescribable, and breastfeeding is indescribable. But I keep trying to describe it. Here is a list that friends and I shared recently about how it feels when the milk "comes in": "Sort of hurts but no matter." "Feels like heaviness." "Most pleasant." "It tingles." "Such a mystery and the sky is the limit." "Like riding down the river and the current swirling all around." "Beneath me I feel an opening, something tearing open, and life is supporting me."

Madonna with Child Abreast

Don't be fooled just because religionists of old and new never called breast-feeding sacred. Musing about it is nothing new. It's neither new nor unknown. I realized long ago my love for fourteenth and fifteenth century altarpieces had something to do with the special nature of this bond. Many of the scenes that move me most depict the Madonna with child abreast. Artists sensed this wonderment. They were conjurers of this magic. Again and again they painted altarpieces depicting a messiah as a tender child at the breast, or touching the breast of the Queen who comforts, who is hopeful, empathetic, reachable. Such scenes leave the viewer peaceful, for they are life-giving, heavenly, awe-filling, celestial.

I felt the force of that same magic when I was giving my baby a bottle. My friend, who thinks breastfeeding is disgusting, said the same thing. Sacred for one woman can be profane for another. Is feeding with a bottle a sacred act? It depends. It has to feel like it is. It has to feel wondrous to watch the infant suckling, get sleepy, smile, and release the nipple. You don't have to be a "carriage peeper" to feel the power of these connections. Just sigh and breathe deeply to transform stress into joy.

Sensuous, Not Sexual

Folklore has it that women can orgasm during breastfeeding. Certainly these are both powerful biological acts. I think those who pass along this information mix up the lexical meaning. For most women breastfeeding is extremely sensu-ous, not sexual. Moms joke about it:

"There's no let-down of milk when a man guzzles."

"There's secretion all right but a foot away."

"It's a close encounter of a second kind."

For women to be in a constant state of arousal or brought to orgasm during breastfeeding would not be a positive evolutionary adaptation; it would be a threat to survival. In the early weeks, mothers feed as often as ten to twenty times each day. In the course of human evolution, such carryings-on would have wiped out our species.

I have been asked by men, "Can I breastfeed as well?" (Have men caught on and want in on this specially private and powerful connection?) I tell them that during the embryonic stage at five weeks or so the development of this mammary gland in males ceases. Some will not take "no" for an answer. Some have admitted that before their baby was delivered, they took prolactin hormones hoping to stimulate some secretion so they too could have this precious experience.

My husband "breastfed." It was like this. I nursed our adopted baby, beginning when she came to us three days old. My younger natural child was then twelve, so I certainly never had sufficient milk. While she suckled me, I pressed a small syringe full of milk into the corner of her mouth. And he did it too. "It sort of tickled," he reported. "That was something special, just the two of us. Everyone was asleep and it was so quiet. I felt a special communion with this kid—I'll never forget it."

A Lesson of Life, a Promise of Peace

I don't cotton to those who would put women and breastfeeding on a pedestal. Beware of such sentimental fineries. They are a frequent technique for covering up contempt. Breastfeeding is a private experience, a sacred love-lesson that made me believe peace is possible and violence not intrinsic to the human condition. It moved me off the plane of everyday banalities and dangers.

I breastfed once for eighteen months and again for ten months—not unusual today for American mothers. Each time I stopped, I knew I was losing something important to me. My love of this function has made me an advocate. I continue to do whatever I can to help other women have the support they need to lactate successfully—in the United States where we breastfeed for this special·joy, this inner calm, and also for our sisters in the developing world where women breastfeed to keep their infants alive.

The Meaning of Eating and the Home as Ritual Space

Sharon Parks

SHARON PARKS was born into a clergy home in which both parents were attentive to the weaving of family life and community life and the importance of special occasions. "So it is not surprising that my professional interests are concerned with the dynamics by which faith is formed and transformed." Her professional field is Religion and Psychology and she is the author of THE CRITICAL YEARS: THE YOUNG ADULT SEARCH FOR A FAITH TO LIVE BY (1986). She has taught for several years at Harvard Divinity School and is now at the Weston School of Theology (a national Jesuit center) and is currently also a visiting associate professor at Harvard Business School. She is a founding member of the Chinook Learning Center and Community "where we have across the last decade and a half worked to recover and renew meaningful ritual and to cultivate new patterns of eating that honor our relationship with the earth and the whole human family."

I invite you to remember a meal you experienced at some time in the past and that you now savor in your memory—a breakfast, lunch, dinner, supper, snack, brunch, or feast—which somehow lingers as important or special. I do not know what comes to your mind, but two occasions come to mine. One was in the summer time. I had returned again to Whidbey Island, just north of Seattle, to the Chinook Learning Center and Community, the spiritual and educational community of which I am a founding member. A group of us stood in a circle of linked hands sharing a moment of quiet around a table laden with heaps of baked potatoes, fresh vegetables, salad from the garden, and Pacific Northwest salmon. As the silence was concluded, a guest among us who knew me well recognized the symbolic power of a gathered, traditional meal, saying simply and rightly, "Sharon is home now."

The second meal that comes to mind is a recent Christmas dinner. For the first time my family had gathered neither in my grandmother's home nor in my mother's home, but in my sister's in Canada. The family, three generations, made our way from California, Indiana and Massachusetts to Toronto for a white Christmas and our traditional Christmas dinner: fried chicken, mashed potatoes, cranberry-orange relish, candied sweet potatoes, a green vegetable, pickles and olives, homemade rolls, molded salads, pies. My sister had made gingerbread placecards for the fourteen of us plus one "in utero."

These meals celebrate the connections among things. They symbolize bonds that transcend geography and generations. They mark the affirmation of a shared way of life—shared commitments and vocation. Each affirms ongoing continuity even in the midst of discontinuity and change.

Food and Meaning-Making

It was the Christmas of 1976; I had just arrived in Boston and I decided to share Christmas with four other friends from the Northwest who would also spend the holidays apart from friends or family. I gathered us together a few days ahead, recognizing that the five of us had never been together before but were now to spend Christmas together. I suggested that we might find out what would be necessary to each of us for it really to be Christmas. What were the family traditions that were important to each one that we could share together?

One of the surprises was how much our traditions had to do with food. Yes, there were readings and music and going to midnight mass which were also important. But we ended up having to spend an extra day together in order to eat all the special foods that five different family traditions could produce. Among the treats were eggs Benedict for Christmas breakfast, fried chicken for Christmas Eve dinner, and, not surprisingly, rich dark fudge.

What we recognize here is that there are finally only three things that human beings need for the basic survival of human life: shelter, food and love. We need protection from the elements. We are dependent upon food and drink for physical nourishment. And we need love—a conviction that we dwell in a mutual recognition and affirmation of connection and belonging. As we weave the fabric of meaning by which we are composed, these essential elements of our existence become the warp and woof of our lives.

This weaving is done with symbol and ritual. Suzanne Langer, the philosopher, has helped us recognize that symbols are objects, acts, signs, and instruments of the sensible world which serve as a key to a pattern of relationships. Words are very economical symbols, she says, but when we want to name more than words can say, we turn to ritual. [1] That is to say, we employ concrete objects and acts in our composing of meaning. Gaston Bachelard furthers our understanding by recognizing that if symbols and rituals are to be powerful for us, they must be resonant. [2] They must have the power to connect with many different parts of our being—our bodies, our feelings, our thoughts, our history, our hopes for the future.

The Symbolic Power of Food and Meals

Food has a particular capacity to serve as a means of more than mere feeding and eating. Food as a common, essential object of the physical world readily links us with the intangible that is also essential, thus lending itself to symbolic use. A home where people share meals together easily becomes ritual space. A home is the context in which food, meals, and feasts repeatedly order the life of our everyday and transmit the stories and expectations of our lives across generations.

We do not have to reflect very long upon the power of food to begin to see why it has such symbolic-ritual power and why meals, whether ordinary or special, can function as complex symbols, keys to whole patterns of relationship between ourselves and other elements of our lives—persons, things, and the source of all food, the earth itself.

Likewise, we begin to see how home is the space where our needs to give and receive shelter, food, and love come together in either a symphony or a cacophony of the demands and graces of life. To prepare for, to preside at, and to participate in a home meal is to create a primary ritual by which, for better or for worse, we weave the fabric of life.

In his book *The Mystery of the Ordinary,* Charles Cummings deepens this insight when he writes: "Eating a meal is first of all an assertion of my will to live and be what I am."[3] He then prompts us to reflect upon the fact not only that we must eat but that we must do so repeatedly and often. We are all aware that we can only go for a short time without food and for even less time without fluids. When we eat, we must very soon eat again. If we dare to contemplate fully the act of eating, we will be led to the unavoidable awareness of our continual desire to live, and also our utter dependence upon the generosity of the earth and its peoples and the power and grace by which our lives are sustained. We will be forcibly led to an awareness of our participation in the mystery of interdependence which we name God. Before the gift of food, we will bow our heads.

Eating Together as Ritual

At the beginning of a Thanksgiving dinner some years ago, when a young child asked why we were bowing our heads and praying before the feast, she was piously told that it was because our food comes from God. She quickly pointed out that this was not so; for instance, she said, "the milk came from a cow." In modern society where few cultivate their own food, we are not only dependent upon the earth and its fruit and the other creatures with whom we share it. We are dependent also upon all those who make it accessible to us— farmers, harvesters, equipment companies, food processing plants, truckers, grocers, chefs, maitre d's, waiters, waitresses, health inspectors, the Food and Drug Administration. But we remain most centrally dependent upon food itself, and we live the mystery of the fact that, across all cultures, we do not typically prefer to eat alone.

Human beings seem to prefer to eat together. Why this is so may be submitted to various types of analysis, but surely a part of each of these is the fact that we are both physical, bodied beings who must be nourished and also inspirited beings who know, who reflect upon, and who suffer the fact that we are not sufficient unto ourselves. We are dependent and vulnerable whether in the womb, or as an infant at the breast, or a child asking for ice cream, or an adolescent hanging out at the pizza parlor, or an adult seeking to impress a client at a new restaurant in town, or a very ill person being sustained by intravenous feeding. Our need to eat is a vulnerability directly related to our vulnerability to love. We need each other to survive. We cannot separate the fact "Because I was loved, I am" from the reality "Because I was fed, I am." We are physical beings made in and for relation, and our word *companion* means "one with whom we share bread."

Erik Erikson's reflections upon the power of ritual in the formation of personality and culture assist us in recognizing the humanizing, civilizing power of the shared meal. He observes that ritualization at its best—that is, in a viable cultural setting—represents a creative form which helps to avoid both impulsive excess and compulsive self-restriction. The shared meal elevates the satisfaction of immediate needs into the context of a communal reality. It tames our eagerness while firmly joining our fragile hope of personal importance to a group's idea of its central place in the natural and spiritual universe.[4]

So the ritual of eating is also a form of teaching. It is a way of learning how to manage some of the most necessary tasks of existence. At the family table we learn to negotiate some of life's most essential skills, especially the ability to balance our needs with the needs of others. We learn that there is nourishment for us and that there must be enough for others too.

We learn that different people have different preferences. We learn to eat at different paces and we have to make time for each other. We learn that we come to the meal from various locations and experiences, in differing moods and bearing different expectations. In the shared meal we weave together those differences of place and preference into a sacrament of belonging together anyway. It is a sacrament from which we gain the strength to move into the future, for we have been both physically fed and also emotionally challenged and confirmed. We have been nourished.[5]

Soul Food

Women in our culture spend a good deal of time being responsible for feeding; indeed, women are the ones who tend to hold primary responsibility for the preparation of food and drink—especially when this is done in the home and without direct financial remuneration and cultural affirmation. We have a difficult time recognizing this daily work of feeding as a sacred activity, and it is inappropriate to sacralize in any glib manner women's roles as traditionally defined.[6] Yet it is essential that we recognize simultaneously that the preparation of meals and the sharing of food can link us with the sacredness of life itself, and *whoever* does the work of it becomes a priest, weaving the fabric of life as the sacred ordinary work of the everyday.

I am aware that there are certain foods or meals I associate with almost all the women who are significant in my life. I find myself remembering Grammie's custard, Grandma's cobbler pie, mother's meat loaf, Patty's chocolate chip cookies, Kristy's custard, Marianne's coffee, Linda's Easter brunch, the warmth of Vivienne's simply and beautifully set supper table, Ineke's tea table, and Roswitha's candlelight European dinners—to name a few. But I also recognize that the same is true for many of the men who are significant in my life. Gramps always mashed the potatoes (or as he said, "busted the spuds") for Christmas dinner. Uncle Ted's peach pie is a special summer treat. My husband Larry can deliver a cheese souffle from a wood-burning cookstove, and no one makes waffles better than my father.

Each of these very different people convey that there is meaning in what they are doing. They prepare food "because it needs to be done." But it is also an act of love and commitment. Each of them serves soul food. And it doesn't "just happen." When we were growing up, I heard my mother ask my father almost daily, "What time will you be coming home for dinner?" We didn't just happen to eat together; it was planned.

The Scope of Our Hungers

Mary Frances Kennedy Fisher, a gastronome and author of several books about eating has written:

> People ask me: Why do you write about food, and eating and drinking? Why don't you write about the struggle for power and security, and about love, the way others do? . . . The easiest answer is to say that, like most other humans, I am hungry. But there is more than that. . . . [I tell about] how I ate bread on a lasting hillside, or drank red wine in a room now blown to bits, and it happens without my willing it that I am telling too about the people with me then, and their other deeper needs of love and happiness. . . . We must eat. If, in the face of that dread fact, we can find other nourishment, and tolerance and compassion for it, we'll be no less full of human dignity. There is a communion of more than our bodies when bread is broken and wine drunk.[7]

Elsewhere Fisher reflects on the relationship between loss and hunger and the "mysterious appetite" that surges in the midst of grief. She believes that it is the wisdom of our bodies calling out for encouragement and strength, compelling us to answer and to eat. She invites us to recognize the truth "that most bereaved souls crave nourishment more tangible than prayers. . . . [For] underneath the anguish of death and pain and ugliness are the facts of hunger and unquenchable life, shining and peaceful.[8]

There is genius in the Jewish practice of centering the weekly observation of shabbat and one of the most central of Jewish holidays, Passover, in a ritual meal shared in the home. These rituals, dwelling in the midst of all that is most familiar and common, are most resistant to secularization and assimilation. They hold the collective identity and memory of a people. Through the gathering around a table, the lighting of the candles, the saying of a prayer and the eating of special foods, they teach the generations that life is lived in the mystery of a covenant, in the mystery of an interdependence with God.

Our lives depend upon this habit of interdependent awareness, this capacity to see the connections between things. We are increasingly compelled by ecological, economic and ecumenical crises to remember that we are interdependent. These words—ecological, economic, ecumenical—have a common root in the Greek word *oikos* connoting environment or household. The single household we share, our small planet home, is threatened with disintegration, the loss of its integrity. In contrast to the eating which nurtures in us the habit of interdependent awareness, there are other ways of eating which have come to dominate our culture.

Eating on the Run

Is it not the case that our faith in technology, the autonomy of the individual, and "busyness" have become ritualized in the forms of our eating?

• Why do we manufacture, much less drink, "instant breakfast"?
• Why have we developed a fast-food industry? Why do we "eat on the run"?
• Why is it that so many in our culture eat alone?
• How has dining become primarily a matter of economic profit, whether for the owner of the restaurant, or for the chef and waiter who prepare and serve the food, or for the company that accomplishes its business over the two-martini lunch?
• How much of our food is manufactured, processed and chemicalized with preservatives and additives rather than simply grown, harvested and seasoned?
• Why have so many women come to feel that preparing and serving a company dinner is a performance by which they will feel judged rather than a sharing of hospitality by which they and others find meaning?
• Why must expensive restaurants promise "personalized service," and why must commercial foods be sold under names such as "almost home"?
• What is the purpose of slogans such as "Nothing says lovin'/ Like something from the oven"? Why do we attempt to sell—and buy—in a commercial package that which can only be embodied in a person and a relationship?

A psychology student at the University of Louvain in Belgium reports a study in which children were shown three pictures and asked which of the three they would like for their own birthday feast. One picture showed a child standing in front of a table piled high with presents. A second showed a small family eating ice cream and cake together, with one large gift package beside the birthday child's place. The third picture showed no presents, just a large group of adults and children eating together around a table obviously decorated for a party. More than seventy per cent of the children studied are said to have chosen the third picture as the one they would like best for their own celebration. Their answers to the question "Why?" stressed the fact that the people were happy, that it was a "real" feast.[9]

Our dilemma is epitomized in the fact that someone has opened recently in San Francisco a successful "stand-up gourmet restaurant." So now we can eat fast, efficiently, standing on our own two feet, alone, trying to be nourished in a way that will satisfy our palate while ignoring our hearts and minds and each other. Meanwhile, Massachusetts General Hospital and other major medical centers are opening "eating disorders clinics."

Our eating really has become disordered. More and more individuals suffer starvation alone in the midst of "plenty" (known as anorexia nervosa) or follow a pattern of gorging and vomiting (known as bulimia). When we try to use food as a means of meeting emotional and spiritual needs for which it can only be a symbol, food becomes addictive. Food becomes destructive.

Eating, divorced from authentic community and communion, becomes just eating. It sometimes turns the potential for nourishment into poison and the possibility of meaningful ritual into the dull boredom of routinization. Human beings caught up in over-industrialized and de-ritualized eating do not learn the balance of needing and sharing, of affirming the self and honoring the other, "the habit of interdependent awareness."

We need fitting rituals, common to all, which order the acts of our every day and teach us the vital nurturing patterns upon which the survival and integrity of our lives depend. In the record of a collective memory and wisdom we read:

> Ho, everyone who thirsts, come to the waters; and ye who have no money, come, . . . buy wine and milk without money and without price. Why do you spend your money for that which is not bread, and your labor for that which does not satisfy? (Isa. 55:1–2)

And the psalmist reminds us: "O taste and see that God is good" (Psa. 34:8).

Yet so little of our shared religious life is about "tasting"; church suppers have evolved into coffee hour after the morning service. We also have given up "seeing" [10] as our worship settings become more and more sparse—while simultaneously our everyday vision is glutted by media images that bombard us. Especially we who are Protestant Christians are reduced to "hearing"—the sense that transcends the concrete embodied stuff of life and best captures our mere abstractions from it. God, who is not only beyond us but also among, within, and beneath us, has been portrayed as so transcendent, so beyond us, that God has a harder time getting inside us and living among us. We do not *taste* that God is good. We do not *see* that God is good. And it is harder and harder for us to believe it when we only *hear* that God is good. [11]

The Politics of Eating and Not Eating

New culture means new food and new eating, new dining and new feasting. One of the signs of religious renewal in our time across Christian denominations has been the return to real bread in place of tasteless wafers for our celebration of communion. But this renewal of communion will not be complete until the quality of our common nourishment is recognized as a primary indicator of the quality of our public, political life.

The politics of hunger determine who does and who does not eat. George McGovern has written:

> Hunger is unique as a public issue . . . because it exerts a special claim on the conscience of the American people. It is the cutting edge of the problem of poverty. Somehow, we Americans are able to look past the slum housing, the polluted air and water, the bad schools, the excessive population growth, and the chronic unemployment of our poor. But the knowledge that human beings, especially little children, are suffering from hunger profoundly disturbs the American conscience. There is a sense, too, in which it outrages the Puritan ethic to have billions spent to stop food from being grown and finance surplus storage while other Americans languish under the blight of malnutrition. [12]

Our eating is disordered. The "Live Aid" concert in the mid-1980s affirmed our humanity in relation to the famine in Africa. But both the "Live Aid" and "Farm Aid" concerts revealed the inability of our government, which is the power of our established collective will, to nourish the human family. In a society in which welfare mothers in Boston must raise children in a single hotel room or worse, living without a stove or a refrigerator, making meals from cans of tuna fish and boxes of crackers kept on the bureau, government officials in Washington, D.C. proposed that catsup be counted a good enough vegetable for children's school lunch programs throughout the country.

An Ancient Wisdom

For a long time my favorite biblical figure has been Esther. I grew up with a fascination for the glamour and edge of terror that marked the story of Esther the Queen. Her father knew their people were threatened with death, and he knew also that she would risk her life if she were to go before the king without being summoned. Nevertheless, asking her to approach the king on behalf of her people, her father said, "Who knows whether or not you have come to the kingdom for such a time as this?" In my childhood understanding of the story, Esther did have the courage to risk her life, the king did receive her and granted her request, and that was pretty much that.

It was only well into my adulthood that I read the story of Esther for myself and discovered that it was not nearly so simple. She did risk her life by going unsummoned before the King. But she did not, or could not, immediately ask him to save her people; rather, she invited him and Haman, the enemy of the Jews, to a banquet—in fact, to several of them. Only in the due course of conversation set in the context of the sharing of food and wine is the truth revealed, power is reordered, and the people are saved through the faithfulness of Esther *and her banquets*.[13]

In the ancient wisdom of Jewish and Christian peoples, God is revealed as the one who provides manna sufficient unto the day and the one whom we recognize in the breaking of the bread. Daniel Berrigan has reflected on this theological truth in *Love, Love, at the End*[14] in a passage I paraphrase here: When I hear bread breaking, it seems almost as though God never meant us to do anything else. It is so beautiful a sound. The crust breaks up like manna and falls all over everything, and then we EAT; bread gets inside humans. It turns into what experts call "the formal glory of God." Sometime in your life, hope that you might see one starved woman and the look on her face when the bread finally arrives. Hope that you might have baked it or bought it—or even needed that bread for yourself. For that look on her face, for your hands meeting hers across a piece of bread, you might be willing to lose a lot, or suffer a lot—or even die a little. "Formal glory." Maybe what we are trying to understand is what they are trying to say, who knows? I do not think they understand, or every theologian would be working part-time in a bread line. Who knows who might greet us there or how our words might change afterward—like stones into bread?

The eating and life of the whole human family is disordered today. We who are women know in our collective memory and practice a wisdom and a talent for composing the ritual meal that heals and nourishes and renews the human family, and the range of our hospitality is being extended and beckoned into a deeper vocation.

Who knows? Perhaps we have come to the "kingdom" for such a time as this.

NOTES

1. Suzanne Langer, *Philosophy in a New Key: A Study in the Symbolism of Rite, Reason, and Art* (Cambridge: Harvard University Press, 1941), chap. 1–3.

2. Gaston Bachelard, *The Poetics of Space*, trans. M. Jolas (Boston: Beacon Press, 1969), p. 39.

3. Charles Cummings, *The Mystery of the Ordinary* (New York: Harper & Row, 1982), p. 105.

4. Erik H. Erikson, *Toys and Reasons: Stages in the Ritualization of Experience* (New York: W. W. Norton, 1977), pp. 75–84.

5. Erikson has observed that it is not enough that children be fed; parents must also be able to represent to the child a deep and almost somatic conviction that there is a meaning to what they are doing. "Ultimately children become neurotic not from frustrations, but from the lack or loss of societal meaning in these frustrations." Erik H. Erikson, *Childhood and Society* (New York: W. W. Norton, 1950) 2nd ed., pp. 249–250.

6. For a powerful description of the negative consequences for women (and men) when women provide nourishment but are not themselves physically, emotionally, and intellectually nourished, see Erika Duncan, "The Hungry Jewish Mother," in *On Being a Jewish Feminist*, Susannah Heschel, ed. (New York: Schocken, 1983), pp. 27–39.

7. Mary Frances Kennedy Fisher, *The Art of Eating* (New York: World Publishing Co., 1954), p. 353.

8. Fisher, *The Art of Eating*, pp. 682–3.

9. See Marianne H. Micks, *The Future Present: The Phenomenon of Christian Worship* (New York: Seabury Press, 1970), p. 151.

10. See Margaret M. Miles, *Image as Insight* (Boston: Beacon Press, 1985).

11. See Micks, *The Future Present*, pp. 141–158.

12. George McGovern, introduction to Nick Kotz, *Let Them Eat Promises: The Politics of Hunger in America* (New York: Doubleday, Anchor Books, 1971), p. xiv.

13. The story of Esther is dominated by the feast motif and is generally considered to be written as a justification of the Feast of Purim. See Sandra Beth Berg, *The Book of Esther* (Missoula, Montana: Scholars Press, 1979).

14. Daniel Berrigan, *Love, Love, at the End: Parables, Prayers and Meditations* (New York: Macmillan, 1968), pp. 114–115.

"Imogen Cunningham and Twinka, Yosemite 1974," Judy Dater photographer

SECTION 7.
OUR BODIES ARE SACRED

7. Women's Bodies Are Sacred

Being Mythed Upon

Women's bodies may be the hardest place for women to find sacredness. For thousands of years men have projected their own dark side upon women's bodies: their fear of mortality and dying, the urgency of their sex drives, the demonic power of their lust, the "evil" which their Genesis mythology created as a category of the "original" human situation.

Women's bodies have been invested with an unholy attraction and power over men. Women's bodies have been objectified in order to sell products, domesticated to clean floors. Women's bodies have been demeaned to "fuck" and "screw." Our vaginas have long been considered the only "natural"[1] receptacle for all the outpourings of male semen. Women's bodies have been cut in clitoridectomy and infibulation, deformed with footbinding.[2] Women's natural body-functions of menstruation and giving birth have been declared defiling of men's sacred space in temple and church.

Women are told by male imagemakers how we should look, by male psychologists how we should feel, by male medicine and male religion how we should understand our bodies.

How can we affirm the goodness, not to mention the sacredness, of our bodies in a woman-denying, woman-denigrating, woman-hating male culture? Emily Erwin Culpepper faces this question in her chapter, "Are Women's Bodies Sacred?: Listening to the Yes's and No's," and portrays this antagonism as conflicting voices: "We face the situation in which women are asserting a deep and holy YES! to our question about our women's bodies being sacred. But we assert this YES! in a nearly overwhelming context of woman-hating that every moment enacts an opposing and cursed NO!" Her chapter is a powerful statement of the tension-filled context in which women today seek to affirm our bodies.

Transforming the Taboo

Women have internalized so many negative cultural attitudes that it is painful and difficult for a woman to find her authentic body-voice. One must reach out with bare hands to seize the hot coal of taboo or degradation and somehow transform that terrible insult to one's self-esteem by embracing it until it becomes a statement of what is good and strong about us.

Carol P. Christ does that for women's sexuality. Our sexuality has long been viewed by males from their perspective; it has seldom been named from our woman's experience of being not for another but simply for ourselves. "I have learned," says Carol, "that my writing is most powerful, most capable of influencing change in the world, when it is most in touch with the power of the erotic in my life."

Jeanne Brooks Carritt also seizes the taboo forced upon women by a youth-loving culture and, looking into the dreaded mirror of age, she dares to affirm the body and the sensuality of the older woman. "The Old Woman is our beginning and our ending, and our beginnings again. Enriched by the experiences of living, she is the missing link in the sacred circle."

Perhaps even harder to confront is the bodily abuse and emotional abyss of low self-esteem which the battered wife and the physically or sexually abused child knows. Laureen E. Smith tells of the horrendous experience of such women, of the bonding between survivors who gather in a support group, and of their discovery of the presence of God in their resistance to battering. "This is for me. You are for me. . . . Can't you see? It's us. We're the Church for me. God is here!. . . . All of us here, we're helping each other, right? We're giving each other the substance of life. We're transforming the pain, right? We are holy."

"The power of the weak"[3] is what Elizabeth Janeway calls this coming together, this bonding of self to self to confront and resist oppression, this joining together to give a spoken name to the suffering in rape, in incest, in battering, even in aging, or simply in being a woman in a male culture which marks each woman with an indelibly stigmatized identity.[4] This naming of suffering is where the healing begins. It is here that we experience the healing transformation of the burning taboo into the glowing coal of our anger, rage and resistance. In this bonding women are beginning to accept and affirm our natural diversity of size, shape, weight, handicap, age, race, and sexual orientation.

Finding our authentic body-voice is a struggle of transformation. It is like taking hard roots or stalks or grains, or tough meat or fowl, and cooking them a long time until they are tender and nourishing. Women have been doing such slow simmering for our families since gatherer/hunter times. Now we are learning to cook a tough body-issue, cook it in rage and in bonding, cook it with the heat of our anger until it yields sustenance for us.

Women's Body-Integrity

As women struggle to get in touch with our own body-integrity, can we exorcise all this negative mental garbage and, looking down at our own breasts and vulvas, see them fresh and new? It is not easy.

Perhaps a true story will help us imagine a new place where our bodies are the only norm for us. Sigmund Freud and other males have assumed that women and girl-children envy the penis men prize so much for themselves. This story gives us an anticipatory glimpse of an "at-homeness" with our bodies which is possible for us.

A little girl, two-and-a-half, raised by her single-parent mother, was unfamiliar with male bodies. Her mother's college roommate, also a single parent, visited with her little boy, also two-and-a-half. After a shared bath each of the children is being put to bed by their mothers. The little girl pulled her mother's head down so she would not be overheard and whispered, "Mother, isn't it a blessing it didn't grow on his face?"

We want to be the norm for our own bodies. We want to forge for ourselves the standards for our lives. We want to myth ourselves free of all that has been mythed upon us. We want to affirm the power of our own subjectivity as active, choosing, sexual and child-bearing beings in a male culture which self-righteous-ly pontificates about pregnancy and birth while doing neither. Louise Hardin

Bray's chapter about her own abortion choice is like a crystal-clear piece of glass, manifesting lucidity and certitude in her decision-making. "I felt then and I feel now that my decision was a loving, caring and responsible one. It was a decision which grew naturally out of a trusting and respectful view of human life —mine, my husband's and my children's."

Many women find body-integrity in their deep resonance with nature. My own chapter about healing suggests the deeply sensual body-wonder of reconnecting with wind and sun and birds after recovering from severe body-trauma: "To be rejoicing, to be able to rejoice, is to be home."

We want our own bodies, our own psyches, our own women's lives, to constitute a plumbline of sacred purpose for us. We want to step into a sacred space where our bodies are inviolate, where our experience is the standard for what is "normal," where our subjectivity is the center of the "naming" universe. Come with us now as we step into that space and name the world anew.

—Elizabeth Dodson Gray

Notes

1. The distinction between "natural" and "unnatural" sexual acts goes back at least as far as St. Thomas Aquinas. "Natural" sex acts were those which could result in procreation. All noncoital sex acts were, in his schema, unnatural. Rape and incest, then, were "natural" sexual acts while masturbation was "unnatural." See Beverly Wildung Harrison, *Our Right to Choose: Toward a New Ethic of Abortion* (Boston: Beacon Press, 1983), p. 143 and p. 296, n. 58.

2. Mary Daly, *Gyn/Ecology: The Metaethics of Radical Feminism* (Boston: Beacon Press, 1978), pp. 134–177.

3. Elizabeth Janeway, *Powers of the Weak* (New York: Alfred A. Knopf, 1980), pp. 168–185.

4. Janeway, pp. 244–248, writes about the "stigma" of being a woman.

Are Women's Bodies Sacred?:
Listening to the Yes's and the No's

Emily Erwin Culpepper

EMILY ERWIN CULPEPPER is a feminist philosopher and theologian, a feminist free-thinker and activist in academia. Her focus on feminist symbols, images and rituals led her to shape her M.Div. thesis at Harvard Divinity School into a film, "Period Piece" about menstruation. She grew up in Macon, Georgia and began being a rebel by challenging segregation there in the 1950s. She earned the Th.D. from Harvard in 1983 and has taught at Harvard, the University of Massachusetts, the University of Southern California, and is currently at the University of California at Irvine. One of the personal accomplishments of which she is most proud is being moderator of Boston's first feminist television series.

As I mulled over this question, "Are our women's bodies sacred?" I became aware of diverse voices in my own mind offering answers. These voices began demanding that I pay attention to different, virtually opposing, realities. There are voices clamoring "YES!" as well as voices clamoring "NO!"

I went to my dictionary and there too I found more than one voice. There is an ambiguity and duality of meaning at the very core of the word *sacred,* for it has root meanings of both "holy" and "cursed," and a sense that what is sacred is something that has been "set apart." [1] Both the "Yes" and the "No" voices in my head grew louder as I pondered these two basic directions in meaning—set apart as holy, set apart as cursed. The voices began to shape themselves into an argument or dialogue, a graphic conversation about this question, a virtual chorus of various Yes's and No's. So that is how I have chosen to present this question, as a dialogue in which I will bring forward many voices for us to hear, both Yes's and No's.

YES—Women's Bodies Are Sacred

This is the answer of many women in the present. In a deep and complex way it is my own most fundamental answer. This Yes is an answer offered by feminism as we discover a great pleasure and power in experiencing our own female bodies as sources of insight, inspiration and worth. This Yes is suggested also by the underlying philosophy of the women's health movement, which approaches health and healing with the affirmation that "Our bodies *are* ourselves." [2]

In my own work on menstruation this Yes is a voice I have heard repeatedly. Some women tell stories about menstruation as a time of meditation; and we find a new consciousness about this basic female body process as a guide for spiritual quest and a source and catalyst for spiritual insight. [3] One such voice is that of the poet and playwright Ntozake Shange. In a poem affirming Black American liberation struggles, we hear:

> Our visions are our own,
> our truth no less violent than necessary
> to make
> our daughter's dreams
> as real as mensis [4]

Dreams as real as menses . . . yes, there is a sense here of invoking a sacredness of women's bodies. Shange's voice is a strong and vibrant one among the Yes's. It is she who dares to say:

> We need a god who bleeds,
> spreads her lunar vulva   & showers us in shades of scarlet,
> thick & warm like the breath of her,
> our mothers tearing   to let us   in,
> this place breaks open
> like our mothers bleeding,
> the planet is heaving   mourning our ignorance
> the moon tugs the seas
> to hold her/ to hold her
> embrace swelling hills/ i am
> not wounded i am bleeding to life [5]

The artist Judy Chicago has presented vulva imagery in ways that convey great beauty, strength and power. In *The Dinner Party Project* she creates an aura of honor for this quintessentially female part of our bodies. Theologian Nelle Morton observes that Judy Chicago's vision offers us an opportunity to "claim unashamedly and proudly what belongs to us." [6] Like the many other women working with woman-identified symbolism of vulva, breasts and women's bodies, Judy Chicago is helping us claim respect for "our own sacred images." Judy Chicago's most recent project brings this same awe and reverence to the subject of birthing. It looks at birthing through woman-created designs, exploring birthing as one part, a powerful part, of many women's personal history. So we can hear in the chorus of Yes's the hundreds and hundreds of women artists who have participated in Judy Chicago's ambitious projects.

Another resounding Yes to the sacredness of women's bodies comes from the thousands of women who participate in the new/old Goddess religion of Wicca or Witchcraft. One representative voice for contemporary feminist witchcraft is Starhawk, author of *The Spiral Dance*. She draws upon the Celtic Oral Tradition which teaches that:

> Women shed their own blood monthly and risk death in service to the life force with every pregnancy and birth. For this reason their bodies are considered sacred, and held inviolable. [7]

Goddess-oriented spirituality, whether practiced as a religion or as a path of meditation, is a phenomenon which is growing. In it many women (and some men) participate in rituals that clearly honor and affirm women's bodies. In Goddess religion the cosmos is modeled on the female body, which is sacred.[8]

With each Yes I let fill my mind, space is opened for hearing other affirming voices join in that chorus. I sense a rising and perhaps endless tide of voices urging, "Yes, Yes, of course women's bodies are sacred. How could it be otherwise?"

In the multitude I can discern the voices of many proud poets singing the beauty and sacred worth of female bodies at work, at rest, at play in all our ages and strengths and infirmities. I catch the music of Casse Culver weaving through these Yes-sayers, singing of a free and delight-full women's sexuality, calling it forth, singing, "flow on sacred river."[9] Hers is one representative of lesbian feminist vision, calling all women to touch a core affirmation of woman-identified celebrating and Self-love.

"Women's bodies are sacred. How could it be otherwise?" This question has opened my shaman's ear to an ocean of affirmation I will never forget, that I realize is always around me if I can remember to dip into it in times of need, in times of celebration.

The Yes's Echoing from the Past

In the background of these many present-day voices is another older Yes. Yes has also been an ancient answer to this question "Are women's bodies sacred?" We are discovering in our own day the extent to which this has been so. Judy Chicago, writing about her discoveries of women's history that inspired *The Dinner Party Project,* reminds us of the ancient sacredness of women that she found:

Ancient people believed the world was created by a female deity. . . . Awe of the universe was transformed into reverence for Woman Herself, Whose body became the symbol of birth and rebirth.[10]

Audre Lorde is a witness to this long-lasting and still surviving meaning in Africa:

. . . the human power to achieve success in practical and material ventures, the ability to make something out of anything. In Dahomey [West Africa], that power is female.[11]

Some of the women who have pointed the way for many more women on a search into the ancient past are Elizabeth Gould Davis (*The First Sex*), Helen Diner (*Mothers and Amazons*), Merlin Stone (*When God Was a Woman*), Marija Gimbutas (*The Gods and Goddesses of Old Europe*), and Luisa Teish (*Jambalaya: The Natural Woman's Book of Personal Charms and Practical Rituals*). What these women have found in the ancient world are many and diverse ways of imaging divinity and sacredness as female.

Letting Ancient Images Speak

Christina Biaggi is a feminist sculptor and scholar who attended a select academic conference in 1984 at Malta, an island in the Mediterranean off the southern coast of Sicily. Biaggi went with a group of women specifically intending to be a feminist presence at the conference, which was called to consider the extremely ancient female figurines and megalithic temples there. These small figures are ingloriously derided in most traditional scholarship as "the fat ladies." Biaggi describes them as sculpting of magnificently large, ample figures. Size is being emphasized artistically to convey an overflowing and powerful sense of abundance. These neolithic figures (3000–2500 B.C.E.) come from still older paleolithic prototypes.[12]

In pondering Biaggi's report I have heard two voices crying Yes! from Malta. One is an ancient voice, pointing us to recognize that the very temples themselves at Malta (and they are the oldest European megaliths) are also in the shape of amply round female bodies.[13] The temples and the female figurines mirror each other's shape. Surely a multiform and profound connection of female body with sacredness is being imaged in these structures arising from earliest European efforts to express in stone its deepest wisdom.[14]

The second voice from Malta comes through a contemporary woman. Another woman with the group in Malta knew that ancient priestesses practiced the ritual of dream incubation there. In keeping with that ritual practice, she lay alone on an altar stone one day meditating, surrounded by an ancient woman-shaped temple. As she felt the fathomless power of this place, she had a sudden vision, a voice—perhaps ancestral, perhaps her own—ringing in her mind's ear saying, "I *am* the oldest temple. This, my female body, is the oldest temple." [15]

Our female bodies, the oldest temples . . . this Yes rises from the dawn of human culture and certainly should carry on into and through new ages of understanding and interpretation. But it is just at this point of core insight, where the Yes! is fundamental and clearest, that I also hear another very different set of voices.

NO—Women's Bodies Are NOT Sacred

This No is also both a present and a past answer. There are many voices crying No. This negative answer is fundamental to patriarchy in its long march through history. It is an answer from the beginning of the traditional world views of Judaism, Christianity and Islam.

> To the woman [God] said, "I will greatly multiply your pain in childbearing; in pain you shall bring forth children, yet your desire shall be for your husband, and he shall rule over you." (Gen. 3:16 RSV)

> When a woman has a discharge of blood which is her regular discharge from her body, she shall be in her impurity for seven days and whoever touches her shall be unclean until the evening. (Lev. 15:19 RSV)

This is the voice of Yahweh, the same warrior god/father who chastises and rebukes his chosen people, Israel, by calling their disobedience and sinfulness "like the uncleanness of a woman in her impurity" (Ezek. 36:17 RSV). In the sacred texts and traditions of patriarchy there are examples without end of this revulsion and repugnance toward female bodies. Our bodies have been so despised that they are perceived as appropriate symbols of sin and degradation.[16]

This ancient NO! echos throughout many cultures. It undergirds those who hold power today. This great NO! is a basic article of faith in what radical feminists have come to recognize as a global religion of longstanding—the rule of men over women, the supposed divine right of phallocracy and gynocide. Mary Daly has put it with brilliant clarity: *"Patriarchy is itself the prevailing religion of the entire planet."* [17]

Vilifying women's bodies is an article of faith as well as an act of faith in this religion. In her book *Gyn/Ecology,* Mary Daly herself is one of those women's voices, feminist voices, calling us to take a sustained look at the NO! which men have enacted on women's bodies throughout history and still enact now throughout every day. Daly examines a representative and graphic Western model of sacred gynocide. The Babylonian myth of Creation tells how the god Marduk rises to supreme power by murdering and dismembering the goddess Ti'âmat.

> He shot off an arrow, and it tore her interior;
> It cut through her inward parts, it split [her] heart.
> When he had subdued her, he destroyed her life;
> He cast down her carcass [and] stood upon it. . . .
> The lord trod upon the hinder part of Ti'âmat
> and with his unsparing club he split [her] skull.
> He cut the arteries of her blood
> And caused the north wind to carry [it] to out-of-the-way places.
> When his fathers saw [this], they were glad and rejoiced.
>
> —Enuma Elish (Tablet IV:101–104; 129–133) [18]

Daly traces the reenactment of this paradigmatic goddess-murder through five diverse global examples of such ritual atrocity against women. She identifies a "sado-ritual syndrome" (a pattern common to diverse examples) of a ritualistic impressing and branding of male domination upon the bodies of women. Daly analyzes five sado-ritual syndromes: *suttee* (and modern kitchen-dowry murders) in India; genital mutilation of women in Africa; Chinese footbinding of women; the burning of millions accused of Witchcraft in Europe; and American gynecology. A terrible part of these patriarchal rituals is that other women are forced to be complicit in them. Women must often be the ones who actually inflict the pain upon other women, thus promoting hatred and misunderstanding and guilt among women, and conveniently hiding male power that underlies and mandates these atrocities.

Hearing the Chorus of NO's—and Continuing to Listen

It is very hard to listen, and continue hearing, voices that cry NO! with this much ancient and present pain. Many feminists are calling us to the task of both hearing and responding to this enormous and longstanding NO! This great NO! sits like a giant stone upon our chests in the manner of one of the medieval Christian tortures of women accused of Witchcraft. A woman-loving ethics demands of us that we face and change this reality.

I hear poet Pat Parker's voice, particularly her poem "Womanslaughter." It is an angry elegy for her sister, murdered by an estranged abusive husband. He was convicted only of manslaughter by a court that saw him as a quiet well-behaved man, guilty only of a "crime of passion." Parker's voice speaks for all our anger at gynocide when she says: "Sister, I do not understand./I rage & do not understand. . . . Was his crime so slight?" [19]

Audre Lorde's voice resounds also as the chorus rises in intensity, pointing us toward comprehending and withstanding the Awe-full Terrible NO's. Lorde warns us that we cannot leap sentimentally into a weak and idealized Yes that does not hear and do justice to this record of women's ongoing pain and torture. In a poem of outrage concerning two young sisters who were returned to their parents after being subjected to repeated incest (and pregnancy) by their father, Lorde laments:

> On the porch outside my door
> girls are lying
> like felled maples in the path of my feet.
> I cannot step past them nor over them,
> their slim bodies roll like smooth tree trunks,
> repeating themselves over and over,
> until my porch is covered with the bodies
> of young girls.
> Some have a child in their arms.
> To what death shall I look for comfort?
> Which mirror to break or mourn? [20]

The record in just the United States is massive, constant, and difficult to keep knowing, to keep confronting: rape (every few minutes), battering (every few seconds), incest (the reported frequency of one in four girls is now found to be one in three), and pornography (increasing both in explicit violence and in liberal legitimation).

Andrea Dworkin is one voice calling us to look at what pornography really is and what it is doing to women.

In the United States, [pornography] is an $8-billion trade in sexual exploitation. It is women turned into subhumans, beaver, pussy, body parts, genitals exposed, buttocks, breasts, mouths opened and throats penetrated, covered in semen, pissed on, shitted on, hung from light fixtures, tortured, maimed, bleeding, disemboweled, killed. . . .

It is scissors pointed at the vagina and objects stuck in it, a smile on the woman's face, her tongue hanging out. . . .

It is the conditioning of erection and orgasm in men to the powerlessness of women: our inferiority, humiliation, pain, torment. . . .[21]

Dworkin is uncompromising in her demand that we face unflinchingly this propaganda for patriarchy and also its effects. Pornography that depicts violence against women is spreading rapidly. The most sophisticated of modern technologies are available to design and promote it. Advertising of the media mainstream is being poisoned increasingly by slick sickening images constructed to elicit violence against women and children.[22] These are the modern texts or scriptures of patriarchy that set women apart as *cursed*.

The debasement of women's bodies is a foundation of global patriarchy, and pornographic images both express and instill a basic belief in the meta-religion of patriarchy, what Andrea Dworkin has called "access to our bodies as a birthright to men."[23] She observes that "The pornographers actually use our bodies as their language. Our bodies are the building blocks of their sentences."[24]

So there are abroad in our world today radically divergent answers to the question of whether our women's bodies are sacred. Women's bodies are *sacred* as holy to ourselves and those who genuinely love us and acknowledge without fear our historical connection as women to creating the life of the human community. In a most profoundly positive and spiritually holy way, then, our women's bodies *are* sacred. But we must also hear ringing in our ears and in our larger world of global culture the NO! that is being aggressively pushed upon the human community. To patriarchists, women's bodies are *sacred as cursed*. The Oxford English Dictionary informs us that *sacred* means "dedicated, set apart, exclusively appropriated to some person or special purpose"—especially "some religious purpose and hence entitled to veneration." Still further on it says, "Secured by religious sentiment, reverence, sense of justice or the like against violation, infringement or encroachment." The root ambiguity and duality we noted earlier in the word sacred *sacred* is reflected and expanded by these very different answers to our question. To the patriarchist, women's bodies are the bodies of Eve, temptress and source of sin, object of fascination and awe as well as of the fear and dread of evil.

The Law and Limiting Pornography's NO!

Recent feminist proposals for limiting pornography and the subsequent debates have sharpened my thinking about this conflict of voices, the YES's and NO's about our women's bodies. Proposals are being made by feminists to prohibit pornography on the basis of civil-rights laws. The intention of these suggestions is to set limits that both protect women and are not based upon community standards of obscenity, however that may be defined by a majority in the community (the current basis of anti-obscenity laws).[25]

The laws being proposed would give women and others harmed by pornography a basis to bring a civil suit to try to prove harm and collect damages. The proposed laws would not propose criminal codes authorizing censorship, prior restraint, or in any way limit the right to publish. The proposals are highly controversial. I consider them a risk, but one I would like to see attempted. There is no social change without risk, and women are already directly at risk from unchecked violent pornography.

Arguments against such legislation have centered on concerns that it would violate the First Amendment guarantee of free speech. Freedom of speech is very dear to me. I see my work as an activist and that of all activists against diverse forms of oppression as safeguarded in important ways by this constitutional guarantee.

But my deepest inner wisdom and my keenest attunement to women's experiences tell me that something is deathly wrong with arguing that the images of violent pornography cannot be limited and must be protected as "speech." Women are enslaved by this "speech." In every other area of life we recognize the necessity to make a social contract, to construct laws we know will be imperfect, to remain vigilant about the proper use and abuse of our legal codes, and to devise laws that admit of the complexity of human interactions and their contexts. For example, we have a variety of laws about taking another human's life. These laws range from recognizing the individual's right to self-defense to distinguishing among homicide, manslaughter, and varying "degrees" of murder. Why should it be too dangerous to attempt the social experiment of enabling women to have civil legal redress if they can prove harm from pornography?

I do not believe laws are the solution to all social ills. I am under no illusion that the legal justice system is equally accessible to all. My expectations of laws and the justice system are actually very guarded and limited. But at this point in our history I see them as one tool we can try to use, and about which we must remain critical and self-conscious. Feminists have advanced a similar perspective about the necessity for rape laws and vigilance regarding their administration.

Asserting a Holy But Critical YES!

I have listened to the arguments (often from other feminists) that freedom of speech must remain inviolable, even when this means the violation of actual women. I have pondered these arguments, wrestled with them, and I have come to realize that the sacrosanctness of free speech is a secular belief which is very consistent with the dominant Western theology.

Opponents of any limitation whatsoever on pornography would demand of us all a literally inerrant faith in the First Amendment, a faith so absolute in its demands that it constitutes a modern secular form of worshiping the Word. In this way the Word functions like the one god above all, most horribly above women, for the ascription of inviolable stature to such "speech" perverts a Constitutional principle (free speech) into an idol (the Word as god). Arguments in this way worshipful of "speech" replicate traditional attributes of the patriarchal Christian god: omnipotent, omnipresent, omniscient.

Of this god the Bible says, "In the beginning was the Word, and the Word was with God, and the Word was God" (John 1:1 RSV). In the world of the New Testament, the Greek word *Logos* (or Word) had complex overtones peculiar to that time. But in American popular preaching, God simply is "the Word." This attitude of reverence for "the Word" serves to undergird a reverence for speech (and for what is written and spoken) that permeates the mentality I am describing. Idolizing the Word, then, is a logical consequence in a society still shaped by patriarchal Christian patterns of thought, now transmuted into the secular debates over pornraphy and free speech. This realization clarified for me why I was so disturbed by the claim that pornographers' "speech"—and the lucrative industry promoting it—has a value so absolute that we are warned of any dilution or restriction.

I was directly aided in this insight by the work of Nelle Morton. When Morton examined the dynamics operating in feminist consciousness-raising, she discovered the pivotal importance and liberating function of women *hearing* each other in new ways. Reflecting on this process, Morton says:

> A fundamental question now insinuates itself: Could the limiting imagery in the word Word—*Logos*—derive from a patriarchal way of perceiving and experiencing the universe? . . . Could it be that *Logos* deified reduces communication to a one-way relationship—that of *speak–ing*—and by-passes the far more radical divine aspect of *hearing?* [26]

So, speech needs to be seen in relation to hearing. And I ask, in pornography *who* is being heard? Whose voices are (and are not yet) in the chorus of voices we hear rising in response to our profound question about whether women's bodies are sacred?

Many more critical questions are needed. We must ask, for example, about *agency:* Whose speech are we talking about? And whose silence? And what is the speech (and silence) about? We must also ask about the *context:* Under what conditions is the speech (or silence) taking place? Also, who has *access* to such speech? These and similar questions can help us establish the critical distinctions and qualifications that characterize our relationship to Constitutional principles. Such questions help us to see guiding principles in their relation to other values and guiding principles, and in so doing help us not to erect one or another of them into an icon or idol.

I believe feminists are on a wise path when we raise questions of who is doing what to whom, and when are they doing it and why? We must also expand and unfold our question about the sacredness of our bodies to ask broader questions. Our bodies are *made sacred by whom?* They are *set apart by whom? Secured by what religious sentiment?* Our bodies are *appropriated to what special purpose?* Such an emphasis upon context and actual function provides essential aspects of overall meaning.

We face a situation in which women are asserting a deep and holy YES! to our question about our women's bodies being sacred. But we assert this YES! in a nearly overwhelming context of woman-hating which enacts every moment an opposing and cursed NO! I conclude with a question and a vision. The question is urgent: Where and how shall we go on together from here? The vision is from French feminist Monique Wittig and is one touchstone that helps sustain me: "They, the women, the integrity of the body their first principle, advance marching together into another world." [27]

NOTES

1. *Webster's Seventh New Collegiate Dictionary.*

2. Boston Women's Health Book Collective, *Our Bodies, Ourselves* (New York: Simon and Schuster, 1971).

3. Emily Erwin Culpepper, "Menstruation Consciousness-Raising: A Personal and Pedagogical Process," in forthcoming proceedings from the Sixth National Conference of the Society for Menstrual Research (May 5, 1985); Culpepper, *Period Piece* (Cambridge, Mass.: Culpepper Productions, 1974). This is a short color film exploring attitudes about menstruation. A flyer describing the film and rental information is available from: Culpepper, 3420 Falcon Avenue, Long Beach, CA 90807.

4. Ntozake Shange, "New World Coro," in *A Daughter's Geography* (New York: St. Martin's Press, 1983), p. 52. Shange's spelling, *mensis,* honors Black English pronunciations.

5. Shange, "We Need a God Who Bleeds Now," p. 51.

6. Nelle Morton, "Beloved Image," in *The Journey Is Home* (Boston: Beacon Press, 1985), p. 122.

7. Starhawk, *The Spiral Dance: A Rebirth of the Ancient Religion of the Great Goddess* (San Francisco: Harper & Row, 1979), p. 32.

8. Starhawk, *The Spiral Dance,* p. 85.

9. Casse Culver, "Sacred River" on *Three Gypsies* (Urana Records, 1976).

10. Judy Chicago, *The Dinner Party Project* (Garden City, N.Y.: Doubleday, Anchor Books, 1979), pp. 10–11, 21–24.

11. Audre Lorde, "Eye to Eye" in *Sister Outsider* (Trumansburg, N.Y.: Crossing Press, 1984), p. 174.

12. Christina Biaggi, "Megalithic Sculptures That Symbolize the Great Goddess," Ph.D. diss., New York University, 1982.

13. Christina Biaggi, "The Significance of the Nudity, Obesity and Sexuality of the Maltese Goddess Figures," (Paper delivered at Harvard Divinity School, November 1, 1985).

14. Traditional scholarship belittles such ancient female representations as "merely" fertility Goddesses, or fertility amulets for the superstitious, or dolls. Many feminists, including Biaggi, Merlin Stone, Starhawk, and Marija Gimbutas point out the gross oversimplification and misogynist misunderstanding underlying this approach.

15. Discussion remarks by Catherine Allport at Dr. Biaggi's lecture, November 1, 1985.

16. See Drorah Setel, "Prophets and Pornography" in *Feminist Interpretation of the Bible,* ed. Letty Russell (Philadelphia: Westminster Press, 1985).

17. Mary Daly, *Gyn/Ecology: The Metaethics of Radical Feminism* (Boston: Beacon Press, 1978), p. 39. Emphasis in the original.

18. Alexander Heidel, *The Babylonia Genesis: The Story of Creation* (Chicago: University of Chicago Press, 1951), pp. 40–42. For a feminist discussion of the prepatriarchal background to this myth and its parallels in other myths, see Barbara G. Walker, "Ti'âmet," in *The Woman's Encyclopedia of Myths and Secrets* (San Francisco, Calif.: Harper and Row, 1983), pp. 998–999.

19. Pat Parker, "WOMANSLAUGHTER," in *Womanslaughter* (Oakland, Calif.: Diana Press, 1978), p. 61.

20. Audre Lorde, "Chain," in *The Black Unicorn* (New York: W. W. Norton, 1978), pp. 22–23.

21. Andrea Dworkin, "Against the Male Flood: Censorship, Pornography and Equality," in *Trivia: A Journal of Ideas* 7 (Summer 1985), p. 18.

22. Gayles Dines-Levy, "Images of Women in Israeli Mass Media," (Slide show and lecture, Cambridge, Mass., February 10, 1987, from a dissertation in progress at Salford University, England.) Dines-Levy has conducted research about the effects of pornography on society at Haifa University, Israel.

23. Dworkin, "Against the Male Flood," p. 19.

24. Dworkin, "Against the Male Flood," pp. 24–25.

25. The "Model Anti-pornography Law" was written by Andrea Dworkin and lawyer Catherine MacKinnon in consultation with numerous feminist and community activists against pornography. It has been proposed in Indianapolis, Minneapolis, and Cambridge, Mass. For one version of the proposed law, see Dworkin, "Against the Male Flood," pp. 30–32.

26. Morton, "Preaching the Word" in *The Journey Is Home,* p. 54.

27. Monique Wittig, *Les Guérillères* (New York: Avon Books, 1969), p. 72.

"We Are Where God Is":
Sacred Dimensions
of Battered Women's Lives

Laureen E. Smith

LAUREEN E. SMITH is a Presbyterian clergywoman ordained to a ministry with women that extends beyond the churches into the Boston community at large. Her undergraduate major in theatre prepared her to write her M.Div. thesis at Harvard Divinity School in the form of a play "Silent Sins" about her work for several years at a battered women's shelter. "I have been honored by many women who were willing to share their life stories with me. I continue to search out ways to portray women's religious experiences for the theatre."

Hurting Women

"I was so ashamed. . . . I thought I was the only woman on God's green earth who couldn't deal with her own problems. I thought somehow I deserved to be beaten. I could never seem to make him happy." [1] These words from a character in my play "Silent Sins" could have been spoken by any number of women I have come to know working in a battered women's shelter near Boston.

Several years ago "Donna" (not her real name) told me the story of how she met and fell in love with her husband when she was seventeen. "Danny was my knight in shining armor, my prince charming," she confided in me. "He was everything that I had ever hoped for. You see, my family didn't have much money, and Danny used to buy me lots of gifts to impress me. Danny promised me the world, and so we got married."

However things soon changed for Donna. On the night of the wedding, Danny began to beat Donna. She had no indication it was going to happen. "I was shocked. I mean, where did this come from? What did I do? I couldn't believe he hit me!" she said. The beatings continued for two years. She sought help during that time, but her friends were too afraid of Danny to do anything. The marriage counselor asked her what she had done to provoke the beatings and insisted that she work things out; the doctor never questioned what had happened to her as she was sitting on his examining table with a broken eardrum, two black eyes, a boot print on her cheek and clumps of hair missing from her head.

Finally Donna went to her parish priest. "As I sat there in the priest's large office, I had the sense that God was speaking to me that day through my priest." Donna told him about her fears, about the threats and about the beatings. "And do you know what he said to me? He advised me to get down on my knees and say the rosary three times a day, so that the fruits of the spirit would come to my house to help Danny and me. Can you believe it?" The priest reminded Donna of Christ's suffering and said that this suffering was her cross to bear.

Donna was confused but did as he said and went home to pray. She lit her candles and got on her knees. While she was praying, her husband came home, demanded supper, and joked about her praying. "Then Danny kicked me until I was unconscious."

Another woman, Sarah, "had been beaten by her husband throughout their married life. She was sixty years old when she finally sought shelter. . . . but then her rabbi telephoned and convinced her to go back home. When she returned to the shelter, she was bruised from another beating. The rabbi called again, and again he persuaded her to give her repentant husband another chance. The third time Sarah returned to the shelter, she had a broken rib. This time the rabbi called and said her husband was so repentant he wanted to take her on a trip to the Holy Land. "[2]

God and the Suffering of Women

These and other stories that battered women have shared with me give some insight into the recurring violence that battered women suffer daily. For the past several years I have been working as a staff advocate with a battered women's service group. I have worked with women like Donna and Sarah who come seeking refuge from the violence in their homes. They come needing emergency shelter, medical help, court and legal advocacy, counseling, referrals, hugs, smiles and friends. The shelter provides all of these. My work has had a unique aspect to it, however, as I am a woman preparing for the ordained ministry.

Profound spiritual anguish accompanies many battered women's physical and mental pain. Often when women learn I am preparing to be a minister, the flood gates open and religious questions come rushing out. "Do you believe God wanted me to suffer? Why did God let this happen? Where was the Church or my community?" Battered women not only struggle with the violence in their lives, but they grapple with the meaning and presence of God in that violence as well. Some may ask what religion or spirituality has to do with violence against women, but I feel that Donna's and Sarah's stories cast light on the important role that religion can have in helping either to perpetuate abuse or to end it.

When we explore the sacred dimensions of women's lives, we see that often these lives of women include violence. The problem of violence against women in our society is overwhelming. The number of women beaten, kicked, threatened, sexually violated, harassed and killed by their partners each year is reaching epidemic proportions. The FBI estimates that in this country a woman is beaten every eighteen seconds. In Massachusetts alone, every twenty-two days a woman is murdered by her partner or ex-partner.[3] While most people would like to dismiss the problem of family violence as associated with only small segments of the population, the truth is that there are thousands upon thousands of women of all ages, races and all economic classes who are being abused each year. Women are suffering. This must be recognized and understood.

God's presence is with these women experiencing violence. This presence is found and experienced by them in various ways which are often significantly different from the traditional understandings of "sacred" that most of us have learned. As battered women articulate their experience of the sacred, their voices must be heard.

The Absence and Presence of God

Many battered women have felt as if God were absent from them, too far away to help or even to care. In "Silent Sins" one of the women says, "I always thought that you were as powerless as me, God, because you didn't do anything to help." [4]

When God seems distant and unavailable to a battered woman, prayer becomes the only way she can reach this "far-away God." A God who is sovereign, almighty and omnipotent is separate from human beings and our nature and daily experience. God is far away "in Heaven" according to these traditional religious teachings. Furthermore, "sin is always ultimately against God," [5] not against the person who is actually being hurt. Sacredness here is distant and separate from the violence a battered woman suffers.

But every day I hear battered women recognizing for themselves a different sense of God and what is holy. Battered women when they articulate their experiences of violence, pain and fear, break the silences surrounding their lives and express as holy what they have experienced.

> "Imagine that I have been thrown to a very hard slate floor several times, kicked in the abdomen, the head and the chest, *and still remained alive.*" [6]

Battered women have survived, have remained alive. We seldom say that those who survive violence have experienced God, but battered women have. God is present with them in the suffering battered women endure and in their survival. To name this endurance as holy allows battered women to move from a place of passive acceptance of the violence and to achieve an active recognition of their power in surviving. Claiming God's presence directly is an action filled with dignity and hope. The battered women in the play "Silent Sins" claim:

> *Naomi:*   I survived. I endured.
> *Alex:*   Survival is holy.
> God is in the pain of that survival. [7]

As battered women realize that God is found in their survival, beliefs shift from accepting the violence as a part of life, to realizing different ways of living. Women start to ask questions about the suffering and the pain that they have endured. The characters in "Silent Sins" illustrate this shift:

Woman #2:   You see, everybody's got this idea that suffering's the hottest thing to come along since Moses himself. . . . But, hell, who wants to be suffering? Women been doing that number for days. See, people got this idea that the Big Man,

Woman #1:   Big Woman,

Woman #3:   Big God,

Woman #2:   wants us all to be miserable. Well, it just ain't so. . . I mean, just why do we want to believe in a God who makes us hurt so much? Huh? Just take a second and think about it. Okay, enough thinking—now let's do something about it.

Woman #1:   . . . What are we supposed to do about this mess? You got women on my right and women on my left getting the message from their priests, ministers, rabbis and congregations that they gotta endure and suffer these beatings.

Woman #2:   Well, the way I see it, you can either go on living in the pain, enduring all the hurt that's heaped upon you or . . . you can change it all and help others to change too. You know, change the suffering of thworld. Transform it. . . . You tell me what you think God would rather have us do?!" [8]

Taking On the Bible

In my work I have met women who have been told to do as Jesus said and "Turn the other cheek"—even if their cheek was already bruised! Women have also been told that this is the cross they must bear, or to pray harder and to accept the violence as God's will for them.

Susan Brooks Thistlethwaite writes, "As anyone who works with abused woman knows, [dealing with the Bible] is not an option. Battered women frequently bring their religious beliefs to the process of working through a battering relationship. . . . I received calls from some women who were experiencing abuse but were reluctant to try to change their situation because they had been told the teachings of the Bible prohibited their protest." [9]

So in addition to challenging concepts of God as distant, all-powerful and impersonal, battered women confront a Bible that is upheld as sacred, holy, and unchallengeable or immutable. Many battered women have had to wrestle with biblical texts that have historically contributed to the violence against them. Women have had preached from the pulpit, have studied in education classes, and have had shouted at them on television and radio such passages as:

> "Wives submit to your husbands."
> "Turn the other cheek."
> "I permit no woman to speak in Church."
> "Woman was made from man to be his helper."
> "Pray for those who abuse you."
> "Deny yourself." [10]

These injunctions have been particularly difficult for Christian battered women who have been taught that believing the Bible literally means they must accept the violence perpetrated against them.

However some battered women have found strength and courage in the Bible. For instance, the Psalms are particularly powerful for some women because several of the Psalms (Psalm 55, for example) speak so truthfully about the emotional experiences of someone in pain. Because of the strong biblical tradition honoring the expression of feelings of injustice, outrage and anguish, battered women can find their own emotions echoed and validated in scripture. Thistlethwaite writes that women "can learn that the scriptures are much more on their side than they dared hope. They can become suspicious of a biblical exegesis [interpretation of a text] that is a powerplay against them. The process of critical interpretation is often painful and wrenching, because new ways of looking at the Bible have to be learned. But it is also affirming because one is telling abused women, 'You have a right to both your religious beliefs and to your self-esteem.'" [11]

Used in this way the Bible can allow battered women to see the image of God within themselves and claim it. The Bible can be a mirror to a battered woman's soul that allows her to see her own worth and dignity which was being thrown away by her abuser. To her pastor, who had warned her that "what God hath joined together let not man put asunder," one battered woman replied "What God has joined together, a man has already put asunder." [12]

Clarifying What Is "Sacred" about the Family

In Christianity, Judaism and Islam the family is often sanctified as a social institution that is a primary foundation of society. It then becomes imperative that the family be kept together at all costs, and most of this responsibility usually lies with women. Relationships and marriage itself are upheld as sacred in a similar way.

For a battered woman, the burden of keeping the family or relationship together often means sacrificing her own personal safety. In "Silent Sins" Jane voices the pain and tensions:

He says that he can't imagine life without me. How do I respond to a comment like that? He hits me and then he says he didn't mean it, that he loves me. With this kind of love, I need a full-time bodyguard. . . . My parents keep telling me that the real problem is that David and I don't have any children. That once we were a real family that everything would be fine. They say I'm disrupting the image of the model couple by not having children. I don't want children. [13]

The family as a unit is more important than the individual members of it. There is much concern for form rather than the quality or actual substance of relationships. Reporting on a recent study of pastors and their handling of battering in marriage, James Alsdurf writes that "Most pastors in this study are more willing to accept a marriage in which some violence is present even though not God's perfect will,' than they are to advise a separation which might end in divorce, also 'not God's perfect will.' To some degree, these pastors are more committed to their concept of Christian marriage than they are to the Christian concept of loving nurture." [14]

Many people, not just the pastors in Alsdurf's study, do not consider the quality of the relating that goes on in a given relationship or family, including (as Marie Fortune puts it) "the presence or absence of consent and the distribution of power." [15] Battered women are often accused of breaking up the family or marriage by seeking shelter from abuse. It should be clear to all that in a violent home divorce is not what is breaking up the family. Violence and abuse are breaking up the family. A divorce is usually the painful, public acknowledgement of what is already an accomplished fact. In short, it is the abuse and the abuser that is violating the commitment of trust and stability in a relationship or marriage.

Redefining Who Is Family

The traditional form of marriage and family has been held up as sacred to most women in this culture. Battered women are indeed claiming that family and relationships include God's presence but they are doing this in a different way. Battered women and their children have struggled to make life better in their families. They have hoped that things would change and often they have worked very hard to facilitate such change. This commitment to love even within a violent relationship deserves recognition as sacred.

But battered women are now affirming also that *leaving* a relationship, mourning its death as well as the loss of security, can also contain the Spirit of God. The ending of one family and the beginning of a "family of choice" is just as sacred as traditional definitions of family. A "family of choice" can be simply the woman and her children. Or it can be the primary caregivers and support systems from religious groups, shelter-based friends, or the wider community that a battered woman and her children choose to surround themselves with in their healing journeys. Such "families of choice" are grounded in love, care and non-violence. The courage, hope and strength that come to a battered woman when she realizes that "family" can mean many different things can only be reverenced as holy. Redefining who is family and living in those relationships with non-violence and commitment is indeed where God's healing love can be found.

Breaking the Silence of "Confidentiality"

Silence is the most "sacramental" tool used against battered women. Confidentiality or silence about the violence, silence about the "imperfect" family, and finally silence about broken relationships and trusts—by these silences battered women have been prevented from experiencing and expressing the depth of emotions that are a part of any violent relationship. Rage, grief, fear and guilt are suppressed by silence in the name of "confidentiality," in the name of protecting and sustaining "the family." These emotions are not valued as holy. The secrets and silences battered women must keep are not acknowledged as places to search out and find God. Instead only the appearance of order and happiness is acceptable and seen as somehow sacramental.

Silence begets silence, so that both victim and society are kept mute. Marie Fortune notes that "Not coincidentally, this silence has served to maintain the status quo of women's oppression and isolation." [16] Silence condones violence and this "holy" silence hurts.

Feelings of isolation and helplessness result from silence and can magnify the suffering and increase the victimization. A friend who is a former battered woman tells me that "the isolation is one of the most devastating aspects of domestic violence. No one is there. No one can help. No one *knows.*"

But as women come together and share their experiences, their isolation and helplessness disappears. In a community of support they find their voices and become able to name their pain and their silenced emotions. When these women come together and "name" as battering what they have been experiencing, they are not only affirming their own power to name what has gone on (and hence their own importance), but they are also seeking together ways to change their lives. As they do this, communities of healing are created. As Alex, one of the main characters in "Silent Sins," realizes,

> That's why I left the Church fifteen years ago. What was there for me? No one nourished me. No one helped me. . . . There was nothing for me. . . . *This* is for me. *You* are for me. . . . Can't you see? It's us. We're the Church for me. God is here! . . . All of us here, we're helping each other, right? We're giving each other the substance of life. We're transforming the pain, right? *We* are holy.[17]

When Silence Breaks

Battered women can claim as sacred the breaking of silences, the bonding with other women, and the expression of their anger, rage, fear, confusion, grief, hope. While many religious traditions urge strength and keeping "a stiff upper lip" as a response to crisis, thus discouraging visible emotional responses, a victim of domestic violence as she rages, as she cries, as she dreams of a different life, as she mourns, can know and affirm that God is there with her in her painful emotions. The natural feelings that emerge in such a crisis are holy and are necessary for healing. The expression of anger and grief allow women to touch the deep places of themselves, to know that what has happened is wrong, and that emotional responses are justified.[18]

Silence is broken as we women wail loudly for ourselves and our sisters.

Donna Rose: Why does he want to control me? Why does he want me to be scared of him? To give away myself? I'm so confused. So damned confused and . . . angry. I am so angry. God!

Alex: And what do I do with this anger, huh? Who listens to it? Who will hear my rage? . . . I want to move on. Feel good about myself, pick up those pieces and move on. No more anger, no more pain, no more fear.

Donna Rose and Alex: No more.[19]

An important and wonderful transformation happens as battered women move through their emotions and come together, sharing their experiences. Listening and understanding each other's difficulties gives women's lives a reality and substantiality that a battered woman in her isolation may feel her own life does not have. Women are helping one another transform the pain that has been their lives. These processes are the essence of the support-group experience. As women claim as holy their lives amid violence, they experience transformations that constitute a pilgrimage from being a victim to seeing themselves as survivors. That transformation is difficult. It is often slow. But battered women recognize that they are healing—and that God is at work on their behalf in that healing.

> It is not just me. It is us. All this time I thought I was the sinner. I was the one who did all the bad things. NO! *I* have been *sinned against. I* have been violated. *I . . . We!*[20]

For me, I find that I am most moved when women realize that God is not only with them in their journeys but that they themselves also breathe the breath of God and God abides in them. The profound transformations, the claiming of God in Self, the active journey of healing, all reveal new definitions of what it means to experience "the holy."

Seeing Our Battered Bodies as Sacred

Granted, most women in this society have learned to devalue and detest their bodies. But women who have suffered violence to their bodies at the hands of someone they trusted, know the humiliation and fear that become connected with one's body. The bruises and the broken bones are looked at by others as shameful and ugly. And they are looked at by the battered woman herself as embarrassing and disgraceful. They are not even battle wounds to show off proudly; they are symbols of her weakness and lack of power, and are to be hidden away and kept secret.

How then can one claim that there is anything sacred about a battered body?

In support groups, in counseling and in classes women are beginning to understand that the journey from victim to survivor includes a slow and often excruciating process of coming to affirm and love one's own body. One comes to accept the scars, remember the beatings, and yet know that, in the midst of all this, there is a body that is holy, given to you by God, and made in the image of the Creator. The process of working all this through is sacred work that women are doing as they reclaim their bodies for health rather than victimization, reclaim their bodies for creativity rather than destruction, reclaim their bodies for life.

Battered women are affirming new perceptions of where God is and what is sacred. They are affirming that at the foundation of what is holy in battered women's lives are battered women themselves. Battered women's experiences are as diverse and as painful as they are holy. Battered women's psyches, no matter how shattered and fragile, still vibrate with God's presence. Despite broken bones and scarred skin, their bodies are holy temples of Spirit. A battered women themselves are sacred, regardless of the messages women receive to the contrary.

The centuries of silence cannot quiet battered women giving voice to the diverse and profound ways they have experienced God's presence. We are hearing the voice of prophecy, the voice that announces the presence of God and denounces in God's name a great injustice. This voice directs us to see the Life of God in and among women who have suffered violence: battered women's lives are sacred, as are all living beings on Earth. Loud and clear it is being proclaimed,

"We are the holy sanctuary of rest. We are where God is." [21]

NOTES

1. Laureen E. Smith, "Silent Sins" (Unpublished play, 1987), p. 42. For more information contact the author at 356A Concord Ave., Cambridge, MA 02138.

2. Rabbi Julie Ringold Spitzer, *Spousal Abuse in Rabbinic and Contemporary Judaism* (New York: National Federation of Temple Sisterhoods, 1985), p. 22.

3. Statistic from the Massachusetts Department of Public Health. In 1984 the U. S. Attorney General's Task Force on Family Violence stated that battering was the "single most cause of injury to women." The National Clearinghouse on Family Violence claims that 1/3 to 1/2 of all co-habiting relationships involve violence.

4. Smith, "Silent Sins," p. 42.

5. Wesley R. Manfalcone, *Coping with Abuse in the Family* (Philadelphia: Westminster Press, 1980), p. 44.

6. Letter of an anonymous battered woman, in *For Shelter and Beyond* (Boston: Massachusetts Coalition of Battered Women's Service Groups, 1981), pp. 6f. Italics added.

7. Smith, "Silent Sins," p. 42.

8. Smith, "Silent Sins," p. 32.

9. Susan Brooks Thistlethwaite, "Every Two Minutes: Battered Women and Feminist Interpretation" in *Feminist Interpretation of the Bible,* ed. Letty M. Russell (Philadelphia: Westminster Press, 1986), p. 62.

10. See Eph. 5:22 and 1 Peter 3:1; Matt. 5:39 and Luke 6:29; 1 Cor. 14:34; Gen. 2:18; Luke 6:28b; Mark 8:34, Matt. 16:24 and Luke 9:23.

11. Thistlethwaite, "Every Two Minutes," p. 100.

12. Joy Bussert, *Battered Women: From a Theology of Suffering to an Ethic of Empowerment* (New York: Division for Mission in North America, Lutheran Church in America, 1986), p. 60.

13. Smith, "Silent Sins," p. 13.

14. James Alsdurf, "Wife Abuse and the Church: The Response of Pastors," *Response* (Winter 1985), p. 11.

15. Marie M. Fortune, *Sexual Violence: The Unmentionable Sin* (New York: Pilgrim Press, 1983), p. 71.

16. Fortune, *Sexual Violence,* p. xii.

17. Smith, "Silent Sins," p. 42.

18. See Susan F. Turner and Constance Hoenk Shapiro, "Battered Women Mourning the Death of a Relationship," *Social Work* (September–October 1986), pp. 372–376.

19. Smith, "Silent Sins," p. 36.

20. Smith, "Silent Sins," p. 44. Italics added.

21. Smith, "Silent Sins," p. 44.

In Praise of Aphrodite:
Sexuality as Sacred*

Carol P. Christ

CAROL P. CHRIST is a leading feminist thinker and writer. She earned her B.A. from Stanford and her M.A. and Ph.D. from Yale. She has taught religious studies at Pomona College, Harvard Divinity School, San Jose State University, Columbia University and Wesleyan University. She is the author of DIVING DEEP AND SURFACING: WOMEN WRITERS ON SPIRITUAL QUEST (1980) and LAUGHTER OF APHRODITE: REFLECTIONS ON A JOURNEY TO THE GODDESS (1987). She is co-editor with Judith Plaskow of WOMANSPIRIT RISING: A FEMINIST READER ON RELIGION (1987) and WEAVING THE VISIONS: NEW PATTERNS IN FEMINIST SPIRITUALITY (1989). She lectures internationally on the subjects of women and religion and Goddesses. Raised as a Presbyterian, she is now a priestess of Aphrodite and a follower of earth religion. "I am presently living in Míthimna, Lesbos, Greece, where I am daily renewed by sea, sky and earth."

AEOLIAN MODE

According to Kay Gardner, the Aeolian or mixolidian mode invented by Sappho was condemned by the church.

> I descend gray cobbled steps
> you await me with ouzo
> we sit and talk   sun setting
> I want to hear every word
> I take coffee   sun setting
>
> sky and sea transform   turn pink
> sun sets   rose gold envelopes
> new moon rising silver.
>
> You tune me like a lyre
> Aeolian melody
> you reveal your deep longing
> to touch   to hold   to be held.
> I open   my body sings.
>
> "This island is so beautiful," I say.
> "This island is so beautiful," you say,
> As if with words we encompass it all.

When I wrote this poem in celebration of love and a deeply transforming sexual relationship, I felt myself to be, as I have several other times during my life, deeply and fully under the power of Aphrodite. I knew myself to be her priestess. I knew her to be Goddess of Love and Beauty, and I understood that Love and Beauty are not the attributes of a trivial divinity, but are the source of all that is creative and life-affirming in the universe. I knew that beauty is not only a matter of cosmetics, jewelry, clothing, and so-called feminine wiles: beauty is a great gift of the bounteous earth. I knew that the rose gold that envelopes the sea each night, like the rosy goldenness which shone from the face of my lover, expressed an aspect of the deepest meaning which can be found in our lives on this earth. My lover and I had come to each other from relationships that had long since lost that rosy glow. And so for each of us our love was a power of renewal. I praised Aphrodite with the poems I wrote and with those of Sappho which I read to my lover while he washed away the heat and dust of summer in a cool bath:

> Thank you, my dear
>
> You came, and you did
> well to come: I needed
> you. You have made
>
> love blaze up in
> my breast—bless you!
> Bless you as often
>
> as the hours have
> been endless to me
> while you were gone [1].

And my lover answered, "Yes, that is exactly how it was, exactly how it is." In that time I lived fully in my body and in intense awareness of the beauty and fragility of the earth. And I knew that this fullness was not only for its own sake, but that it was opening wells of creativity that would flow into my poetry, would transform all the writing I did afterward, enabling me to trust and to write what I knew at the deepest level of my being. I knew that in some deep way that I did not understand, I was being initiated into a new stage of my life.

Audre Lorde has written:

> The erotic is a resource within each of us that lies in a deeply female and *spiritual* [my italics] plane, firmly rooted in the power of our unexpressed or unrecognized feeling. In order to perpetuate itself, every oppression must corrupt or distort those various sources of power within the culture of the oppressed that can provide energy for change. For women this has meant a suppression of the erotic as a source of power and information in our lives.[2]

At the time when I met my lover, the power of the erotic was very much suppressed within me. I found little joy in my work or in my relationships, and I had been unable to write for several years. I had lost touch with the creative center which is the source of my power in the world. Lorde says that the erotic is "an internal sense of satisfaction to which, once we have experienced it, we know we can aspire," "a question of how acutely and fully we can feel in the doing." [3] Though I had no idea where the re-initiation into the power of the erotic which I experienced with my lover would lead, I knew at some depth of my being that my life would change dramatically. I would no longer be able to continue to do work that did not give me joy, and I would no longer settle for relationships in which the erotic's power was not manifest.

Like all lovers, I prayed that the relationship we had would last for us. And when it didn't, at least not in the way I had imagined it would, I was devastated. It was little consolation to remind myself that the reason Aphrodite's powers are called "divine" is because they are transformative, not because they promise the "happily ever after" of a fairy tale. I felt betrayed: I had only begun again to trust the power of the erotic in my life, and the relationship was terminated by factors which were beyond our control and by my lover's choice in response to them. I felt angry with Aphrodite, like Sappho who wrote:

> Last night
> I dreamed that
> you and I had
> words: Cyprian [4].

And:

> Tonight I've watched
>
> The moon and then
> the Pleiades
> go down.
>
> The night is now
> half-gone: youth
> goes; I am
>
> in bed alone [5].

Now as I look back on the relationship I had with my lover, I understand that Aphrodite brings transformations in our lives that are deep and lasting—but not necessarily those we would knowingly choose. Since the time of my re-initiation into the power of the erotic I tried unsuccessfully and with a great deal of pain to reinfuse an old relationship with Aphrodite's power. And at the moment, I, like Sappho in the poem, am in bed alone. And at the same time, I know more deeply than ever that I am Aphrodite's priestess. I am learning, not without difficulty and a great deal of stumbling along the way, to trust the power of the erotic in my life. And I am learning that though for me the power of the erotic is experienced most intensely when I am involved in a passionate sexual relationship, the power of the erotic is not encompassed by sexuality, nor does it require a constant sexual relationship in order for its transformative power to be experienced. As Lorde writes:

> When we begin to live from within outward, in touch with the power of the erotic within ourselves, and allowing that power to inform and illuminate our actions upon the world around us, then we begin to be responsible to ourselves in the deepest sense. For as we begin to recognize our deepest feelings, we begin to give up, of necessity, being satisfied with suffering and self-negation, and with the numbness which so often seems like their only alternative in society. Our acts against oppression become integral with self, motivated and empowered from within.[6]

Since my re-initiation into the powers of the erotic, I have found a new voice in my writing and have begun to understand that my writing is at the center of my creative work. I have learned that my writing is most powerful, most capable of influencing change in the world, when it is most in touch with the power of the erotic. My writing has become more fully embodied. I have learned not to fear, but to celebrate, the rooting of my insights in the story of my life. I have learned to trust that when my writing is most open and vulnerable, it is also most powerful, most likely to touch a chord and to influence change in others. This is not because all of our stories are the same but rather because we are all embodied: the telling of one story opens a space for the telling of another.

The outer contours of my life have changed radically too. I used to live in a big house with bevel leaded glass and two Victorian fireplaces. Fixing up that house took a great deal of my time, energy and money. I thought I would live there forever. I used to live in the United States. I used to be in a relationship that was comfortable and friendly, but which had lost the power of the erotic. I thought that was the most one could hope for in a relationship. I used to work at a job that drained the life force out of me. I used to come home from work too tired to do anything but watch television. I used to live in a culture of the automobile, even though I knew that driving in city traffic and on freeways made me tired and irritable. My relationship ended, the house had to be sold, I took an extended leave from my job, and eventually resigned from it, and I have chosen to live for now in a simpler way, in a Greek village that is not paradise but is still extremely beautiful. I don't have a car; I can't afford one, and I don't want one. I am able to spend my time on my writing. I experience daily the erotic power of the sea, sky, sunset and cobbled streets. I am stimulated by living amongst people whose life stories are very different from my own. I am very lucky to be able to live from my writing, to have found friends in another culture. And I also thank Aphrodite for awakening within me the power of the erotic which forced me "to give up, of necessity, being satisfied with suffering and self-negation, and with the numbness which so often seem like their only alternative in society." [7]

Aphrodite is a great power, a great Goddess. And yet she has been much maligned, trivialized, misunderstood. Why is it that when we say in a Christian context that "God is love," we understand love to be the greatest gift, the source of life, but when we say Aphrodite is Goddess of Love and Beauty, we say yes, but really there are more important things in life: what about morality and law?

Is it because we prefer to think of love as an abstract force, dissociated from the joy we take in each other's physicality? Is it because we prefer to think of love as an abstractly masculinized force? Do we fear the naked female body of this Goddess whose physical presence reminds us that love is intimately bound up with our bodies, our finitude, our mortality? Is it because we cannot help but associate Aphrodite's nakedness with the nakedness of Eve, which we have been taught is shameful, which we have been taught brought sin and death into the world? Is it because, as Audre Lorde has written, the suppression of the erotic is one of the "master's tools" which holds together a patriarchal and hierarchical society?

Though Christianity and the ascetic body-denying and life-denying culture it spawned in Europe played a great role in the suppression of the erotic, the erotic had begun to be suppressed earlier. In the *Iliad* of Homer (c. 800 B.C.E.) which is often said to be the foundational work of Western culture, Aphrodite is subordinated to the Father God Zeus. Each of the Goddesses is given a separate and limited sphere: Aphrodite gets love and beauty; Artemis, the wild animals and the wild places; Athena, the city and the crafts, including warcraft and the female crafts such as spinning and weaving; Hera, marriage and the life cycles of women, and so on. Behind each of these differentiated Greek Goddesses lies the pre-Olympian Goddesses of Old Europe whose spheres were all-encompassing. According to archeologist Marija Gimbutas, the Old European Goddess was Giver and Taker of All and the principle of Renewal and Regeneration. Old European culture began to change following a series of invasions which began as early as 4400 B.C.E. By the time of Mycenean Greece (c. 1600–1200 B.C.E.) the Indo-Europeans had established themselves in Greece. Homer looks back to the time of the Mycenean warrior-kings and celebrates the Indo-European Gods. Gimbutas sums up the change which led to the creation of the mythos and ethos celebrated by Homer:

> The new ideology was the apotheosis of the horseman and warrior. The principal gods carried weapons and rode horses or chariots; they were figures of inexhaustible energy, physical power, and fecundity. In contrast to the sacred myths of the pre–Indo-European peoples which centered around the moon, water, and the female, the religion of the pastoral semi-sedentary Indo-European peoples was oriented toward the rotating sky, the sun, stars, planets, and other sky phenomena, such as thunder and lightening. Their sky and sun gods shone "bright as the sky"; they wore starry cloaks. . . . They carried shining daggers, swords, and shields. The Indo-Europeans glorified the magical swiftness of arrow and javelin and the sharpness of the blade. Throughout the millennia, the Indo-Europeans exulted in the making of weapons, not pottery or sculpture. They believed that the touch of the axe blade awakened the powers of nature and transmitted the fecundity of the Thunder God. . . . [8]

Homer's Zeus who rules from atop Mount Olympus (hence the name Olympian) is the prototypical Indo-European warrior-god. In the *Iliad* the powers of love and beauty, the powers of Aphrodite represented in the love affair of Paris and Helen, start the Trojan war, but it is the warriors and their champions, especially

Zeus and Athena, who win the day. Aphrodite is wounded by a mortal soldier and helplessly limps off the battlefield. The Homeric ethos might be summed up as "Make war, not love." The ethos of the warrior is not only patriarchal and hierarchical but also profoundly antithetical to the ethos of eros. War requires the warrior to set aside the deep erotic feelings which bind him to family and homeland. Warriors must also deny the erotic bonds which tie them to other human beings, so that they can kill other men, rape women, and take women and children of the "enemy" into slavery, as was the common practice throughout the ancient world. In other words, warriors must learn not to feel the ordinary feelings of human beings. In our own time, anti-war protesters of the Vietnam era proclaimed "Make love, not war" in recognition that the ethos of eros is incompatible with the ethos of war. And some soldiers of the Vietnam era have begun courageously to speak of the dehumanizing process the warrior undergoes.

Sappho, who lived approximately two hundred years after Homer, celebrated, as we have seen, the ethos of eros. She was aware that the powers Aphrodite represented were far from trivial, as can be seen in the following fragment where she asks:

> What, Sappho, can
> you give one who
> has everything,
> like Aphrodite? [9]

Reacting against the Homeric denigration of Aphrodite, Sappho remembers that Aphrodite "has everything" because she *is* everything, the Giver and Taker of All, the power of Regeneration and Renewal. In one of the longest surviving fragments of her poetry, Sappho attacks directly the Homeric ethos:

> Some assert that a troop of horsemen,
> some footsoldiers, some a fleet of ships,
> is the most beautiful thing on the dark earth.
> But I assert that it is whatever anyone loves.
> It is quite simple to make this intelligible for all,
> for she who was far and away preeminent
> in the beauty of all humanity,
> Helen, abandoning her husband, the . . .
> went sailing to Troy and took no thought
> for child or dear parents.

Homer above all asserted what Sappho contradicts, that armies are the most beautiful thing on earth. Unlike Homer, Sappho praises Helen's choice to follow the one she loved. In the final fragment of this poem, Sappho compares Helen's love for Paris to her own love for a woman named Anaktoria:

> . . . reminds me now of Anaktoria
> absent: whose lovely step and shining glance of face
> I would prefer to see than Lydians' chariots
> and fighting men in arms. [10]

Sappho asserts that what one loves, man or woman, is more "beautiful"—a greater good—than war. In her critique of the ethos of the warrior she reminds us that to worship Aphrodite, to celebrate eros, one cannot remain within a so-called limited, so-called trivial, so-called female world. The celebration of Aphrodite and of eros requires that the fundamental values of patriarchal war society be challenged. Aphrodite calls us to transformation not only of ourselves and our lives but also of our world.

There is one further issue raised by the power of Aphrodite, by the power of the erotic. Lorde writes that the power of the erotic stems from our "deepest *nonrational* [my italics] knowledge." [11] Sappho, for example, reminds us that Helen abandoned her husband, her children, and her dear parents when she sailed with Paris to Troy. When we are under the power of Aphrodite, our conventional judgments, even our conventional moral judgments, are suspended. Sappho wrote:

> Without warning
>
> As a whirlwind
> swoops on an oak,
> Love shakes my heart [12].

There is something not entirely rational about love, about passion. Neither its beginnings nor its endings can be rationally chosen. Deeply passionate love is something we must simply live through. No matter how much we calculate, imagine, hope, attempt to control it, we cannot. Erotic love simply is. And when it is present in our lives, it seems like the most important thing there is. Perhaps this is why the Greeks called Aphrodite Goddess and Eros God. Love calls us out of ourselves, out of our ordinary contentment, out of our ordinary lives. And let us not mince words: love can cause great pain, not only to ourselves and our lovers, but to others who had no direct part in its joy and whom we did not consciously intend to hurt. Recognizing this, some have argued that disinterested love, self-giving love, compassion, *agape*, is superior to *eros*, which is always interested, even self-interested. Eros reminds us of our embodiment, our finitude, our mortality, our inability fully to control the circumstances of our lives. But this is precisely its form of transcendence: eros gives meaning through depth of feeling, through our physicality, to our finite, mortal lives.

In a polytheistic world, Aphrodite and Eros are not the only divinities. There are other great powers in the universe, and they too are worthy of honor, respect, celebration. And in a polyvalent world, we are free to worship Aphrodite, while recognizing that she brings both joy and pain. With Sappho, we are free to say:

> With his venom
>
> Irresistible
> and bittersweet

> that loosener
> of limbs, Love
>
> reptile-like
> strikes me down [13],

and with other lovers to admit that we too know what Sappho meant when she wrote:

> Now I know why Eros,
>
> of all the progeny of
> Earth and Heaven, has
> been most dearly loved [14].

NOTES

1. Mary Barnard, *Sappho: A New Translation* (Berkeley and Los Angeles, Calif.: University of California Press, 1958), #46.

2. Audre Lorde, *Sister Outsider: Essays and Speeches* (Trumansburg, N.Y.: Crossings Press, 1984), p. 53.

3. Lorde, p. 54.

4. *Sappho,* #63.

5. *Sappho,* #64.

6. Lorde, p. 58.

7. Lorde, p. 58.

8. Marija Gimbutas, "Women and Culture in Goddess-Oriented Old Europe," in *The Politics of Women's Spirituality,* ed. Charlene Spretnak (Garden City, N.Y.: Anchor Press/Doubleday, Anchor Books, 1982), p. 31.

9. *Sappho,* #4.

10. Jack Winkler, "Gardens of Nymphs: Public and Private in Sappho's Lyrics," in *Reflections of Women in Antiquity,* ed. Helene Foley (New York: Gordon and Breach Science Publishers, 1981), p. 71. Winkler's interpretation of the poem differs from mine.

11. Lorde, p. 53.

12. *Sappho,* #44.

13. *Sappho,* #53.

14. *Sappho,* #48.

Body-Decisions as Sacred

Louise Hardin Bray

LOUISE HARDIN BRAY was born into the home of a Methodist minister and grew up in Texas. She married an economist and they had two children before they faced the decision about which she writes. "I wrote this chapter because the decision to have an abortion was made within the context of a family attempting to live faithfully." She has her M.A. in social work from the University of Chicago and has been an active volunteer in her community. She says of herself, "It appears that the first half of my life was filled with learning to love with abandon and the second half is filled with learning to let go."

Abortion Story

It is during the end of the life of my father and in the high-school senior year of my daughter that I have been collecting my thoughts to tell this story. I can see clearly now that my decision to have an abortion was only one in a long series of riveting acts of faith characteristic of my own and other women's lives, from which both the growth and the consequences are unknown at the time.

A wife and mother makes choices on a daily basis in which life is affirmed. I believe that many decisions in my life have been taken as seriously as my decision to have an abortion. I have decided over and over again to value and respect the lives of our family members. Society however feels that the abortion decision is one in which women need particular guidance. I wonder why society is not more helpful when the questions loving parents must address are choices about feeding, housing, educating, caretaking?

My decision fourteen years ago to have an abortion was made with a clear vision of what it meant for me to be a faithful parent and wife. It was 1973 and I was able to decide to have a legal abortion with the full support of my physician and my husband and my own conscience. I felt then and I feel now that my decision was a loving, caring and responsible one. It was a decision that grew naturally out of a trusting and respectful view of human life—mine, my husband's and my children's.

Part of a Family and a Generation

I had been reared to care deeply about other people's lives and opinions, so I have wondered since why I was not then, and am not now, more troubled by the question of abortion which sends so many people to outrage and to their knees. At the time I had the abortion I felt a sense of disbelief that anyone could question our decision. Our decision grew out of a deeply grounded view of what it meant to love and to be related. I do not remember any language about law or God or ultimate reality being part of our discussion.

It was a personal matter based passionately on a whole view of hope for a family that nurtured and cared for each of its members. My husband and I felt keenly that each member of our family deserved the support and affirmation of all others. It was only out of this conviction about life and our commitment to each other that we even thought of creating a family.

Some background is appropriate at this point. My sister and I were raised in a home heavily influenced by the fact that my father was a liberal Methodist minister and that my mother was devotedly focused on the family. I have no memory of any discussion about family planning at home, and I remember my excitement in a college ethics class when I was writing a paper about planned parenthood. That paper was probably my first sanctioned attention to sexuality, since I had chosen the "goodie-goodie" route throughout my growing up as a preacher's kid during the 1940s and 1950s. As a result of writing that paper I developed an outspoken commitment to all parents being able to choose the *number* of children they want to try to have, as well as their being able to choose *when* they want to try to have them.

I grew up as part of a generation from the southwestern United States that came along with post–World War II technology, including the birth-control pill. I shared with my generation an amazing audacity. I thought all problems were soluble and that my generation would have what it wanted. I assumed with amazing hope and trust that my life would unfold along paths that would be interesting, peaceful and serene.

Miscarriages and Two Children Later

David and I were married in 1964 and we lived near Washington, D.C. I had worked for two years at an uninteresting job when, following up on my earlier ethics paper, I found a job with Planned Parenthood. In 1967 David and I decided I would stop taking the birth-control pills so that we could begin our carefully planned family. I was astonished that I did not have a baby nine months later. In fact I had two heartbreaking miscarriages before our daughter was born in 1969.

The anguish around those miscarriages as well as the joy of new life in Louisa were laced with an intensity of emotion I had not known before. I was one of those women who had seen her destiny completely connected to her being a mother and wife. I felt myself naturally equipped for these parts of my life. I felt the importance of these tasks for myself and for the world, They were tasks in which I felt very much at home. I felt a joy at being a homemaker.

I took being a mother more seriously and more completely than any other part of my life. I took on with certainty the role of being the heart of a family. As I look back now upon my mistakes in those early years, I believe they grew out of my claiming for myself the role of parent and homemaker—to the exclusion of my husband. I relished being the mother of a small child, and even now I look back with awe on the blissful naivete and emotional high of those years. I felt I had a mandate from the universe for the task of motherhood.

When we were ready to have another baby and I had a third miscarriage, I was once again astounded. I was very lucky; each of the miscarriages occurred mercifully early in the pregnancies, and I had a doctor by this time who gave me hope that we could resolve the problem. Andrew was born in 1972. We felt we had the perfect family. We were part of the strong Zero Population Growth generation, and we felt terribly lucky and grateful to have two healthy children. We felt we had the capacity to deal with our lives with grace, commitment, plenty and joy.

Abortion Decision

I was paying particular attention to birth-control, and when Andrew was six weeks old I had a Lippes Loop put in place because we wanted the surest and safest method. I do not remember our considering my having a tubal ligation or my husband a vasectomy at that time. It seemed a cruel irony when early in 1973 I became pregnant with the Loop in place. The Loop was removed and I stayed pregnant.

I felt wrenching disbelief. Each day I expected the miscarriage which had become so familiar. I realize that we were arrogant and naive to think we could be completely in charge of a process so complicated as pregnancy. However David and I had no dilemma about my having an abortion, and thanks to the *Rowe* v. *Wade* decision the previous January mine would be a legal abortion.

I did not have to convince the State of the rightness of my decision. We felt we had been careful and responsible about birth control and we felt that two children was the number we could care for and love. I had private thoughts about the capacity of our marriage to sustain another child, and David was clear about his wish not to have more babies. We were certain together of our decision in a way I realize now was luxurious. We acted out of our sense of responsibility to the wider global community, to our own beloved and lively children, and to each other. We knew we had a choice to make, and we were comfortable making it. We felt clear-eyed, clear-headed, and clear-hearted.

After My Abortion

I had an afternoon of sadness after my abortion. I also had a couple of angry reactions to comments made by a doctor and by a friend. But we had made a decision which we have always felt we would make again. For myself I cannot think of a more autonomous or responsible decision. I felt free to make the decision, free to carry it out, and free to live with the consequences. The decision and the action grew out of a sense of self that has never been more strong or focused. I do not remember any thoughts of myself as a feminist at the time, but I felt sure of my judgment in a way that only recent discussions of my value as a women have truly awakened and consolidated.

There were moments in family relationships all through the year 1973 when the central elements in our abortion decision, our capacity to love and to act, were tested. We responded with clarity about relationships and life and support. But there was more pain in the rest of that year as we watched those we loved in very difficult situations. My memory of the love and strength in our family system that year gives me hope today as we all live with my father's dying. Loving and letting go are again the primary themes in our family life, and we recognize that these are themes which will continue as we ourselves get older.

Looking back now to 1973 I can see that because we were fourteen years younger we were most sensitive to the decision to love and to act. From today's perspective we can see as an additional dimension to our decisions to love, the decision to let go. We have let go in other ways in the years since 1973, and once again new life-forces are forcing upon us heightened awareness of family decisions made in love.

The Continuing Impact

Last November I stood at the polls on a cold day holding a sign which read "Vote Pro-choice, Vote No on [Proposition] One." I was there because there was a referendum threatening the freedom to have a legal abortion in Massachusetts. During those chilly hours I talked with another woman also standing in the cold. That woman was also a mother. She was a strong Catholic and she disagreed with my sign. However we talked about being mothers.

We listened attentively to the route each had taken, and we heard the other's faithful attention to her view of loving herself and loving her family. We did not agree on public or private policy about "choice," but we felt linked by our roles of having children, being women, being wives. We each valued the struggle of the other. We felt hopeful about being heard and being able to listen. We felt the freedom to share our questions, our growth and our upbringing.

We felt more. We felt the need and freedom to talk to each other and not be rejected. We felt sure that in our private decisions about pregnancy we were serving ourselves and those we loved with all the positive energy we had. We felt we were using the language of our lives to sing the song of the universe. To be faithful women, wives and mothers was the way we saw our connection to the world. My decision to have an abortion grew out of that belief about my relationship to the universe, to myself and to my family. And her decision to have four children grew out of her understanding of her relationship to the universe.

We grew on that day in November by listening to and sharing with someone who had radically different understandings. We began to establish a relationship with another who shares the struggle to talk about the various ways we care about being alive.

Our Bodies Are Still Ourselves as We Age, and They Are Still Sacred

Jeanne Brooks Carritt

JEANNE BROOKS CARRITT *is seventy-two, an Oberlin College graduate with advanced degrees from Smith College and the University of Massachusetts, a wife, a mother and grandmother. A lifetime of work as an educator enables her to be the vigorous and sensible advocate she is today. "I have always been a feminist although until recently I never had a name for it. By the time I was ready to be a more 'organized' feminist I was an 'old' feminist. I found that I had also become invisible to feminists and nonfeminists alike—both male and female. When I discovered the problem was not me but my age, I was really angry. My commitment is to help raise the consciousness of other older women to their personhood, their self-hood, and to help restore the wise older woman, the Crone, to a place in the life cycle of the broader community, but most particularly to the women's community."*

Searching and Self-searching

Pulling my thoughts together to speak about my aging body has been a slow and painful process. I know that I am not exceptional in that. Religious and cultural taboos have prevented most women of my generation from speaking about feelings and experiences associated with our bodies. Female sexuality and original sin had been divinely connected. Like all self-searching, however, the gains have finally outweighed the losses.

I would go to the literature, I decided. Certainly someone had written about older women's bodies. A first look yielded nothing. Thanks to the current feminist movement, younger women have begun to share bodily feelings and experiences more comfortably. This is evident in the tradition-breaking book, *Our Bodies, Ourselves.*[1] But I was thwarted even here. The women in the Boston Women's Health Book Collective spoke from their own experiences, making their original (1971) edition applicable only to those in middle-age and younger. The 1984 greatly expanded edition, with the title *The New Our Bodies, Ourselves,*[2] includes a chapter of thirty-seven pages on "Women Growing Older." I awaited with eagerness their next book, *Ourselves Growing Older: Women Aging with Knowledge and Power.*[3]

The works of feminist artists and poets are rich in female imagery, sacralizing the vulva, the menses, the breasts, mother's milk and mother's blood. There are many images of the Virgin and the Mother, but nowhere did I find any mention of the third member of the goddess trinity, the Crone or Wise Old Woman. Listening to our female bodies is a relatively new experience, and these younger artists are rejoicing in their discoveries. A further search was more fruitful. May Sarton, an older woman herself, has shared her experiences in *At Seventy,*[4] and Florida Scott-Maxwell's journal *The Measure of My Days*[5] is pure poetry.

The Crone

It is not surprising that in Western societies the Crone aspect of the goddess of earlier times has never existed in any of her forms except in a negative way. The Crone has been as an image of evil, old age and death. For earlier societies the Crone was not a problem. Death for them was a part of the sacred cycle by which human life related to the cosmos. Their deity, the Goddess, was sexual and destructive as well as generative. The Christian church fathers of the first centuries had a lot of difficulty with that. Barbara Walker, in *The Crone: Woman of Age, Wisdom, and Power,*[6] says that "until the Crone figure was suppressed, patriarchal religions could not achieve full control of men's minds." Thus in the formation of Christian doctrine, the soul was seen as separate from the body; sexuality in women of child-bearing age was seen as being for procreation only; and any sexuality at all was simply unacceptable for older women. The earlier triple-goddess was replaced by Mary, the image of divine womanhood and the virgin mother of men's dreams, while virginity became the highest degree of sacredness that a woman could achieve. A woman's body as a sacred process at any age was simply out.

The bleakest chapter in the story of old women in the Christian West was the witch mania. It began in Europe in the fifth century, peaked in Europe in the sixteenth and seventeenth centuries, and spread to America in the eighteenth century. Tens of thousands of mostly old women were burned at the stake for doing what old women had always done, doctoring and healing, ministering to the dying, and tending to the dead. Before it all ended, witch-burning became political as well as religious, a way of getting rid of old women who could no longer look after themselves.

The Grandmother

"Why do you have hairs on your chin, Grandma?" my six-year-old grand-daughter asked. "Grandpa has hairs on his chin too," I tell her. But she quickly responds, "But he's supposed to. Hairs make you look like a witch." The stereotype of the wicked old witch is still alive and well. However the old witch is not burned at the stake any more. She has been replaced by the benign grandmother who, unlike the witch, is perceived as a useless object. Immersed in silence, often alone and in financial straits, she waits without complaining for some demonstration of interest and concern.

Recently I heard a grandmother story which warmed the cockles of my heart. The son of one of my friends waited until the day before Thanksgiving to phone his mother to ask what time he and his family should arrive for dinner, Thanksgiving dinner being Grandma's traditional yearly task. Instead of her voice, he got a recorded message which said, "I have gone to New York for the weekend. If your message is urgent, I can be reached at the following number. Please do not call unless you are in dire straits. I have an appointment with my publisher on Monday, and will return on Tuesday, or maybe later if I'm having a good time. Love, Grandma."

I visited another friend who was alone on her ninetieth birthday. I expected to find her sad but she was in high spirits. She told me that she had decided many years ago to give her body to a medical school but that she had heard nothing from them. "I suppose they thought I had died," she said. So she called them on her birthday. "When they asked my age, I told them I was ninety. The man on the other end of the line hesitated. But when I said I was in excellent health, he said, "All right, we'll take you." She chuckled and said, "Well, I've finally found a way to be useful."

Getting Old and Wearing Out

I have thought a lot about this bittersweet story and the consequences of living in a culture that pushes old people and particularly old women to the periphery, making us feel useless and unwanted. What a condemnation of a society that it leaves such an old woman able to feel useful only by dying.

As I reflect upon my own situation, I ask whether I feel useless too, and am I just braving it out? Why do I feel apologetic when I call my children and have nothing in particular to say? How do they feel about me, really? Am I ashamed of being old? Am I trying to pass as a younger person than I really am? Why do I mind being called a senior citizen? If I have to be pigeon-holed by age-cohort, I wish there were a better term for it.

I am not overly fond of my aging body when it complains to me too often and I find it difficult not to dislike my appearance and that of my contemporaries, as our faces and bodies respond to the accumulation of years. It would have been easier to have grown old in a culture in which wrinkles and sagging skin were an affirmation of accumulated wisdom, as it was in some North American Indian cultures. Nevertheless, overall I am rather enjoying the aging process. This body is still me, the one I entered the world with, and the one I will take with me when I leave. In the deep lines on my face I can now see my brother, my father, and my maternal grandmother, none of them now living. Yes, my body is myself, and related to the universe. It is indeed sacred.

The dictionary says *sacred* refers to "not secular, or not to be profaned; hallowed by association with the divine." An old dictionary, this. I need a definition that resonates better for me. I found it in some hand-scribbled notes, the author's name forgotten, "Sacred is that which takes us out of our little selves into the larger self of the Whole Universe." Here is a definition I can go with. It meets a growing need I have to search for ways of shared wholeness, to move toward more connectedness, both in relationships and in the natural world.

Living in a Time When the Sacred Has Been Lost

This need of mine has been trying to get my attention for a long time, for it speaks to a need for spirituality in my life. It seems to me that democracy has become synonymous in our time with patriarchal capitalism, and that democracy has become the religion of our society. This civic religion worships success; the acquisition of money is its gauge. Sacred connections with the cosmos are all gone. The rituals and symbols which used to connect humans to each other and to the universe are nothing more than hollow remnants of a lost time. It is all Christmas presents without the spirit of Christmas.

Our lives have become linear. We ignore the past and fear the future. Man has become the creator of himself. He sees life as a continuum in which he comes in at one end and goes out the other. He fears death. But if death must come, let it be a hero's death—a single event and not a life-process. This gives us violence and war, death on the battlefield or in some shoot-out. And always men assume that it will be the other fellow, the enemy, who will be shot. Or there is the more benign violence of racing cars, fighting bulls or climbing Mount Everest. Nature has become to us a death agent who must be defied. But unlike merely mortal woman, nature goes its own way, treating everyone the same, building and destroying and building again. Men build houses on the edge of the sea or on the banks of rivers, and storms and floods wipe them out. Winds blow in spirals at high speeds, sinking ships and splintering towns. Men cut down trees and the rain then washes away the topsoil so that millions starve. They take uranium from the earth, and use it to build weapons of massive destruction.

What Has Been Lost

The circle of life and death and again life has been broken. And we have lost the sacred, our connections with the whole. With this we have also lost the Wise Old Woman, the Crone. If we look back through time we find her in Sumeria in myths two thousand years older than the Bible. She is in the three-headed trinity of early Greece. She is in the Wise Old Woman of American Indian cultures.

When the Old Woman or Crone disappeared from our world, the sacred knowledge of life as a process and not a product disappeared too. It was the Crone and not the benign grandmother who was "the ancient funerary priestess who controlled the circumstances of death as she did of birth" and who took us "through the dark spaces of non-being." [7] The tasks she used to perform have been handed over to professionals now; doctors for healing the body; psychiatrists for healing the mind; priests for healing the spirit; obstetricians for midwifing; cosmeticians and undertakers for preserving the dead. Millions are spent to extol, preserve and glorify youth. Advertising hucksters sell older women creams to replace lost hormones, dyes to cover the gray in the hair, health clubs and diet centers to slim us down, while such ads as those for Pepsi-Cola and Miller's Lite tell us that no matter how much we try, youth in its brilliance and its *joie de vivre*, has passed us by.

Aging and Self-esteem

"You have really beautiful legs for a . . ." a young friend said to me. She then interrupted herself and blushed.

"It's all right," I said, to relieve her dis–ease. But I looked at her youthful body with skin smooth and eyes shiny, and then looked at my hands covered with brown spots. "Liver spots," my grandmother called them, "They're in the family, honey," she would say to me, "You'll have them too when you get old." I felt anger at my young friend and I felt self-pity. I yearned for my lost youth. I can't talk myself out of it. My consciousness has been shaped the same as everyone else's. To be old is to be at the bottom of the ladder. Hierarchical assumptions that value some and diminish others permeate so totally our understanding of reality. Why can't being old be not better or worse, but simply different, another stage in life?

I have been revisiting Imogen Cunningham today, re-enjoying her, as I often do when I am feeling sorry for myself. She was a fine photographer who did not receive much recognition until she was over eighty. She applied for and received a Guggenheim Fellowship when she was eighty-seven, and when she was over ninety she decided to do a book on old people, which she completed before she died at the age of ninety-three. "People don't like themselves very much, but photography reveals them," she said at one time. An examination of the faces in *After Ninety* [8] certainly supports her observation, for it is surely possible to read the stories of their lives in their wrinkles and creases. About one woman's face she comments, "When she asked to be photographed I told her that I wasn't taking commissions any more but I did it because she didn't care if she looked old, and she didn't hate her face."

And neither did Imogen. Although she had always been homely, she had always enjoyed being photographed herself. Lee Witkin, director of the Witkin Gallery in New York City, was a great admirer, both of her work and of her personally. In *Imogen Cunningham: A Portrait* he says of her, " . . . there are ugly beautiful and beautiful–ugly people, and Imogen was one. It was amazing that, given her physical appearance, she could really be so beautiful. Beauty really is inside." [9] Imogen would have liked that. Such acceptance by the young has to be earned. It is not easily come by.

Barbara Macdonald is a feminist activist. When she was sixty-five she wrote powerfully about how the women's movement has been silent about older women's issues. [10] She says that younger women see us as men see us—as women who used to be women but are not women any more—they ignore us, render us invisible. How I can relate to that. A feminist all my life, I have sat in so many meetings and felt alienated, a stranger, surrounded by members of my own sex with whom I could not identify, feeling like everybody's grandmother, useless and cast aside. I don't attend those meetings much anymore, for I can be useful in other ways which are not so damaging to my self-esteem.

Some years ago I attended a lecture for which Bella Abzug, that grande dame of politics and tireless advocate of women's rights, had been invited to speak. I still remember with anger how the audience of mostly younger women who were politically active trashed her from the floor, saying that she never did anything for women. They even ridiculed her clothes. She was finally forced to sit down without finishing her talk. When I looked at her closely I could see that her eyes were full of tears, tears of confusion, anger and disbelief. My effort to support her earned me nothing but catcalls.

But there is a brighter side. Much of the harassing has ceased, though not always the conspiracy of silence. For myself, I count among my friends many younger women, and I believe the relationships are as rewarding for them as they are for me. One of the most cherished gifts that I have received in a while was a Mother's Day card from a fifty-year-old friend of some means who had sent a donation to the National Women's History Project in my name, and the greeting on the card read "To help carry on the important work of remembering and recognizing countless numbers of older women who, like yourself, have touched and inspired many generations." How important it is to feel useful. This is progress indeed.

The Fear of Older Women's Sexuality

One of the most upsetting and misunderstood aspects of the Crone is the fear of her sexuality. Older women sexual? Doesn't sensuality stop at the menopause? A resounding NO! For as long as we are alive our bodies are still ourselves, and we are sensual. Why does society clamp down anew on women just at the time when we are relieved of the responsibilities of childbearing and are free to enjoy and explore our bodies and our sensuality? The appropriateness of sexuality in older women is denied by common consent, a consent promoted by the media and supported by the cultural mores and the Church. Consider the plight of the widow who remarries. Seldom is she in the good graces of her children, nor in the good graces of her new husband's family, who all too often feel that their own mother has betrayed them. Why? Is sexual ecstasy to be reserved only for the young?

But now there is a new hype. The real estate developers move in to extract their pound of flesh. As they manipulate us into fancy retirement compounds and the leisure life, they tell us we have earned the right to become obsolete. In these times when many people are alive and active well into their nineties, most of us, if left to our own devices, are not ready for checkers and shuffle-board at fifty-five. Our sensuality is alive and well and does not take kindly to being disenfranchised. In spite of our longer life spans, however, the denial of positive embodiedness which is handed down to us over many centuries by the Church is widespread today in our culture. It continues to exist and indeed to intensify—it is particularly hard on older women for whom, by unspoken constraints, sensuality's expression is considered ugly, grotesque, and inappropriate. A sexual older woman is still a witch.

Sexual intercourse may become less frequent, but the need for touching and being touched increases as we age, for touching is an acknowledgement of our being in the world. Our need for physical intimacy does not diminish as we grow older, Beverly Harrison tells us, and "unless we learn to overcome our historic negativism toward embodiedness and learn to celebrate sensuality, we will continue to perpetuate the isolation, exclusion, and devaluation of those no longer young. . . ." [11] How freeing this is! It is all right to have sexual longings and fantasies, to wish for a kiss or an embrace, whether from spouse, from friend, from daughter or from son. For as long as we are alive, each of us is an energy system of which our bodies are one manifestation, and through which we are connected in some way with the whole. The body is no less sacred in the winding-down time than in the coming-up time.

The Kind of Power Women Need

Time slows us all down. But it provides us with opportunities for reflection, for gathering up the pieces of our lives, for weaving them together into a sacred whole. The chlorophyll of spring and summer covers up the red and gold, but what a glorious surge there is in autumn when the chlorophyll disappears and the red and gold is revealed in all its brilliance before the leaves turn brown.

Life truly is a cycle. But we can't complete it until we bring back the Crone, for without her we have no continuity. The Old Woman is our beginnings and our endings, and our beginnings again. Enriched by the experiences of living, she is the missing link in the sacred circle. In this time of near holocaust we need her knowledge and her holy fury, for "most of all," writes Barbara Walker, "the Crone can represent precisely the kind of power women so desperately need today, and do not have; the power to force men to do what is right, for the benefit of future generations and of the earth itself . . . but she had better do it soon, for he is already counting down to doomsday." [12]

May Sarton draws upon the wisdom of the Nootka tribe of British Columbia in a recent poem:

"When a woman feels alone, when the room
Is full of demons," the Nootka tribe
Tells us, "the Old Woman will be there."
She has come to me over 3000 miles,
And what does she have to tell me, troubled
"by phantoms in the night"? Is she really here?
What is the saving word from so deep in the past?
From as deep as the ancient root of the redwood,
From as deep as the primal bed of the ocean,
From as deep as a woman's heart sprung open
again, through a hard birth or a hard death?
Here, under the shock of love, I am open
to you, Primal Spirit, one with rock and wave,
One with the survivors of flood and fire.
We have rebuilt their homes a million times,
have lost their children, and borne them again.
The words I hear are strength, laughter, endurance.
Old Woman, I meet you deep inside myself.
There, in the rootbed of fertility,
World without end, as the legend tells it,
Under the words, you are my silence. [13]

As the young goddess merges with the old goddess, should we not search for a ritual to mark the passing?

NOTES

1. Boston Women's Health Book Collective, *Our Bodies, Ourselves* (New York: Simon & Schuster, Touchstone Books, 1971).

2. Boston Women's Health Book Collective, *The New Our Bodies, Ourselves* (New York: Simon & Schuster, 1984).

3. Boston Women's Health Book Collective, *Ourselves Growing Older: Women Aging with Knowledge and Power* (New York: Simon & Schuster, 1987).

4. May Sarton, *At Seventy: A Journal* (New York: W. W. Norton, 1984).

5. Florida Scott-Maxwell, *The Measure of My Days* (New York: Alfred A. Knopf, 1969).

6. Barbara G. Walker, *The Crone: Woman of Age, Wisdom, and Power* (San Francisco: Harper & Row, 1985), p. 29.

7. Walker, *The Crone*, p. 32, p. 33.

8. Imogen Cunningham, *After Ninety* (Seattle: University of Washington Press, 1977), p. 66.

9. Judy Dater, *Imogen Cunningham: A Portrait* (Boston: New York Graphic Society, 1979), p. 105.

10. Barbara Macdonald with Cynthia Rich, *Look Me in the Eye: Older Women, Aging and Ageism* (San Francisco: Spinsters Ink (sic), 1983).

11. Beverly Wildung Harrison, *Making the Connections: Essays in Feminist Social Ethics*, edited by Carol S. Robb (Boston: Beacon Press, 1985), p. 164.

12. Walker, *The Crone*, p. 175, p. 178.

13. May Sarton, *Letters from Maine: New Poems* (New York: W. W. Norton, 1984), p. 23.

Why Do the Birds Sing?:
Healing after Trauma

Elizabeth Dodson Gray

Awakening

This morning is an extraordinary morning for me. But in order to understand that, you have to understand my last two-and-a-half years.

I came awake slowly, aware of how cool the summer air was and how good it felt to snuggle my body close up against my husband/lover/colleague. How purringly lovely it was to be so close and so contented as I stirred from sleep on a morning cool enough to subdue my hot flashes. My skin, smooth now from too many showers and therapeutic hot baths, luxuriated in touching our skins from toe to shoulder. We moved and turned together in our bed, resting like nesting spoons.

This was the first morning in two-and-a-half years that, when I came awake, I was not in pain. I was reveling in my newly regained abilities to feel totally sensual and be without pain, when I noticed the birds singing. I glanced at the digital clock; it was 8:50, yet they were singing as though it were dawn.

You need to understand that here in New England in recent years we have heard very few birds, what with the ravages of DDT and more recently the spraying to control the ravages of the gypsy moth. So until this morning the only such outpouring of birdsong I could recall ever hearing had been from a remarkable phonograph recording that consisted of an LP-length recording of midday sounds in an August rural meadow.

Another Time, Another Place

But today I heard again. The birds really were singing. And as I lay there listening, I remembered another time, another place. I was near the Delaware Water Gap atop a mountain in eastern Pennsylvania. It was the time of morning meditation at Kirkridge, an ecumenical retreat center, and as a sun-lover I chose to do my quiet time outside on the deck of the lodge with a 240-degree unobstructed view of the horizons all around me.

As I was settling into a comfortable position in the sun, I noticed that there was a bird perched on the very top of each of four tall trees whose tips were near the deck of the lodge. And those birds were all singing.

As I "centered in" to meditate, I suddenly came to the strangest feeling, that I was coming late to prayers and that the birds were already deep into their morning praise and I was being privileged to join them, except that I did not know how to sing.

So today, listening to the birds through my open bedroom window, I again felt as though I were somehow slipping late into a pew and joining a celebration already in progress.

The Flow of Being in the Universe

But this time I asked myself a new question—"Why do the birds sing?" The answer came to me strong and clear from someplace deep in me or deep within the universe—"Birds sing because rejoicing is the center of the universe."

It was a deep-gut feeling embodied in a new set of words. I had known that feeling before. I had felt that deeply in some non-verbal interior way. But I had never formulated it into those particular words.

And then suddenly I knew why I had felt so alienated from the center of my life and from the center of the universe by my last two-and-a-half years of pain. Before my pain I had rejoiced, and I had felt deeply centered and connected. But then the pain, the anxiety, and the despair had been like some terrible filters which had distorted everything and had made it impossible for me to rejoice in creation.

I could not look up at the stars and marvel in simple amazement. I could not look at a sunset in a winter sky and lose myself in pure joy. I could not feel the sensual luxury of my woman's body. Always there was intervening, like a nightmare filter, the distraction of physical pain, the diminishment of my feeling tortured, and the threat of my own not-being in death.

I hope that someday I can discover the secret, if there is one, of rejoicing in creation while in pain, and while dying. I don't know how to do that yet. But my bird-filled reentry into wonder this morning allowed me to put into words something I have always known, that *rejoicing is the flow of Being in the universe.*

Stepping into the Flow

This rejoicing, this flow of being, is the intention of creation. This is the intention of the overflowing and bubbling up energy of creativity which has brought everything in this 193-billion-galaxy universe into being. It is rejoicing, it is wonder, it is beauty, it is flow, it is energy, it is creativity, and it is good.

And when we step into that flow of rejoicing, whether alone or in the company of other celebrants, we are connected, we are home.

I have always felt this. It goes back with me at least to my early teenage years. But I could seldom put it into words. So imagine my delight and surprise a few years ago when I heard theologian Margaret Miles put this into her words in talking about "The Courage to be Alone, In and Out of Marriage." She was pondering Augustine's statement about "loving the other in God." "Augustine speaks," she said, "from a world view which assumes a center of being, of value, and of reality that the individual has access to only through her personal center." [1]

I was awestruck. She had said what I had long felt. You connect to the center of reality when you deeply connect to yourself, so being alone is coming home.

The Perfect Place

I remembered now my earliest childhood recollection. I was sitting underneath my grandfather's hydrangea bush in my backyard. I was about three and I was alone, "playing house." I was bathed in warm sunshine, and I felt very happy and deeply companioned in my aloneness by the sun, the air, the bush and the flowers. I was deeply, blissfully, contentedly at home.

Suddenly there is another memory, this one a recent one, from this spring's recuperation. This was in a time of diminishing pain as I would exercise and stretch and break adhesions. It was a time of daily struggle but with each broken adhesion I was becoming a little more free of pain, a little more free to use the muscles of my shoulder and move. I was getting well. This particular day was Memorial Day weekend and we were taking a three-hour cruise on an inland lake in New Hampshire, Lake Winnipesaukee, aboard a large ferryboat.

I was prowling the decks looking for the perfect spot to feel the wind and sun on my body and to contemplate the wonder of the very blue sky and the sun-dancing glimmer on the water. I finally found it, and I put my face up to the sun, feeling its warmth bathe my face while the strong breeze caressed my whole body. I gave a big shuddering sigh, and I knew I was back home.

Back to the sun and wind, back home to wonder and celebration, back home to my deeply integrating connection to my own center and to that center of reality which grounds my life in Being itself.

The Constancy of Change

Suddenly the ferry's direction had changed. We had left Center Harbor and were heading for Wolfeboro about an hour's ride away. My old perfect spot was no longer perfect. The sun was coming upon the boat from a totally different angle, and I had to put sun and wind and location together in a totally different way to approximate the previous hour's contentment.

The sun-glimmer on the water was different now. We were no longer moving closely through passes and islands and my perfect place for sun and shielding from too much wind gave me suddenly a vastness of view and horizons. I settled in again.

It was only after letting off passengers at Wolfeboro and the ferry's heading off in still another direction to complete its triangle-like course—and my having to find a third perfect place on the same boat and on the same day with the same weather and wind and sun—that I began to think about the perfect places in my life and how they were constantly changing. As the journey goes on, I thought, even with much staying the same, I have to stay in touch with myself and my center in order also to stay in touch with the equivalent of that sun and wind and sun-glimmer on water and shelter that made for a perfect place on our ferryboat ride.

To stay the same in the rush of change I had to adapt. The ferryboat ride was a metaphor for my life. It had perfect places but I had to seek them out and enjoy them and make use of them. Then like the birds and their nests, I had to sense changes and know I'd seek other perfect places, other places to sing and to be.

Recognizing Home

But amid the change I knew the center, the grounding, the pulse, is rejoicing. To be rejoicing, to be able to rejoice, is to be home. And all the famine in Africa, all the suffering of the Holocaust, all the pain humans cause one another —that is aberration. That is not the norm, not the pulse of creation. Suddenly I am remembering George Burns in the movie "O God" saying, as God, "It's all here. It all works."

Life is brought into being in joy, in rejoicing. The pain of childbirth is not the theme of the melody, rejoicing is. Celebration is. The energy that creates the atoms and that flows through the chemical processes of the burning stars and galaxies flows in rejoicing.

I heard the words and song of an old hymn suddenly:

> The spacious firmament on high
> with all the blue ethereal sky
> And spangled heavens, a shining frame . . .
>
> What though in solemn silence all
> move 'round the dark terrestrial ball,
> What though no real voice nor sound
> amidst their radiant orbs be found,
> In reason's ear, they all rejoice
> and utter forth a glorious voice,
> Singing as they shine . . . [2]

I thought to myself, Someone else besides me has had ears to hear that silent but profound rejoicing. Then my memory suddenly caught up another fragment of melody and words:

> Mortals, join the happy chorus
> which the morning stars began.
> Stars and angels sing around thee,
> field and forest, vale and mountain,
> Flowering meadow, flashing sea,
> chanting bird and flowing fountain,
> Call us to rejoice in Thee. [3]

A Microsecond Out of Phase?

It is clear to me that the pulse of rejoicing is there in the whole of creation. It awaits only our joining in.

George Leonard, in *The Silent Pulse: A Search for the Perfect Rhythm which Exists in Each of Us,* suggests that "perhaps, after all, perfect rhythm is always present in our every action and relationship, and it is only our awareness of it that is a microsecond out of phase. Could it be that we miss the experience not because it is so distant but because it is so close?" [4]

What if the rhythm we sense is the rhythm of rejoicing? Perhaps that is what holds the stars and planets on their course and centers the animals and birds. Perhaps we have only to step one microsecond to the side, into our own centeredness, to find that deep connectedness to the whole chorus, and to come home again to ourselves.

NOTES

1. Margaret Miles, "The Courage to be Alone—In and Out of Marriage," in *The Feminist Mystic and Other Essays on Women and Spirituality,* ed. Mary E. Giles (New York: Crossroad Publishing, 1982), pp. 96–97.

2. "The Spacious Firmament on High," words by Joseph Addison (1672–1719) based on Psalm 19.

3. "Joyful, Joyful We Adore Thee," words by Henry Van Dyke (1852–1933).

4. George Leonard, *The Silent Pulse: A Search for the Perfect Rhythm Which Exists in Each of Us* (New York: E. P. Dutton, 1978), p. 131.

Coming Home

Refrain: We're coming home to the spirit in our soul ____ We're coming home and the healing makes us whole ____ Like riv-ers running to the sea ____ We're coming home, we're com-ing home ____ 1. As the day is wo-ven in-to night, ____ As the dark-ness lives within the light ____ As we o-pen vi-sion to new sight ____ We're coming home, we're com-ing home ____

2. Bearing words born new unto each day
   Speaking bold where only silence lay
   as we dare to rise and lead the way

3. As the full moon waxes into wane
   Changing, yielding all that she did gain
   as from death she dares be born again

4. To reclaim the thinking of our mind
   Leaving shackles lying far behind
   bearing hope for every soul confined

5. To create a world of joy and peace
   where the power of justice does release
   love abounding, wars forever cease